UNCONQUERED

THE STORY OF KENT
AND ITS LIEUTENANCY

David McDine

THE ALLAN WILLETT FOUNDATION

Dedicated to the people of Kent, past, present – and future.

First published 2014
by THE ALLAN WILLETT FOUNDATION

Willett Family Office, Cumberland Cottage, Chilham, Canterbury, Kent CT4 8BX
©The Allan Willett Foundation
ISBN 978-0-9928348-0-7

Design and layout by Chris Michael
Page furniture by Danny Michael

Printed and bound in Kent by Headley Brothers
The Invicta Press, Queens Road, Ashford, Kent TN24 8HH

WHY UNCONQUERED?

In his book *Kent, A Royal County*, the late H R Pratt Boorman OBE DL, Kent Messenger Editor-in-Chief and a Deputy Lieutenant of Kent, told the story of the *Invicta* memorial that now stands near Swanscombe Church:

> The monument recalls how the Men of Kent and Kentish Men met William 1st at Swanscombe in 1067 (after he had been crowned in London), with boughs on their shoulders and swords in their hands, and offered William peace if he would grant their ancient rights and liberties 'otherwise war and that most deadly.' William yielded to their request and the Men of Kent and Kentish Men gained their motto '*Invicta*' – Unconquered – and were the only people to retain their ancient privileges.

Former Lord-Lieutenant Allan Willett helped keep the tradition alive with a pilgrimage to the memorial in 2006, saying: 'This monument is hugely symbolic – a reminder that our Frontline County, once a kingdom in its own right, has remained unconquered for more than a millennium.'

A PRAYER FOR KENT

**by the Very Reverend Dr Robert Willis, Dean of Canterbury
and a Deputy Lieutenant of Kent**

Almighty and Everlasting God, you have made our County of Kent throughout the history of this nation to be both a symbol of the strong defence of its sovereignty and also a sign of its welcome to those who journey here. We give you heartfelt thanks for the abiding beauty of this 'Garden of England', of marsh, down and weald, dockyard and Medway town, white cliff and pilgrim way, and pray that the daily life and work of our communities may demonstrate an equal beauty in the welfare, development and care of every member. Bless this county and prosper with your grace all its creative endeavours, that in their upholding of truth, justice and liberty its people may ever remain '*Invicta*' – Unconquered – an encouragement of service to our nation and a beacon of hope for all humanity, through Jesus Christ our Lord. Amen.

CONTENTS

Foreword by His Royal Highness The Duke of Kent KG

Introduction by Allan Willett CMG CVO, former Lord-Lieutenant of Kent

Appendix A: Kent's Lord-Lieutenants

Appendix B: Serving Deputy Lieutenants

Appendix C: Supplemental List Deputy Lieutenants

Acknowledgments, Source Notes, Picture Credits, Index

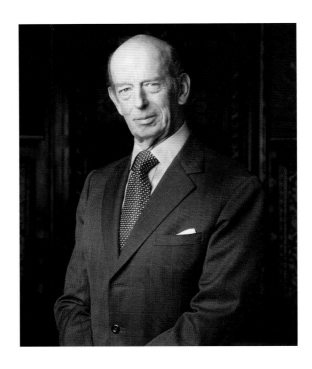

FOREWORD

by His Royal Highness The Duke of Kent KG

When my late father was made Duke of Kent he and my mother quickly developed a great affection for the county and its people – a feeling my family and I still share today.

For our many visits, the Lord-Lieutenant, carrying out his duties as representative of the Crown in the county, is invariably on hand to ensure that everything runs smoothly.

Kent has always been in the vanguard of the nation's history and from Tudor times the Lieutenancy played a crucial part in the maintenance of law and order, local defence – and many other functions that have since devolved to other bodies.

For more than 300 years successive Lord-Lieutenants and their Deputies performed the defensive task faithfully and effectively, as Kent's proud motto *Invicta* – Unconquered – testifies.

In the modern era the Lieutenancy has evolved in line with the Monarchy, and now plays an increasing and significant role in serving the Sovereign in the county, celebrating Kent's unique identity – and projecting the interests of its people.

The fascinating story of the Lieutenancy of Kent is chronicled for the first time in this book which covers not only its colourful history but, most importantly, what it continues to do today to enrich the lives of Kent's communities. I commend The Allan Willett Foundation for making this publication possible.

INTRODUCTION

by Allan Willett CMG CVO

Throughout history, Kent's exposed geographical position has made it the obvious stepping stone for would-be invaders. From the time of the Armada, whenever danger threatened this Frontline County, the Lieutenancy of Kent was there to organise its defence and maintain law and order.

Historically the Lieutenancy fulfilled a great variety of other roles, ranging from overseeing surveys of the Monarch's woodlands to supervising the Magistracy.

Eventually the changing nature of warfare dictated the need for defence of the realm to be organised on a national basis, and many of the Lieutenancy's other duties devolved to the county, district and borough councils.

Nevertheless, the close association with the Armed Forces, and especially the Volunteer Reserves and Cadets, continues – as does the relationship with the Magistracy. As the Sovereign's representative in the county, the Lord-Lieutenant's primary duty is to uphold the dignity of the Crown and, with the help of an influential network of Deputies, to promote voluntary service and encourage the industrial and social life of the county. Above all, the modern Lieutenancy seeks to engender pride in Kent's unique history and confidence in its future.

If the Lieutenancy is to continue to be an asset to Kent it is important that people understand its origins and modern role: hence this book which is dedicated to the people of the Frontline County – past, present and future.

~ ONE ~

GUARDIAN, GARDEN – AND ROYAL GATEWAY

**T**here is a buzz of anticipation as the shiny deep maroon limousine, with Royal Standard fluttering, approaches sedately. Excitement mounts, schoolchildren lining the route wave their Union Flags frantically, and there are cheers and applause from the expectant crowd as the car glides to a stop and The Queen alights. And first to greet and welcome her to Kent and present a line-up of people eager to meet their Sovereign is Her Majesty's representative in the county – the Lord-Lieutenant.

His navy blue military-style uniform, with peaked cap, scarlet-striped overalls, crimson and silver waist sash, sword and spurs, is a reminder that for centuries the Lieutenancy of Kent's role was to protect what can proudly claim to be Britain's Frontline County against invasion and insurrection.

Now, in an era of upheaval, rapid change and globalisation that makes many feel insecure, the Lieutenancy seeks to protect the county's identity and keep alive the indomitable Spirit of Kent that has carried its people through thick and thin. Like the Monarchy, it is part of the glue that binds society and communities together.

Excited children line the route to catch a glimpse of their Queen

RIGHT: Honouring the Dunkirk Little Ships – wishing Steve Norris, of Faversham, 'bon voyage' for the 70th anniversary crossing from Ramsgate to France in 2010 in his sailing barge Greta, the oldest active Dunkirk Little Ship, were the then Lord-Lieutenant, Allan Willett, and the then Vice Lord-Lieutenant, Lord De L'Isle

Members of the Women's Land Army, including Mrs Freda Murray (92), of Birchington, whose wartime service, often under enemy fire, had finally been recognised by the award of special badges, were honoured at the Lieutenancy's 2009 Civic Service

Just as the Monarchy they serve does nationally, the Lord-Lieutenant and his network of non-political, unpaid Deputies who make up the Lieutenancy provide a focus for county identity, unity and pride, foster a sense of stability and continuity, recognise achievements, success and excellence, and support and promote the ideal of voluntary service.

Where once they raised troops to defend the county they now encourage legions of volunteers to work for the good of their communities.

With no axes to grind other than love of Kent, their aim is to celebrate the county's unique history and culture – some say safeguard its very soul – serve its diverse mosaic of communities and contribute positively to its future.

The story of the Lieutenancy over the past five centuries *is* the story of Kent and its people – and of the extraordinary part the county has played in the nation's destiny.

It is the story of how – peasant, yeoman and nobleman alike – they flocked to the colours ready to do their utmost to throw the Spaniards and later Bonaparte's soldiers back into the sea if they had managed to win control of the Channel and land on the Kentish coast.

It is the story of Kentish soldiers – including the Lord-Lieutenant of the day – marching to the Channel ports to endure the horror of the World War I trenches. Every town, village and hamlet in Kent sent its young men, and the guns firing in Northern France shook the very earth of their home county.

And it is the story of how Kent's ports sent their little ships and pleasure boats to bring back survivors of the World War II miracle of Dunkirk to be welcomed with tea and wads as they returned through the county; of how the people reacted to the Battle of Britain that was fought in Kentish skies by supporting the Lieutenancy's appeal and donating whatever they could to fund a

County of Kent Spitfire squadron; and of how the Land Girls braved enemy fire to bring in the harvest – momentous events still commemorated by the Lieutenancy today.

But it is also the story of happier times – and especially of the royal visits so enjoyed by the people, whether experiencing the excitement of a wartime morale-boosting visit, receiving Maundy money from The Queen, welcoming a 21st Century countess to a school for disabled children or a prince and future king for the enthronement of an archbishop.

Inevitably Kent's destiny – to be in the vanguard of the nation's history – was shaped by its geography. Jutting out into the English Channel and the North Sea like a defiant jaw, this ancient county and one-time kingdom was *Guardian* of the nation's gateway long before it became known as the Garden of England.

As Britain's Frontline County, it bred a hardy people determined to defend its shores. Yet, as keepers of the stepping stones to and from the Continent, they have welcomed peaceful newcomers and are ever willing to adapt to new ideas.

In war and peace, the people of Kent can be justly proud of their county's story, centre stage in England's history. And Winston Churchill, on his installation at Dover as Lord Warden of the Cinque Ports, so aptly described their peninsula, surrounded on three sides by water, as:

> This glorious foreland of England, the shrine of its Christianity, the cradle of its institutions, the bulwark of its defence…

Romans, Jutes and Vikings came here to raid or colonise, but throughout the past millennium Kent has remained *undefeated* and significantly Duke William is known to the Men of Kent and Kentish Men not as the Conqueror but as William the Norman because he did *not* conquer their county.

Later the Spaniards, with their vast yet fatally flawed Armada, Napoleon with his prematurely vaunted 'Army of England' and Hitler and his Nazis all sought to exploit the narrowest stretch of the English Channel in order to defeat our nation, with Kent as their entry point and springboard. But all failed.

Others have come in peace. It was here that St Augustine's mission arrived in 597 A.D to begin the Christianising of England, from which sprang our language and laws, his teachings inspiring the building of the great Cathedrals of Canterbury, which over time was to become the world centre of Anglican Christianity, and of Rochester.

Newcomers also brought fresh agricultural and industrial ideas, techniques and products that were refined and passed on by the versatile people of Kent – England's leading innovators in everything from market gardening to hops and beer, paper and print.

Sir Winston Churchill is his uniform as Lord Warden of the Cinque Ports

'This glorious foreland of England, the shrine of its Christianity, the cradle of its institutions, the bulwark of its defence'

A stained glass window at Dover's Maison Dieu commemorates Henry VIII's visit en route to the Field of the Cloth of Gold

In addition to its Frontline fame, Kent has long won the right to be called a *Royal* county. Through the centuries Kings and Queens have passed back and forth between London and the Continent – Kent's ports the Royal Gateway.

- It was to Kent that Henry II came to do penance for the murder of an Archbishop.
- Henry V returned here following his triumph at Agincourt, his victorious army including 300 Kentish bowmen.
- Elizabeth I progressed majestically through the county with a huge entourage as voracious as a plague of locusts – as she arrived in Dover the tail of her procession was still toiling up the hill out of Folkestone.
- Henry VIII sailed from here, first to war, and then to seek peace on the Field of Cloth of Gold – and he wooed that ill-fated Kentish Maid Anne Boleyn at Hever.
- A French King's daughter, Henrietta Maria, arrived here to marry Charles I in Canterbury Cathedral.
- Charles II returned from exile to Dover for the Restoration of the Monarchy following the Civil War and Commonwealth.
- The fleeing James II was detained at Faversham by 'rude Kentish fishermen.'
- And, like other royal spouses, Prince Albert landed in Kent on his way to marry Queen Victoria.

Foreign Heads of State from the Sultan of Turkey and the Shah of Persia to the Czar of Russia and most of the crowned heads of Europe have come and gone via Kentish ports, and in more recent years members of our own Royal Family have made frequent visits – on average a dozen a year – for all manner of great occasions from the opening of the Channel Tunnel to the first-ever visit of a Pope, and to honour and encourage community volunteers, give a boost to worthy causes and celebrate their achievements.

Over the centuries three ancient offices have played key roles in protecting the county – pivotal to the defence of the realm – and in modern times they continue to work closely together for the good of Kent and its people.

Oldest by far is the Shrievalty. The Sovereign's 'Shire Reeves' – now called High Sheriffs – have operated in English counties since Saxon times and were originally responsible to the Monarch for all matters judicial, military and financial within their shire, or county.

This included organisation of the county levies of men at arms, originally the Anglo-Saxon 'fyrd', who were to rally in defence of the homeland when needed. Sheriffs were also responsible for maintaining law and order and collecting taxes due to the Crown.

But by the 16th Century their powers had declined and their military function was transferred to the Lieutenancy. Nevertheless, the appointment has survived

High Sheriffs are appointed annually and wear Court Dress on formal occasions. Lord Colgrain, who was appointed High Sheriff in 2013, with Lady Colgrain, who is a Deputy Lieutenant of Kent

LEFT: A morale-boosting wartime visit to members of the National Fire Service at Dover and Folkestone by the then Queen, who later, as Queen Mother, was the first woman to be appointed Lord Warden of the Cinque Ports

into the 21st Century and today's High Sheriffs, appointed annually, still have a valued role in supporting the Crown and the judiciary – and encouraging emergency, probation and prison services, and voluntary bodies involved in crime reduction. The Shrievalty's annual Justice Service brings together those connected with law and order county-wide.

Another of the great ancient military appointments, based in Kent, but with wider responsibilities and influence, is the combined office of Lord Warden, Admiral of the Cinque Ports and Constable of Dover Castle – the Key of England. Of the 14 members of the Confederation of the Cinque Ports, four of the five ports: New Romney, Hythe, Dover and Sandwich, are in Kent, as are all the seven limbs: Lydd, Folkestone, Faversham, Margate, Deal, Ramsgate and Tenterden; the other port – Hastings – and the two 'Antient towns' of Winchelsea and Rye, being in Sussex.

The Cinque Ports' origins lay in the strategic importance of the Channel coastline – the invasion coast. They supplied the Crown with ships and men and the Ports can justly claim to be the cradle of the Royal Navy that was to be the foundation of the nation's global power – and empire.

In return they were granted privileges and rights which included freedom from tolls and customs duties, freedom to trade and to hold their own judicial courts. Their status also entitled them to send Barons to carry the canopy over the Sovereign at coronations.

The office of Lord Warden and Constable of Dover Castle is a royal appointment, for life, and the post has been held by, among others, the royal princes who became Henry V and Henry VIII, later by the victor of Waterloo, The Duke of Wellington, who lived his later years and died at Walmer Castle, and more recently by Churchill, who made his home in Kent, that great Australian Sir Robert Menzies – and Queen Elizabeth The Queen Mother, the

The Duke of Wellington – one of the many illustrious Lord Wardens of the Cinque Ports

only woman to have held the appointment, and still so affectionately remembered in the county.

The present holder is, appropriately, a distinguished naval officer and former Chief of the Defence Staff, Admiral the Lord Boyce, who took office in 2004, charged with maintaining the Portsmen's ancient rights and privileges.

Like the Shrievalty, the Cinque Ports' powers had also declined by the 16th Century to the point when they could only muster half a dozen small ships for the Armada fleet, and today the Lord Warden's role is purely honorary and ceremonial. Nevertheless the present holder plays an important part not only as 'a constant anchor' in fostering local identity, unity and pride in a fast-changing world, but also does much to encourage youth achievement.

The other great ancient military office is the Lieutenancy. And for much of the past five centuries the Lord-Lieutenant and his Deputies have been at the centre of Kent's fortunes – the link between the Monarch, its defence and its people, playing a key role in ensuring that the county's proud claim, to be Unconquered in the modern era, endures.

The appointment of Lieutenants, so called because they are *tenants* of a position, standing in *lieu* – or in place – of the Monarch in each of Britain's counties, was born of necessity in Tudor times. Before the days of nationally-organised defence and effective local government, Monarchs looked first to the Sheriffs and later to trusted senior noblemen with strong Court and Privy Council connections and large estates – and therefore strong vested interests – to represent the Crown at county level.

Initially these county Lieutenants were appointed to serve on an occasional basis to deal with a particular emergency – from within or without. The office represented a delegation of the royal will or prerogative and gave the Lieutenants enormous power in their counties.

Each in turn appointed a number of Deputies, who acted as subordinate military commanders in the different lathes of the county.

They were usually themselves landed gentry, exercising great power locally, and were able to draw on considerable administrative support. At the time of the Armada threat Sir Thomas Scott was able to gather 4,000 armed men near the East Kent coast within 24 hours, and Sir John Leveson left 70 boxes of papers – much of it concerned with the Lieutenancy in West Kent.

Foremost among Lieutenancy responsibilities was raising, training and commanding levies of local men to defend their counties and, collectively, the realm. And nowhere was this role more crucially important than in the Front-line County.

But when each crisis was over their emergency powers were invariably withdrawn as promptly as they had been granted: jealous Monarchs ever fearful of leaving too much influence in hands other than their own for too long. However, the complex and largely efficient defensive arrangements exercised by the county Lieutenants in response to the Armada threat – and the growing usefulness of the office in managing the Monarch's business and justice at county level in an age when there was little effective local government – resulted in the appointment being made permanent.

Defence was far from being their only role. Their officials were used for the collection of loans under privy seal, for the supervision and disarming of Catholics – known as Recusants – and for such tasks as enforcing prohibition of the export of cannon forged with Wealden iron.

Importantly, they were also responsible for issuing proclamations regulating the economic life of the county:

> Such as those forbidding the eating of meat in Lent and for the equitable distribution of grain in times of scarcity.[1]

In the early years of his office, the county's first permanent Lieutenant, William Brooke, 10th Baron Cobham, also held the other great military appointments as Lord Warden and Admiral of the Cinque Ports and Constable of Dover Castle, as did a number of his successors, making them among the most powerful military commanders of their time.

STYLE

A reference to more than one Lord-Lieutenant is sometimes styled Lords Lieutenant, but their national Association follows the Lieutenancies Act of 1997 in referring to Lord-Lieutenants, although the hyphen is often dropped in unofficial usage

FACTFILE

■ Lieutenants have been appointed by the Monarch since Tudor times to organise defence of counties when danger threatened

■ The office became permanent from the 1580s when held by William Brooke, 10th Lord Cobham, during the Armada threat

■ Today the Lord-Lieutenant represents the Sovereign in the ancient and ceremonial County of Kent which includes Kent County Council and Medway Council administrative areas

■ The Lieutenancy maintains close relationships with the Armed Forces, reflecting the ancient office's original responsibility for the maintenance of order and defence

■ Duties include looking after members of the Royal Family and Heads of State when on official visits to Kent, and presenting honours and awards on behalf of the Crown

■ The Lord-Lieutenant chairs the county's Advisory Committee on Justices of the Peace and their appointment – and there are more than 850 JPs in Kent

■ The role of the Lieutenancy is entirely non-political. There is no pay

Times change, and in the modern world it no longer makes sense for the Lord-Lieutenant and his Deputies to organise defence. Over the years this and a great many duties were rightly taken over by Government departments and other bodies, and, like the other ancient offices, the Lieutenancy's role became largely social and ceremonial.

But to this day the Lieutenancy has continued to perform many useful functions – especially in representing the Sovereign and looking after royal visitors. And in Kent and elsewhere it has been modernised, with the active encouragement of Buckingham Palace and the Prime Minister's office, to continue to serve the Monarchy and the community effectively in the changed world of the 21st Century.

In 2009 the Ministry of Justice produced a protocol identifying the modern role of Lord-Lieutenants. First and foremost, it emphasised, they must uphold the dignity of the Crown, but ceremonial is stated to be only one part of their duties. They are also to:

> Promote and encourage voluntary and charitable organisations, and take an interest in the business, urban and rural and social life of the county.[2]

The protocol allows wide discretion in how they carry out the tasks expected of them – and also in those they choose to undertake. However, duties expected of them are:

- **Arranging visits of the Royal Family, including planning, security, briefing on local issues and welcoming and accompanying the royal visitor.**
- **Supporting and promoting a wide range of voluntary, civic and social activity both publicly and behind the scenes.**

- Encouraging local business.
- Supporting and liaising with the Armed Forces, their associated Cadet Forces and the Territorial Army.
- Playing an active part in the honours system, especially raising public awareness and encouraging nominations, and presenting Queen's Awards for Voluntary Service and Enterprise, and honours such as the Elizabeth Cross for the families of those who have died on active service since World War II, and the recently reinstated British Empire Medal for local community service.
- Leading the Magistracy as Chairman of their county's Advisory Committee on Justices of the Peace.

In a nutshell, Kent's modernised Lieutenancy follows the example of the Royal Family in fostering a spirit of community and co-operation, encouraging voluntary service and taking a close interest in business, industrial and social life, celebrating all that is good about the county – and adding value to people's lives.

In doing so it maintains close relationships with the Armed Forces and Cadets, the Magistracy, and Kent's many voluntary organisations and its great army of community volunteers. And in recent years it has led successful campaigns encouraging greater public support for the Armed Forces and their families, celebrating youth achievement, and fostering community volunteering.

A simple announcement in *The London Gazette* recorded the appointment of the present Lord-Lieutenant:

The Queen has been pleased by Letters Patent under the Great Seal of the

Realm dated 1 September 2011 to appoint The Viscount De L'Isle MBE to be Lord-Lieutenant of and in the County of Kent.

Among Lord De L'Isle's ancestors is the Elizabethan soldier poet Sir Philip Sidney, and he is the son and grandson of Victoria Cross winners. He and his wife Isobel live at Penshurst Place, near Tonbridge, home of the Sidney family since 1552.

He saw active service with the Grenadier Guards, for which he was made MBE, but gave up his Army career in 1979 to manage the Penshurst Place Estate, a popular tourist attraction.

A former Honorary Colonel of the County Territorial infantry battalion and of the Army Cadet Force, he is Chairman of Canterbury Cathedral Trust, and is president, patron or a member of a score of Kent organisations and voluntary bodies.

He was appointed a Deputy Lieutenant in 1996, Vice Lord-Lieutenant in 2003, and, after playing a major role in helping the then Lord-Lieutenant Allan Willett to modernise the office, succeeded him in 2011.

The workload of a modern, active Lord-Lieutenant in such a large and populous county – and Kent's population exceeds 1.6 million – is demanding in time and dedication, but Lord De L'Isle regards it as a great privilege to serve Queen and county.

He says: 'The Lieutenancy is the link between the Monarchy and the county, and having been a Guardsman I feel strongly that I owe allegiance to my Sovereign and that it is my duty and my honour to serve The Queen.'

Every county in England, Wales and Northern Ireland has a Lord-Lieutenant – as does each local government area in Scotland. They are appointed by The Queen on the advice of the Prime Minister and are the Sovereign's representative in their ceremonial county or area – in this case the ancient and ceremonial County of Kent which includes the Kent County Council and Medway Council administrative areas.

Being appointed as a Lord-Lieutenant does not make anyone a member of the nobility or give them the right to be addressed as 'My Lord' although some, like Lord De L'Isle, *are* peers of the realm. Nor are they all men. For many years 'lord' was merely a courtesy title recognising the dignity of the office, and did not become official until 1974. And today the appointment is far from being an all-male preserve.

The first female Lord-Lieutenant, Lavinia, Duchess of Norfolk, was appointed in West Sussex in 1975 and of the 55 Lieutenancy administrative areas in England and Wales 20 are held by women. But, male or female, all are addressed as Lord-Lieutenant. In Kent, the first female Deputy Lieutenants were appointed by Lord Astor of Hever, in 1973.

One of the most frequently-asked questions regarding Lord-Lieutenants is: 'How are they chosen?' Precisely how is likely to remain a mystery to all but

The Lord-Lieutenant is appointed by Letters Patent under the Great Seal of the Realm

the Prime Minister's appointments office and Buckingham Palace, and the process is akin, it has been said, to the selection of a new Pope without the telltale smoke. One thing is certain: anyone who seeks the office is unlikely to be offered it.

Traditionally, in past centuries, those chosen were invariably already knights or peers of the realm on appointment. They came from wealthy landed, often aristocratic, families who had an obvious vested interest in protecting and maintaining order in the counties where their largest estates lay.

In Kent they included members of the powerful Brooke, Finch, Sackville, Sidney and Camden families. But in today's more egalitarian society being

RIGHT: Three of Kent's Deputy Lieutenants, Mrs Ann West, Lady Nelson and the late Lady Pender, observe first aid training during a Cadet visit

high-born or 'landed' is not necessary. The Prime Minister's office seeks to nominate for Her Majesty's approval people who more closely reflect modern society, coming from many backgrounds, well known in their county, having given signal service there – or nationally – and prepared to encourage all manner of activities in support of their communities.

Nowadays the Cabinet Office carries out confidential consultations with a wide cross-section of community leaders and others involved in everything from education and the church to agriculture and industry, the Volunteer Reserve Forces and voluntary bodies such as St John Ambulance and the Red Cross.

Theoretically anyone can be appointed. However, an obvious requirement is a close connection with the county and there is a genuine effort to appoint whoever is best suited for the role, be it a self-made businessman like the previous incumbent Allan Willett or the present holder, Lord De L'Isle, who proved his suitability during what he calls his '15-year apprenticeship' first as a hard-working Deputy and then as Vice Lord-Lieutenant.

The role of Lord-Lieutenants is entirely non-political. The *Best Practice Guide to Civic Life* states simply that they 'stand aloof from politics'. Another positive is the fact that they are *not* a burden on the public purse. There is no pay and only minimal allowances for the ceremonial uniform for male Lord-Lieutenants, some secretarial help and official travel expenses.[3]

Deputies, who like the Lord-Lieutenant are expected to remain on the active list until the age of 75, are chosen for the contribution they have made – and will continue to make – to their county and the nation. Kent can appoint up to 70, one for every 25,000 head of population, and they come from every part of the county and many different walks of life.

Kent's current DLs, as they are known, include social care expert Mrs Nadra

LEFT: The Lieutenancy still maintains close relationships with the Armed Forces, reflecting the ancient office's military origins

Ahmed, musician and big band leader Jools Holland, Kent Scouts Commissioner Kelvin Holford, brewery chief executive Jonathan Neame, philanthropist Sir Roger De Haan, farmer George Jessel, former head teacher Mrs Rosalind McCarthy, the Dean of Canterbury Cathedral, the Very Reverend Robert Willis, and former Kent Messenger Group business editor Trevor Sturgess.

They are among those appointed by the Lord-Lieutenant on the recommendation of a knowledgeable selection panel subject only to Her Majesty 'not disapproving' the commission.

The Vice Lord-Lieutenant, currently former High Sheriff Richard Oldfield, was appointed by the Lord-Lieutenant from among the Deputy Lieutenants.

The undoubted honour a Lieutenancy appointment brings carries a commitment to serve the Monarch and community at one's own expense, and Lord-Lieutenants and their Deputies fund Lieutenancy activities in their counties personally in a spirit of altruism.

For royal visits and other formal occasions the Lord-Lieutenant wears his official military-style uniform, reflecting the appointment's military origin. Some of the Deputy Lieutenants, particularly those with military service, wear a similar uniform but with a leather Sam Browne belt rather than a sash.

Non-uniformed Deputies wear either their county badge of office – and Kent was first to commission one, bearing the famous prancing white horse and the *Invicta* motto – or since 2011 the newly-instituted national version which incorporates the Tudor rose, a reminder of the office's 16th century origins.

The non-political, non-sectarian and unpaid nature of the county Lieutenancies is their greatest strength. It has been said that in Kent, no doubt as elsewhere, members of the Lieutenancy have no agenda other than promoting and projecting the interests of their county and its communities.

As in some other counties, the Lord-Lieutenant of Kent holds the appoint-

The Vice Lord-Lieutenant, Mr Richard Oldfield

The Tudor Rose cap-badge surmounted by a crown worn by today's Lord-Lieutenants echoes back to the office's 16th Century origins

ment of *Custos Rotulorum* – or Keeper of the Rolls – the most senior civil officer in the county.

Historically the holder had the power to appoint senior officials, but that is no longer the case other than in his role as Chairman of the Lord Chancellor's Advisory Committee in the county for the appointment of lay Justices of the Peace.

This function is of special importance in Kent which has more than 850 lay magistrates and the Lieutenancy has taken an active part in recruiting new JPs from all backgrounds and all parts of the county to replace those retiring from the bench.

Lay magistrates represent local, visible justice. Today they continue to try more than 90 per cent of criminal cases, just as their forerunners have done ever since Magna Carta stressed the importance of trial by one's peers. Without them, as His Honour Judge Jeremy Carey, now himself a Deputy Lieutenant, has said, the justice system simply would not work.

As Chairman of the Advisory Committee, the Lord-Lieutenant is, in effect, the county's chief magistrate, and attends the swearing-in of all new JPs when they take both the Oath of Allegiance to the Sovereign and the Judicial Oath.

The close ties between the Lieutenancy and Magistracy over many years are evident from the fact that a great many Deputy Lieutenants have also been magistrates, and still, today, more than a dozen of Kent's serving and retired DLs are proud to include JP among their post-nominal letters.

Like many other ancient institutions, the Lieutenancy has changed out of all recognition over the centuries, but is still doing a great deal of worthwhile work and adding value to communities in ways that no other organisation could.

But to understand how the Lieutenancy has evolved from its original mix of military, civil, judicial and administrative duties to its 21st Century role of providing a focus for county identity, unity and pride and promoting service to others, it is necessary to turn the clock back to the Tudor era.

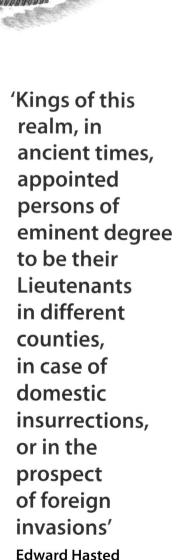

~ TWO ~
DEFENDING THE
FRONTLINE COUNTY

**M**oving menacingly up the Channel in tight defensive formation, a huge crescent-shaped fleet of enemy warships – the much-feared Spanish Armada – was approaching. The great three-decked galleons making their way eastward dwarfed the defending English ships, and eyewitnesses spoke of them as giant floating castles.

The plan was for the Armada to defeat the English fleet, secure the North Sea end of the Channel, allow troops from the Spanish-occupied Low Countries to cross in barges, land them on the thinly-defended coast, and strike for London. It was August, 1588. England's fate hung in the balance, and once again Kent, the Frontline County, was in the firing line.

Since Henry VIII's break from the Roman Catholic Church, the annulment of his marriage to Catherine of Aragon and his destruction of the monasteries, England had feared an invasion by Europe's Catholic powers. And now Philip II of Spain's dream of reclaiming England for the Catholic Church had become Elizabeth I's nightmare.

As ever, the navy was the nation's first line of defence, but if the Spaniards succeeded in seizing control of the Channel, only barely-trained and untrained ragamuffin bands of men, many armed only with bows, billhooks or scythes, stood ready to face Philip's battle-hardened troops.

Reacting to a threat in the days when the fastest means of communication was by horse meant that defence of the realm could not be managed centrally on a national basis. So, as the great Kent historian Edward Hasted noted, in times of danger Monarchs appointed prominent noblemen to act as their temporary Lieutenants in the counties to organise local defence and maintain law and order. And nowhere was the role more important and the threat more serious than in Kent, which offered the shortest sea route and closest proximity to the seat of power in London, making it first stop on the invasion route for Continental enemies.

For England's southern maritime counties, the approach of the Armada was to be a severe test of the ability of Elizabeth's Lieutenants to organise defence of the coast in the face of the greatest threat to our shores since the Norman invasion. Indeed, the origins of the office lay in systems of local government and military control introduced by the Normans and previously exercised by the annually-appointed Sheriff.

'Kings of this realm, in ancient times, appointed persons of eminent degree to be their Lieutenants in different counties, in case of domestic insurrections, or in the prospect of foreign invasions'

Edward Hasted

Assizes of Arms, essentially a re-creation of the general levy of the Anglo-Saxon fyrd, dated back to Henry II's time and required free men – and later villeins subject to their local lord – to equip themselves with weapons to serve the King.

From the reign of Edward II Commissions of Array were issued in time of war, threatened invasion or civil disturbances to 'trusted noblemen, ordering them to obtain, by impressing them or otherwise, a specified number of men from particular counties…'

These men, along with the normal county levy, were placed under a county 'Capitaneous', seen as the forerunner of the later Lieutenant.[1] The cost of raising local troops in this way fell on the locality.

By Henry VIII's time Commissions of Lieutenancy were being used in emergencies giving temporary Lieutenants, generally landed noblemen with a vested interest in maintaining stability, the authority to muster troops in the counties. But there was no provision – or stomach – for a standing army, and because of the natural concern about leaving too much armed power in the hands of ambitious noblemen once the external threat had disappeared, such commissions were deliberately only temporary:

> The dangers of establishing a permanent, and possibly a hereditary, Lieutenancy were manifest.[2]

An early example of one such a temporary commission was that granted to George Neville, 3rd Baron Bergavenny, later styled Abergavenny:

> Commissions of Array were issued on August 28, 1512, [Old Style, OS] to Lord Bergavenny… and to the Justices of the Peace and Sheriff of Kent, to take steps for the defence of the coast against the French. Another was issued on Jan 28 1513, directing the Sheriff of Kent to make proclamation for all males between sixty and 16 to take arms and be in readiness at an hour's warning to report by February following to such place in the said county as shall be assigned by Lord Bergavenny, who is deputed for the shire and sea-coast to resist the invasion of France. This appears one of the earliest instances of the appointment of a Lieutenant for the county, but it will be observed that the appointment is temporary, and only to resist the threatened invasion.

Hitherto '…the military command of the shire remained in the hands of the Sheriff until the appointment of Lords-Lieutenant' [sic][3] but this commission made it clear that although the Shrievalty, which changed hands annually, continued to have a role in issuing the Monarch's proclamations, command of the forces was now in the hands of the Lieutenant.

Abergavenny, who had been a favourite of Henry VII and holder of the

'The dangers of establishing a permanent, and possibly a hereditary, Lieutenancy were manifest'

Baron Bergavenny

quaintly-named office of Chief Larderer – literally chief of the royal larder – was an experienced soldier who had fought against the Cornish rebels at the Battle of Blackheath in 1497.

His 1512 Commission of Array to resist the threat of a French invasion covered not only Kent but Sussex and Surrey, and the following year he became Lord Warden of the Cinque Ports. When the invasion scare subsided his commission lapsed, but he played a leading role in Henry VIII's expedition into France the following year.

Some idea of the available forces that could be called upon in Kent are shown in an early 16th Century muster record listing 1,624 archers, 4,760 billmen, 272 'ablemen with neither bills nor bows' and 1,619 with harness, indicating what were later referred to as light horse, and later yeomanry cavalry. The unarmed 'ablemen' were required to undertake manual labour in support of the armed force, and were in effect a makeshift pioneer corps.

Although Welsh-born, as his title suggests, Abergavenny had many Kentish connections and when he died in 1535 his body was buried at Birling and his heart at Mereworth.

In the turbulent times following Henry VIII's death, Sir Thomas Cheney, who was already Lord Warden of the Cinque Ports and Constable of Queenborough Castle, was given a Commission of Lieutenancy in Kent. Cheney was a soldier, diplomat, and a favourite of Henry VIII, referred to as one of the King's 'henchmen' – a trusted follower rather than a partner in crime which tends to be the modern connotation.

He had served as Treasurer of the Royal Household and was a Privy Councillor and Knight of the Garter. Although his role as Treasurer meant that he spent a great deal of time at court in London, he was reportedly fond of his home in Sheppey, the ancient Shurland Castle near Eastchurch where the Cheneys had lived since around 1300.

However, he was not satisfied with Shurland Castle, or Hall as it came to be called. Between 1510 and 1518 he demolished the Hall and built a new and splendid mansion on the site, or near the first site. It has been suggested that he was influenced by Hampton Court, and the remaining buildings at Shurland bear that out.

He owned Chilham Castle, and it is alleged that he removed stone from there to rebuild Shurland. Apparently the keep at Chilham proved too strong for him and is still there, and in use, today.

The new hall at Shurland was described as 'a stately mansion, comparable with any other gentleman's residence in Kent...' In October, 1532, Sir Thomas entertained Henry VIII there with great ceremony and the King was said to have enjoyed banquets in elegant, comfortable surroundings, and sport in the well-stocked deer park.[5]

An Act of Parliament of 1571 declared the longbow to be 'God's special gift to the English nation.' But muster rolls reveal that the number of Kentish archers halved by the 1580s, due to the increasing use of firearms over the traditional longbow[4]

Sir Thomas Cheney wearing the insignia of a Knight of the Garter

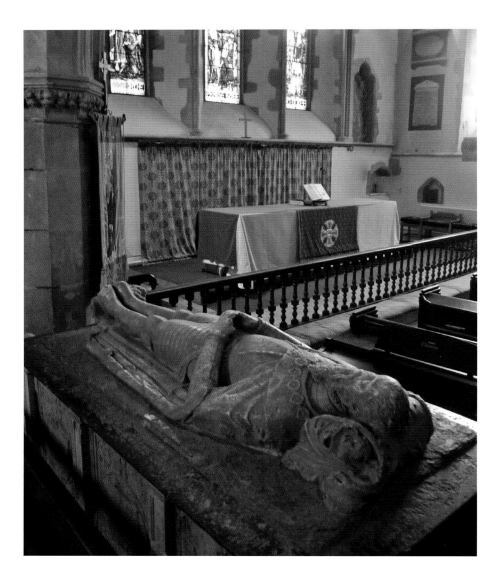

RIGHT: Sir Thomas Cheney's tomb in the Abbey Church at Minster, Isle of Sheppey

DATING STYLE

The 'Old Style' Julian Calendar was used in England until 1751, and there was much confusion when the 'New Style' Gregorian Calendar came into force on 1 January 1752. The change led to rioting by those who thought they had been cheated and demanded, unsuccessfully: 'Give us back our 10 days.' Dates before the change are given here in the New Style unless quoted in the Old Style – OS – in contemporary documents.

The young King Edward VI's brief reign was a time of great religious and social turmoil, with a strong whiff of revolt in the air, hostility on the Continent and the Scots gathering on the border. Cheney's was one of a series of commissions granted in 1547 to local magnates throughout England, and gave him power to raise and train levies within their counties and liberties.

All other officers were 'to be obedient to the Lieutenant in the exercise of the said commission.' And that included the Sheriff, still legally the only one empowered to summon the *posse comitatus* that had hitherto kept the peace, yet now placed under the orders of the Lieutenant.[6]

In Kent Sir Thomas was ordered to raise troops and to array and try - that is, to train them – see them 'furnished' – armed – and use them to resist or repress rebels, enemies, and invaders of the realm. And, just in case they had not understood the chain of command, *all* other county officials were again 'commanded to give obedience to Sir Thomas Cheney.'

This emergency-only commission soon ended and although Cheney was again appointed in 1551, he was imprisoned in the Tower during the nine-day reign of Lady Jane Grey.

However, he escaped and was present at the accession of Queen Mary I – 'Bloody Mary' – and was responsible for the organisation of opposition in Kent to the Sir Thomas Wyatt's rebellion against Mary in 1554, although he came in for criticism for his delay in attacking the rebels.

Cheney's land holdings in Kent were substantial. Following the Dissolution of the Monasteries he had acquired the Manor of Minster, including the site of the Monastery, and eventually owned the greatest part of the island, as well as property on the mainland. Dying a rich man in 1558,

> He left instructions that he was to be buried in 'his Chapel' of St Katherine, in the Church at Minster, near his first wife, Frydewith. The wife of his second marriage was ignored, and his son from that union was not impressed. All Sir Thomas's property was inherited by this son, and attempts Sir Thomas had made to prevent the estate being divided up proved useless. His son, Lord Henry Cheyney, known as 'the extravagant Lord Henry', left Shurland at once, and moved to his mother's property at Toddington, which he proceeded to renovate lavishly. Shurland Hall was left abandoned…[7]

Cheney's impressive tomb can still be seen in the Abbey Church at Minster on the Isle of Sheppey.

At the very end of Mary's reign, on 31 March 1558, the year Calais was lost and there was a strong possibility of a French invasion, Sir Henry Jerningham, Master of the Horse and one of the Queen's favourites, was appointed as her Lieutenant in Kent – again on a temporary commission – but served only briefly.

> That commission treated the county as a compact whole and upon enquiry the Lieutenant was told that his jurisdiction included Rochester and the Cinque Ports. The enquiry had been necessitated because his powers had been disputed by the authorities of both districts and notably, as was inevitable, by the warden of the Cinque Ports.[8]

Such turf wars were indeed inevitable when the offices of Lieutenant and Lord Warden were in different hands. However:

> The Tudors had a favourite and short method of dealing with such questions, and the disputants were curtly advised to settle their differences

amiably if they could, but anyhow to settle them unless worse things should befall them.[9]

This particular case, which brought the Lieutenant into conflict with the Lord Warden, opened up another question, namely:

> The relationship of the Lieutenant, not only to a liberty which claimed independence of him, but to another Royal officer. The Master of the Horse (Jerningham) was told that while his Commission undoubtedly extended to the places named, yet he was to write to the Lord Warden concerning the mustering of the Cinque Ports, and they were to settle the matter between them. There was to be no quarrelling, private interests and ambitions were to be subordinate to the service of the Crown and the welfare of the State.[10]

Jerningham came from a staunchly Catholic Norfolk family and, following Edwards VI's death in 1553 at the age of 15, he had emerged as one of Queen Mary's most ardent supporters. Like Cheney, he had opposed Wyatt's rebels, routing them on their way to Rochester.

Mary rewarded Sir Henry's devotion by making him a Knight of the Bath at her coronation, and appointed him Vice-Chamberlain, Captain of the Guard, Master of the Horse and of the Household, and a member of the Privy Council.

In his Lieutenancy role he deputed Sir Thomas Moyle and Sir Thomas Kempe to see to the beacons and muster, levy and arm men ready for war. However, he had failed to win support in the county and the majority of office-holders refused to cooperate with him at all, but by late October 1558, the danger of revolt or French invasion no longer posed an immediate threat during the winter months, and commissions of Lieutenancy, including Jerningham's, were terminated.

When Mary died on 17 November and her half sister Elizabeth came to the throne, Jerningham was deprived of his other high offices and all his manors and other properties were confiscated.

·~~❋~~·

Significant legislation known collectively as the Arms Act of 1558 laid down detailed scales of arms contributions and was followed by a stream of orders about the conduct of the Militia. This was the forerunner of the later Militia Acts and a century later it was control of the Militias that sparked the Civil War.

In May 1559, in the face of renewed invasion fears, the newly-crowned Elizabeth I placed 17 counties under Lieutenants, and the natural choice for Kent was William Brooke, Lord Cobham. Now there would be no conflict, because he also held the appointment of Lord Warden.

In effect, he had already played himself into the county-wide military role

'Turf wars were indeed inevitable when the offices of Lieutenant and Lord Warden were in different hands'

when invasion threatened in the last year of Edward VI's reign and as Lord Warden Cobham warned 'that ther be many sayles at the Northforland'.

The King ordered him 'to be in a readiness with a good companye of sodiars' and to put the county in a state of defence 'with all diligence possible,' but 'without making any fiers' (i.e. lighting beacons), unless he found it 'very neadfull.'

The commissions of Lieutenancy granted in 1559 were dispensed with two years later, but issued again in 1569 when there was rebellion in the north led by Catholic Earls in an abortive attempt to free Mary Queen of Scots and restore Catholic worship. Again, Cobham was the natural choice for the Kent Lieutenancy, and was in office until 1570 when Elizabeth I wrote to all the lieutenants informing them that:

> As the danger of rebellion was over there was no need for them to remain in office any longer.[11]

William Brooke, Lord Cobham, Kent's first permanent Lieutenant

The Lieutenancy/Cinque Ports relationship across the Sussex border had not been cosy, and there was 'a great to-do' when Winchelsea and Rye, claiming privilege as Cinque Ports, refused to recognise Lieutenancy authority.

Cobham was Lieutenant again… in 1587, and may well have been so in between these years. But during all the earlier period of the reign the commission were issued, renewed and terminated at erratic intervals according to political exigencies.[12]

Notwithstanding the on-off nature of commissions of Lieutenancy in Tudor times, what is abundantly clear is that throughout the period from 1559 onwards Cobham, a man of immense power and influence in Kent, was the natural first choice as Lieutenant when peril threatened the Frontline County. In effect, he was the military head of his home county from the time of his first commission to his death in 1597. Certainly the eminent Kent historian William Lambarde recognised him as such in his *A Perambulation of Kent*.

The growing threat of a Spanish invasion prompted a new commission of Lieutenancy for Cobham in the warrant of 1585, and was renewed two years later naming Cobham's brother Sir Henry Cobham, who used the family title as his surname rather than Brooke, Sir Thomas Vane and Sir Thomas Scott as his Deputies. It appears that these were the first officially recognised Deputy Lieutenants, as previously justices and other significant landowners had been expected to assist the Lieutenant without being given the actual title of Deputy.[13]

Now, as the Queen's Lieutenant in Kent, Lord Warden and Admiral of the Cinque Ports – the foundation of England's maritime power and birthplace of the embryonic Navy Royal, as it was known in Tudor times – Cobham, who was also a substantial landowner, wielded great power in the county and at Court.

A well-known Cobham family group portrait shows him as a stern, confi-

'William Brooke, Lord Cobham, was a man of immense power and influence both at Court and in Kent'

dent Elizabethan nobleman. Born William Brooke on 1 November 1527, he was the eldest son of George, ninth Baron Cobham and his wife Anne, herself the daughter of a nobleman. He was enrolled at Queen's College, Cambridge, with an exhibition from King's School, Canterbury, but went to Italy on the Grand Tour.

He succeeded to the Barony on the death of his father in 1558, and proved to be adept – unlike some of the Brookes – at avoiding political mantraps, even when temporarily finding himself backing the wrong side.

Life at the top in the mid-16th Century required considerable acumen and dexterity in tip-toeing through the maze of complex succession intrigues, religious, domestic and foreign policy issues. Henry VIII's break with Rome and his failure to sire an effective long-term male heir, had created rifts and schisms that would take decades to heal. The brief reign of his only son Edward and the even briefer occupancy of the English throne by Jane, 'The Nine Days Queen', and then the tempestuous five-year rule of Catholic Mary, naturally caused great uncertainty and juggling of loyalties that did not end with the coronation of Queen Elizabeth I.

In a sense, throughout that time the Brookes had managed to have a foot in both camps. When Sir Thomas Wyatt led his Kentish rising involving Cobham's uncles against Bloody Mary, William had retreated into Cooling Castle, now the home of Jools Holland, one of today's Deputy Lieutenants.

Cobham surrendered, but escaped to London. The influence of his in-laws, the Nevilles, stopped proceedings against two of his uncles, even though his marriage to Dorothy, daughter of George Neville, third Baron Abergavenny, who had been, briefly, Henry VIII's Lieutenant in Kent, had broken down.

Again, in 1571, the Brookes were to dice with danger. It was a period of international intrigue and Cobham, exercising his offices of Lord Warden and Constable of Dover Castle, succumbed to a plea by his younger brother Thomas to keep apparently incriminating Ridolfi Plot letters seized at the port, 'for he said they would otherwise be the undoing of the Duke of Norfolk and himself'.

Granting his brother's request was 'a perilous step for Cobham', especially as malicious rumour would claim – almost certainly without foundation – that he had offered the Cinque Ports for an invasion. Instead, his accidental involvement in the plot was 'treated with quite astonishing indulgence': seven months' house arrest; hardly a severe imposition for a wealthy man with an income rising to £5,000 a year, a sprawling mediaeval mansion at Cobham – now an independent school for girls, and a substantial town house at Blackheath.

His background was immensely privileged. He was well connected within the labyrinthine Tudor era network of titled families of noble and landed gentry. At Elizabeth's court he had the ear of the Queen herself and of the leading players on the political stage. Such influence gave him a succession of key appointments, the ability to dispense considerable patronage, and extraor-

1558
Calais is lost; death of Mary I; Elizabeth I ascends the throne

1576
William Lambarde publishes his Carde of Beacons

1585
War with Spain as England supports Netherlands' rebellion against Spanish rule

1587
Execution of Mary Queen of Scots; Francis Drake 'singes the King of Spain's beard' at Cadiz

1588
The Armada sails

ABOVE: Jools Holland, in his uniform as one of today's Deputy Lieutenants, at his Cooling Castle home, ancestral seat of the Brooke family

dinary power in his home county of Kent – including control of the Cinque Ports parliamentary seats.

It was said by Lord Howard during the Armada crisis that at Dover, with his long-standing appointment as Lord Warden and Constable of Dover Castle, 'they rely so upon my Lord Cobham, that without his warrant they will do nothing'.[14]

So it was that, as the mighty Armada gathered in Spanish and Portuguese ports, Elizabeth's Lieutenant in Kent was the ideal man to put the defences of the Frontline County in good order.

In October 1587 the Privy Council wrote to Cobham:

The Queenes Majesty beinge sundrie waies at this present enformed of the great preparations nowe presentlie made readie in Spayne for the furnitureof a mightie armie with a navie to come presentlie into the Seas and haveinge great cause to doubt not of some attempte; it is most necessarye that the whole realme sholde be forthwith well guarded and in readiness in such strength as God hath given unto Her Majesty both by land and sea…

'They rely so upon my Lord Cobham, that without his warrant they will do nothing'

The letter, requiring Cobham to report urgently on the strength of the Kentish forces, would have come as no surprise. Reports of Spanish preparations for an invasion of England had been reaching the Privy Council since the beginning of 1584, and Cobham's early duties as Lieutenant of Kent were to report in detail on the strength and state of readiness of the Frontline County's forces. The report he submitted to the Privy Council was positive:

> There are trained in this county 2,500 men and put under captains; to which His Lordship hath added 700 more with the good liking of the county. 300 horse put in readiness under captains; to each captain 50, with a lieutenant, trumpet, cornet and all in suitable cassocks. There are appointed to each company of 300 trained men, 50 pioneers; and to every company of 200 men, 39 pioneers furnished under the leading of the head constables of the place where they are levied, and to every companie two carts. The Justices will see 300 shot mounted upon ordinarie nags for the firing of the beacons, viz. 50 out of each lath.

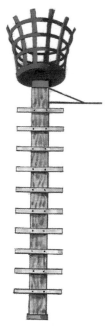

Early beacons were merely piled brushwood, but by the time of the Armada threat most were iron baskets containing 'pitch pots' atop poles

The report added that the Justices had agreed to find petronels – large pistols as used by mounted men. Cobham and his Deputy Lieutenants then sent orders for the intensification of military preparations throughout the county including the setting of watches from Sheppey to Sandgate, and for putting the beacon system into a state of readiness.

The beacons were the early warning system used since ancient times to transmit warnings of danger. Today's instant satellite communications make it difficult for us to visualise a time when the fastest means of alerting the country to an imminent invasion threat was to set fire to piled brushwood; when written messages had to be sent via horseback and foot-soldiers trudged their way to the scene of action at no more than four miles an hour.

In his *A Perambulation of Kent Written in the Yeere 1570*, which was not published in printed form until 1576, the antiquarian and lawyer William Lambarde wrote:

Kent's light cavalry or 'horse' were armed with the petronel, a large pistol kept in a holster attached to the saddle

> As in warre celeritie availeth no lesse than force itself, so the Right Honorable Sir William Brooke, Lord Cobham, and Lord Chamberlaine of hir Majesties household (who hath been sole Lieutenant of this shyre since the first of hir Majesties raigne), fore-seeing how necessarie it was to have the forces of the countrie speedily draw together, for the encounter of any hostilitie: and finding, that upon the fiering of the Beacons (which are erected for that service) not only the common sort, but even men of place and honour, were ignorant which way to direct their course, and thereby through amasednesse are likely to run from the place affected, as to make the succour of it, caused the true plaes of the beacons to be plotted in card, with directorie lines; so many sundrie waies, as any of them did respect

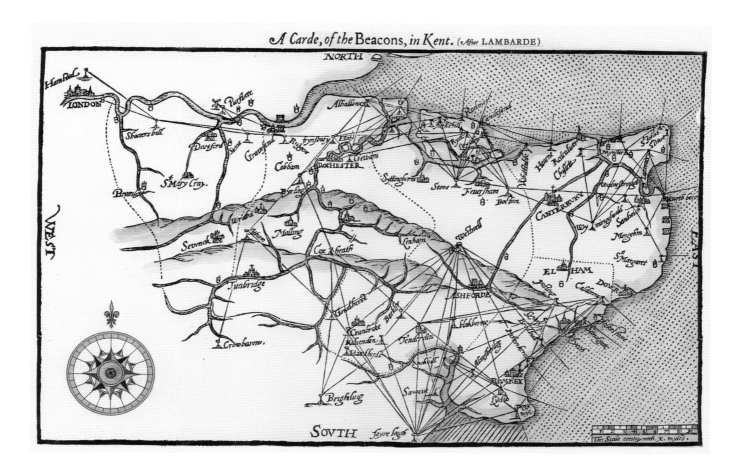

A Carde, of the Beacons, in Kent. (*After* LAMBARDE)

the other; by which any man, with little labour, may be assured where the danger is, and thereof informe his neighbours.

For example: suppose our first beacon, standing on Shooters-hill, to be light: he that will go thither may know by the watchman from whence they received their light; which must be either from the west neare London, or Hamstede; or else from the east, by warrant of the fiered beacon at Stone neare Dartford; of that which is neare to Gravesende.

In later years publication of such a map – showing the 52 sites of the Tudor version of our early warning system – might have become a matter for the D Notice Committee and might even have led to a prosecution under the Official Secrets Act.

But Lambarde, with Cobham's backing, was adamant that it was more important for the defenders to know where the beacons were and how they were linked in order to speed the mustering of forces than to worry about what benefit the map *might* be to invaders. He argued:

And now; if any man shall thinke, that this laying open of the Beacons, is a

Lightly armed horsemen, known as hobelers or hobeliers, were used along with the beacon system to spread warnings of invasion

William Lambarde, historian and lawyer, and producer of the controversial Carde of Beacons

point not meete to bee made publike: I pray him to give me leave to dissent in that opinion from him. For, as the profit to the Realme and subject is manifest, in that it speedeth the service, where speed is most profitable: so there is no secret hereby disclosed, whereof the enimie may take advantage, seeing that beacons stand open to the eie, and all men know the end for which they be advanced, though few know the best use and advantage of them. Yea rather, the enimie is prevented, when he seeth that we can and do make so good and readie use of our Beacons.

Speedie knowledge of the danger, is all alike profitable... otherwise it must follow that there will be no use for the beacons at all: which if it be, the countrie might well be delivered of that continuall and great charge, which it sustaineth by the watching of them.

But as (no doubt) the necessitie of them is apparent: so were it good, that for the more speedie spreading of the knowledge of the enimies coming, they were assisted with some horsemen (anciently called of their hobies or nags, Hobeliers) that besides the fire (which in a bright shining day is not so well descried) might also run from Beacon to Beacon, and supply that notice of the danger at hande.[15]

In early times beacons were piled brushwood, but in Lambarde's day tall poles were used with an iron basket at the top in which pitch could be burnt. Detailed instructions concerning the watch and firing of the beacons were issued by Cobham and he was also involved in a complex legal dispute with the men of Lydd, who challenged his order for them to provide a constant watch as being too much of a drain on local resources.

However, that was a mere irritant, and generally throughout the county preparations were well under way, with the Deputy Lieutenants and captains ensuring that troops could quickly be at readiness to march with their arms and equipment 'to such places as occasions shall require to withstand all manner of attempts by anie enemie.'[16]

The stage was set. The most powerful armada ever assembled was making its way up Channel and the fate of England hung in the balance. But Kent stood ready.

~ THREE ~

'THE SPANISH DID INTEND TO LAND AT DUNGENESS'

From Dungeness in the west to the North Foreland in Thanet, beacons flared and the warning was quickly taken up by others in the line of sight until Kent was criss-crossed with news of the Armada's approach.

The alert was hardly a surprise. In reality the coming of the Spaniards had been so long-awaited, certainly since Elizabeth's exhortation to her Lieutenants nine months earlier to place their counties at readiness, that the only unknown was the precise timing of its appearance in the Channel.

The Spanish plan was simple. Philip II's Armada was to sweep English resistance from the Channel and allow the Duke of Parma's Netherlands-based army to cross in barges. But as other later would-be invaders including Napoleon and Hitler have learned to their cost, its execution would be far from simple.

Preparations in the Armada's main embarkation port of Lisbon and other Iberian Peninsula harbours had been dogged by problems of command, bad

Far on the deep the Spaniards saw

Along each southern shore

Cape beyond cape in endless range

Those twinkling spots of fire...

Lord Macaulay

A contemporary playing card showing Drake's ships harassing the Armada

weather, desertion and disease, which forced the planned January 1588 sailing to be delayed.

What has been claimed as the greatest logistical operation of the 16th Century continued into July before the huge Armada sailed – vessels ranging from mighty galleons, galleasses and rowed galleys to pinnaces used for communications and a score of stores ships. Manning them were 7,000 mariners and on board were more than 17,000 soldiers.

Off the Cornish coast the defenders were gathering. The Lord High Admiral of England, Lord Howard of Effingham, took command of the combined Western squadron of 90 ships. His Vice-Admiral was Francis Drake, the man who had 'singed the Spanish King's beard' with his attack on Cadiz in 1587, delaying the projected invasion of England by a year. Frobisher and Hawkins were there too, and although the English were heavily outnumbered by the Spanish numerically they were more closely balanced in terms of effective fighting ships.

A squadron of 30 ships under Lord Seymour was stationed in the Downs off the Kentish coast.

At this critical time Kent was without its main military commander. As both Lieutenant of the Frontline County and Warden of the Cinque Ports, Lord Cobham was arguably the most influential and powerful guarantor of the nation's cross-Channel defences. But he was taken out of Kent for another mission – sent with others as special ambassadors to the Duke of Parma in the Low Countries where the Spanish commander was marshalling the invasion army ready for action when the Armada had secured the Straits of Dover.

The decision to remove Cobham at such a time cannot have been an easy one, but it reveals how highly he was valued and what trust was now placed in him at the highest levels.

The negotiations with Parma had been initiated by Sir James Croft, but,

> …whereas Croft went beyond his instructions in trying to negotiate peace by offering concessions, Cobham soon advised the mission's termination. Thus he was unavailable during the Armada crisis…[1]

Fortunately Kent was not left leaderless: cometh the hour, cometh the man, and Cobham had chosen his Deputy Lieutenants with care. Sir Thomas Scott and Sir James Hales were to command the eastern division, with his brother Sir Henry Cobham and Sir Thomas Fane in the west. Of them, Scott was to play the key role in the unfolding drama.

The Queen's spymaster Sir Francis Walsingham had received reports from agents that the Spanish 'armie of fflanders' was being prepared and if the Armada could secure command of the narrows, Kent – and in particular Sheppey, Thanet and the beaches from Hythe to Dungeness – was the obvious and convenient launch-pad en route to London.

Kent's contribution towards the defence of country at this time was greater than any other, with subscribers putting up £5,025 compared to the £4,535 pledged by the next highest, Sussex, and a mere £900 from Cornwall. Contributors included yeomen and townsmen as well as the county gentry and the totals give some indication of the population and comparative wealth of the counties at the time.[2]

Lord Cobham had been scrupulous in putting his county on a war footing. Two years before the coming of the Armada he had reminded the justices of the shire of their duty:

> To provide petronells, to watch the beacons, to disarm all ill-affected persons, to prevent rumours and to make sure in the viewing and training of the men that a proportion of the archers was transferred to muskets.[3]

As late as April 1588 the county sent a return to the Privy Council detailing the number of weapons available for its foot-soldiers as:

Muskets and calivers (infantry handguns)	6354
Corsletts (armour for a pikeman)	1762
Bowes	1662
Bills and halberds	1189

The return demonstrates the ascendency of the musket but also shows that the English longbow that had dominated Continental battlefields for so long was far from dead.

The coastal forts were inspected, training of the shot (foot soldiers armed with firearms) was ordered to be carried out by the corporals in every band on the holy days after prayer, and an express warning was issued that those who had become retainers to noblemen and gentlemen were not to be exempt from service in the trained bands 'no matter to whom they belong.' Constables of the hundreds were charged with viewing 'all between the ages of 16 and three score years, except spiritual persons, the lame and impotent.'

Kent led the way. The defensive procedures followed in this most important of the maritime counties were used as model instructions elsewhere, as in Northamptonshire, where the Lord-Lieutenant sent his Deputy Lieutenants a copy in order that they should know 'precisely what the forme of theire traynynge' was to be.[4]

Cobham's *Directions for the Musters in Kent* gave detailed instructions to the captains for the mustering and exercising of the trained bands in the lathes of Sutton at Hone, Aylesford, Scray, St Augustine's, Shepway, and in Canterbury, Rochester, Sheppey and Thanet.

He named the commanders, assigned them places to rendezvous when invasion threatened and reported that consideration had been given to 'all

The English longbow was being superseded by matchlock firearms for the infantry – the caliver, left, and the longer and heavier musket, which required a forked rest to steady it while firing

'All between the ages of 16 and three score years, except spiritual persons, the lame and impotent were eligible to serve'

RIGHT: This image of members of musketeers of the London Trained Bands at Sir Philip Sidney's state funeral shows them at their smartest. Their Kentish counterparts were less well-trained and probably somewhat scruffier – and their *untrained* comrades were ragamuffins, armed with little better than farm implements, and were likely to have been of dubious value in battle

places of descent', although these had not been thoroughly viewed. However, he was specific with his instructions concerning the most probably potential landing areas such as the Isle of Sheppey.

If an attempt were to be made there, he ordered that the three trained bands numbering 700 under John Cobham, Thomas Fane and John Leveson were to hasten there, followed by general bands within reach; and:

> For their more convenient and spedie passage into the Ile, all the baotes of Gillingham, Rochester and Milton are appointed to transporte them.

Sir Thomas Scott, with Edward Boys and Henry Palmer and the 700-strong trained bands from the lathes of Shepway and St Augustine's, were assigned along with the local – untrained – bands to oppose any landing between Sheppey and Dover. Scott, with Sir Richard Baker and 600 men of the trained bands backed by the local untrained men, was also ordered to resist any attempt between Folkestone and Rye.

Cobham ordered the residue of the trained bands not near any enemy landing to remain at their rendezvous until directed forward, lest if 'all ronne to one parte of the Shire the enemye give attempte upon some other.' Beacons were to be erected and watched, Justices of the Peace were to disarm 'papistes and suspected persons', and a general order was made that only 'such as are farmers or owners or their sons' were to be enrolled in the trained bands – all of whom were to swear an oath of loyalty at the musters. The rationale was that such men with a vested interest in the land and maintaining stability could be trusted to do their duty more so than common labourers, and were therefore worth extended training and better arms. Nevertheless:

> It is important to remember that the phrase trained band meant a band

that was to be trained, not a band that *had* been trained. In fact, the training was both infrequent and inadequate.[5]

Finally, Cobham reported that he had written to all towns to make provision of powder and match, stored and ready for distribution and use.

Command of Kent's defence forces was delegated by Cobham to Sir Thomas Scott, because he could be relied upon to do all that was necessary to counter the threatened invasion. He wanted to deploy his 4,000 men along the coast, but others prevailed to whom it made greater sense to mass the Kentish Militia, and await intelligence of Spanish intentions rather than spreading them too thinly. The plan was for the coastal forces to delay the enemy for as long as it took for the inland forces to intercept and prevent him marching on the capital.

Scott's portrait shows a confident man of distinguished, if perhaps rather haughty good looks, with close-cropped hair, high forehead and sideburns that continued into a narrow, neatly-trimmed beard and moustache. As befitted a senior commander and man of considerable wealth, he is wearing richly engraved armour and a fashionable ruff – every bit the Elizabethan gentleman soldier.

He was a remarkable man and if there had been no Cobham he could easily have assumed the mantle of Lord-Lieutenant in Kent, where he had an extensive power base. His success as a commissioner both for the improvement of sea defences between Romney, Lydd and Dungeness and for the construction of Dover harbour had led his contemporaries to dub him 'Father of Romney Marsh and the Founder of Dover Haven.'

> In the county and in Parliament he was ever attentive to his duty; as a magistrate he was wise, just and indefatigable… Possessing such an exalted and at the same time so amiable a character, it is no wonder that he had no known enemy in England… he said little, but when called upon he was eloquent as well as wise.[6]

He had rebuilt his ancestral home, Scot's Hall, a grand mansion at Smeeth (which was pulled down in 1808), and at 53 was a man of many parts. Knighted in 1571, he was a former High Sheriff, Knight of the Shire in two Parliaments and – according to the Scott family's chronicler – was the largest landowner in the county, 'being possessed of upwards of thirty, or parts of thirty, manors in that county alone, besides other lands in Sussex and Essex.'[7]

Scott was known for his generous hospitality, his home a magnet for the many 'who came from affection, duty and business', and 'his Christmasses were beyond belief splendid.' By his first wife Elizabeth, daughter of Sir John Baker, of Sissinghurst Castle, Sir Thomas had fathered 17 children 'all virtuous' and all of whom – remarkably for that time – survived infancy. He was also an expert horseman and author of an influential report on the desirability of improving the breed of English horses.

Sir Thomas Scott, commander of Kent's anti-Armada forces

Sir Thomas Scott was rightly dubbed: 'Father of Romney Marsh and the Founder of Dover Haven'

His skill in whatever related to war was so great, especially in horsemanship, that he was fixed upon to govern the camp at Northbourne, where he acquired great commendation.

He also had an intimate knowledge of the coastal early warning system. Nineteen years before the Armada he had been appointed with Lord Cobham and others as a commissioner for the defence of the coast:

> …concerting arrangements for the firing of beacons throughout Kent, and providing 'hobelers' – light horsemen – to act as scouts night and day, to give the earliest warning of the approach of a hostile fleet then expected from the coast of Spain. The Commissioners met at Ashford on 1ˢᵗ October 1569 (OS), and the report made on this occasion to the Privy Council, is a long and careful document, and many precedents embodied therein were, upwards of two centuries afterwards, considered and adopted, when a descent on the English coast was in contemplation by the first Emperor Napoleon.[8]

It was that experience as a commissioner that made him an ideal choice to command the Kentish forces gathered at the Downs Camp when the Armada threatened, and he won praise for 'the expedition with which he equipped and assembled four thousand men on… the day following the receipt by him of letters from the Privy Council.'[9] Gathering such a sizeable force so speedily was a remarkable feat considering the relatively primitive communications, both in sending out the call to arms and the travel time involved, that existed at the time.

It was no doubt Scott's energy and powers of command exhibited at that time of peril that inspired one of the verses of his apt epitaph:

> When any servis shold be doun,
> He liked not to lyngar,
> The rich wold ride, the poor wold runn,
> If he held up his finger

29 JULY
Armada enters the Western Approaches; running battle ensues up-Channel

5 AUGUST
Kentish forces make a show of strength on the Downs as the Spaniards pass

7 AUGUST
English fireships attack the Armada anchored at Calais

9 AUGUST
The storm-battered Armada is pursued up the North Sea

18 AUGUST
Nevynson meets Drake on board Revenge at Margate

19 AUGUST
Scott's report that the greater half of the Armada is defeated reaches the Privy Council at Tilbury; but Elizabeth I still makes her defiant 'heart and stomach of a king' speech

Dates here are given in the New Style

As the invasion threat heightened the vital importance of coordinating defence of the southern maritime counties had led to the appointment of Sir John Norris as Royal Commander-in-Chief over Kent, Sussex, Hampshire, Dorset, Essex, Suffolk and Norfolk. He favoured an orderly retreat in the event of a landing, and to counter-attack when it suited the defenders. Scott, who preferred 'answering of the enemy at the seat of fire before they can be with any forces on land' resented the overall command being given to Norris – and what he saw as a change in strategy – and took up his pen to complain about the plan and about a force of 2,000 foot leaving the county 'to guard the Queen's

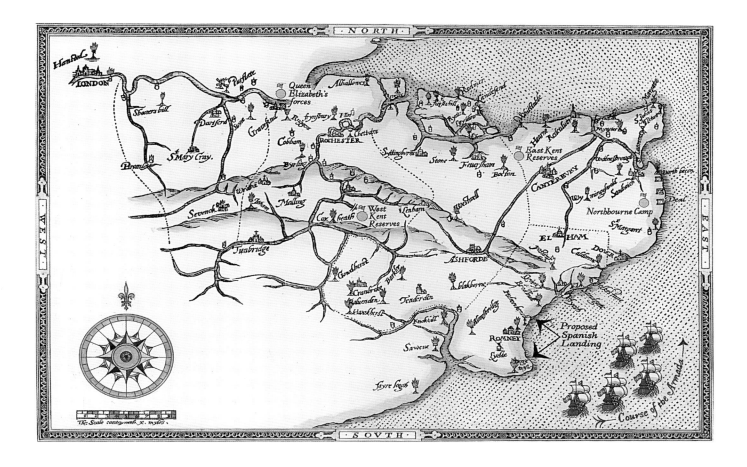

person'.[10] One of the captains of this force was Sir Robert Sidney, ancestor of today's Lord-Lieutenant, Viscount De L'Isle. Scott wrote:

> Whereas by occasion Sir John Norreys and wee ourselves were much busied yesterday in viewing, martialling and trayning of the most part of the select and trained bands of this county… it was not remembered to answer a letter sent by the Lords of the Council a good tyme synce conceryning the sending forth of 2,000 out of the county to attend Her Majesty's person and 4,000 to make head against the enemy after he is landed. In answere whereof we are nowe bound to signifie unto your good lordshipps we thincke it verie meete that out of the number of 2,500 trayned soldiers, 200 of the best to be sent to attend Her Majesty and 500 of the worst to be drawn equally out of everie band and left to join with the other bands to the 4,000 we verily thincke may be sent to make head as aforesaid.

Scott was quite naturally concerned at so large a force being taken out of the county should Kent's coast be attacked. He clearly thought the best way to protect the Queen was to oppose the enemy on the coast rather than wait

Pikemen of the trained bands. Only one in eight of foot soldiers at the Northbourne Camp was properly trained

to hit them as they advanced on London. Despite his misgivings, he was ordered to concentrate his force at Northbourne, where he gathered 500 foot-soldiers fully armed and trained with musket and pike, and 3,500 armed, but untrained, foot. The untrained men were armed with a hotchpotch of bows, pikes, halberds, billhooks – normally used for hedge laying – and a variety of early firearms including the already obsolete arquebus.

In addition there were 713 horsemen, armed with a variety of lances and firearms and led by Sir James Hales, and the force was supported by 1,077 pioneers – labourers who could be used for everything from digging latrines to throwing up earthwork defences or carrying loads, but were not equipped for fighting.

Some 2,020 East Kent reserves were held between Canterbury and Faversham, and the West Kent reserves of 2,800 gathered to the south of Maidstone.

From the Downs Camp Scott could march his men westward to Dungeness or eastward to Thanet or Sheppey in little more than a day – and the beacons and associated horse-back hobeler early warning messenger system should give them time enough to deploy. However,

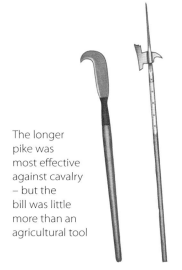

The longer pike was most effective against cavalry – but the bill was little more than an agricultural tool

> …had the Spaniards landed where Scott was prepared to meet them, the planned orders were that both Scott and Hales should retreat from the seat of fire once contact had been made and then join the reserve force of over 2,000 from East Kent, who were then assembling at Canterbury. Both forces were to meet either there or at Ashford.[11]

With a mere one in eight of the men at Northbourne assessed as fully effective, the camp seethed with activity as Scott's captains strove to instil rudimentary training into men who only a few days earlier had been labouring in the fields or following their trades in towns and villages throughout the county. While they drilled, unknown to them a great drama was being played out at sea.

The 'Invincible Armada' had entered the Channel, its great three-decked Spanish galleons dwarfing the defending English ships such that eyewitnesses spoke of them as giant floating castles. But they were fatally flawed. Their towering superstructures with raised gun-decks made them vulnerable to attack from their smaller, lower opponents.

For days the English warships shadowed, harassed and fought a series of battles with the Armada, picking off what they could. Then, on 5 August, Scott reported to the Secretary of State, Lord Burghley, that the Spanish fleet having been seen off Boulogne, he had 'drawn all the forces within two miles of the shore, to make a show upon the Downs in sight of the enemy.' He also warned that the Isle of Thanet, still thought of as a likely invasion target, lacked its military commanders and was vulnerable.[12]

The Halberdier was effective against horse or men at arms

However, the situation was rapidly swinging in England's favour. The fresh Eastern Squadron under Lord Seymour that had been guarding the straits joined battle. And on the night of 7 August and the early hours of the following day fireships were sent among the Spanish at Calais, driving the Armada from its anchorage.

Before it could reform, five Spanish ships became embroiled in a fierce battle with the English off Gravelines. Others joined in and fearful damage was inflicted before a strong north-westerly wind threatened to force the Spaniards to destruction on the shoals.

They headed into the North Sea and with the wind now swinging round to a hard south-westerly they headed northward, pursued by the English, except for Seymour's Eastern Squadron which was held back to guard against any attempted crossing Parma might make from the Low Countries, however unlikely that now was. Effectively the invasion threat was dead, although those ashore did not yet know.

Although the Kentish forces in the Downs camp had seen for themselves that the great Armada had arrived up-Channel and made their show of defiance on the clifftops, there was still no reliable news. Rumour and counter-rumour flew, and Scott sent his scoutmaster – in modern terms his chief intelligence officer – Sir Thomas Nevynson to Thanet to try to discover what was happening.

Nevynson, whose home was in nearby Eastry, was not only the Lieutenancy's Scoutmaster for East Kent, but also Provost Marshal and captain of the light horse for the Lathe of St Augustine's, from the area around Canterbury. So he was not only gatherer of intelligence but the Kentish force's policeman, appointed to punish by martial law both civil and military offenders in such times of emergency, and also commanded a unit of light cavalry – each a demanding enough role in itself.

He rode to Margate where he found Drake's flagship, the 46-gun galleon *Revenge*. Drake, already famous as the first English circumnavigator of the world and for the Cadiz raid, had sensational news: mauled all the way up-Channel, severely damaged by the fireships off Calais, and battered by gales, the mighty Armada had been pursued in complete disarray up the North Sea.

The immediate invasion threat was well and truly over. And despite all the rumours, claims and counter-claims then and later, Nevynson reported that Drake revealed to him, presumably from information obtained from prisoners, what Parma's true intention – by now clearly an impossibility with the Armada wounded and scattered and the English firmly in control of the Channel – had been.

As was already known, the plan had been to seize control of the narrows and embark his troops from the Netherlands. What was not known but now revealed was that Parma intended to land at Dungeness, create a beachhead resupplied from the Continental ports, and march on London. The scoutmas-

This Elizabethan propaganda playing card shows the English making a show of strength as the Armada passed

Sir Thomas Nevynson

Sir Francis Drake

ter hastened back to Northbourne to report Drake's sensational news that the Spanish had been severely mauled, chased beyond Scotland and were highly unlikely to be able to pose a further threat to England that summer.

Scott wrote immediately to his cousin the Earl of Leicester encamped at Tilbury where he had gathered 17,000 men to counter the expected Spanish approach to the capital:

My especial good Lord

Being certified this morning by Mr Nevenson, our scoutmaster, who was on board this last night with Sir Francis Drake at Margate, that Sir Francis did inform him that the Spanish army did intend to land at Dungeness, near Lydd, and there to entrench themselves, and to be supplied from time to time out of France with victuals and all necessaries, I have thought it very meet to certify your Lordship thereof, to the intent that I, by your Lordship's directions, may draw either the forces here, or some part thereof, towards that place when your Lordship shall think it meet.

Hindsight confirms that in view of Drake's report such a re-deployment was totally unnecessary, but at the time there could be no absolute certainty that Parma would not make some attempt by barges despite the Armada's defeat. Scott described Dungeness in unflattering terms:

The nature of the place is as followeth:- Lying between New Romney and Rye Camber; compassing about in manner of a half island; good harbour for ships at all winds except one point, which I take to be some part of the north; four miles in breadth; very deep at the shore, whereby men may be landed without help of longboats; this half island containeth by estimation six or seven thousand acres, all of loose beach. The next ground adjoining to the same consisteth of 50 thousand acres of marsh, inhabited with few other than shepherds and herdsmen; so as it is a place of all this shire farthest from aid of men, and the greatest desert.

Sir Francis Drake reporteth that the greater half of the Spanish Navy is defeated, and that, so far as his judgment and skill doth serve, he left them so far beyond the farthest point of Scotland as they cannot return to do any hurt in England this summer. Nevertheless, he will not warrant it but that they may return.

Here are landed at Margate, as I am informed, six or seven hundred musketeers out of the Low Countries. We humbly pray your Lordship's direction for them, and that they may be joined to this camp here, except your Lordship have otherwise disposed them. And so, recommending your good Lordship to the protection of the Almighty, I most humbly take my leave.

From the camp at Northbourne, this 9th of August (OS), in haste, 1588.
Yours Lordship's to command during life,
Thomas Scott.[13]

It has been argued that Nevynson must have misunderstood what he had been told about Dungeness being the Spaniards' intended landing site, as by then 'Drake knew perfectly well that they had no such intention.' That may well have been the case, but although the Armada was scattered the possibility of Parma attempting an invasion could not have been totally ruled out at the time. In any event, it is clear from Drake's report that Dungeness *had* been the intended invasion point, even if a landing was by then no longer viable.

Queen Elizabeth appeared at Tilbury on 18 August to the firing of a royal salute, the shrill of fifes and beating of drums, and the cheers of her soldiers gathered there to defend the capital and their Sovereign.

> 'The barrier of boats intended for use as a carriageway for troops to cross from Tilbury Fort to Gravesend should Kent be the point of invasion (as, of course, it was intended to be) was not yet complete.'[14]

The following day, mounted on a white palfrey horse, wearing white velvet and a silver breastplate she appeared among her troops, many of whom had been sent there from Kent.

The scene has been captured by many an artist and film-maker and heavily romanticised. But there is no doubt that it was a highly dramatic episode, described by contemporary historian William Camden, who may well have been present, or certainly have heard from eyewitnesses. He wrote: 'Her presence and her words fortified the courage of the captains and soldiers beyond all belief.'

The rank and file would not have had detailed knowledge of the Armada's fate, but the Queen and her Privy Councillors certainly did, having received Drake's report via Nevynson and Scott before the Tilbury review and reliable intelligence from Seymour and others.

Nevertheless, her oratory clearly fired up her soldiers just as Churchill's wartime speeches rallied the nation almost four centuries later – and still reverberates down the years. Elizabeth opened by placing her complete trust in her soldiers and people, thus endearing herself to them:

My loving people, we have been persuaded by some that are careful of our

THE OATHE OF A TRAYNED SOULDIER

'I ---- ---- doe utterlye testifie in my conscience that Queene Elizabeth if the only supreme governour of this her realme of England, and of all other her dominions as well in Exclisiasticall as temperall causes, and that no forene person hath or ought to have any manner of power within any of the same.

And I doe promise that from henceforth I shall bear faythe and true allegiance to Her Majesty, her heirs and lawfull successors. And that in the place and dutie of a souldier I will readily and faithfully serve Her Majesty against all her enemies, traytors, rebels whatsoever aswel in this realme, and for the preservation of her said person as also for the safetie of any her Realmes or dominions, so often as I shalbe thereunto appointed by Her Majesty, or by suche as shalbe lawfully auctorised under her in that behalf. So help me God through Jhesus Christe.'

safety, to take heed how we commit our self to armed multitudes, for fear of treachery; but I assure you, I do not desire to live to distrust my faithful and loving people. Let tyrants fear. I have always so behaved myself, that, under God, I have placed my chieftest strength and safeguard in the loyal hearts and good will of my subjects, and therefore I am come amongst you, as you see, at this time, not for my recreation or disport, but being resolved, in the midst and heat of the battle, to live or die amongst you all; to lay down for my God, for my kingdom, and for my people, my honour and my blood, even in the dust. I know I have the body but of a weak and feeble woman, but I have the heart and stomach of a king, and a king of England, too, and think it foul scorn that Parma or Spain or any prince of Europe should dare to invade the borders of my realm; to which, rather than any dishonour shall grow by me, I myself will take up arms. I myself will be general, Judge and rewarded of every one of your virtues in the field. I know, already for your forwardness, you have deserved rewards and crowns; and we do assure you on the word of a prince, they shall be duly paid to you. In the mean time, my Lieutenant General shall be in my stead, than whom never prince commanded more noble or worthy subject, not doubting but that by your obedience to my General, by your concord in the camp and your valour in the field, we shall shortly have a famous victory over those enemies of my God, of my kingdom, and of my people.[15]

Her speech, in the version handed down, had everything: praise for and trust in her troops, a promise to reward them, and an emotional call to patriotic duty that none could ignore. It was a masterful exhortation and superb showmanship. The words may well have been embellished over the years, but certainly the only known eyewitness account by James Aske, although incomplete, confirms that the sentiments expressed and the pledge to march beside her men into battle *were* used in her iconic speech.

But of course, thanks in large part to Nevynson and the Kentish Deputy Lieutenant Sir Thomas Scott, her Privy Council was already well aware that the threat had passed. What was left of the mighty Armada was scattered to the four winds and there would be no invasion that year. Her 'famous victory' had already been won at sea. So was her exhortation simply an early example of political 'spin'?

If the Spaniards *had* managed to seize control of the Channel, establish a beachhead in Kent and bring troops across from the Low Counties, it would have been a close run thing. The Spanish troops were no doubt far better trained than the part-time, part-trained defenders. But Sir Thomas Scott in particular had already proved himself a resourceful commander, and he had all the advantages of home turf and could no doubt have inspired in his men the necessary determination to protect property and womenfolk.

It had not come to that, but nevertheless the Lieutenancies in Kent and elsewhere had done what was required of them in organising the defence of the counties and passed their first major test.

The fact that the command and control system had worked – coupled with the continuing Spanish threat – confirmed the county Lieutenancies' value and necessitated a move away from temporary arrangements to meet a specific or particular threat to a permanent quasi-military structure and chain of command in the counties.

The Lieutenancy's crucial involvement in defence of the realm at that critical time had confirmed its value beyond doubt and ensured its continuation. And so, with justification, William Brooke, Lord Cobham, is recorded by Hasted as the first *permanent* Lord-Lieutenant of Kent.

'I know I have the body but of a weak and feeble woman, but I have the heart and stomach of a king'

Queen Elizabeth's exhortation

ABOVE: Kent's first permanent Lord-Lieutenant, William Brooke with his family. His son Henry was to succeed him, only to end up accused of treason

FOUR

'THE PRICE OF PEACE – ETERNAL VIGILANCE'

Although the immediate danger of invasion was over, the Spanish threat was to remain for a further 15 years and for Kent's Lord-Lieutenant and his Deputies 'the price of peace seemed, indeed, to have been eternal vigilance!'[1]

For now, there was a brief respite for some. In mid-August Sir John Norris, the Queen's overall commander in the south-eastern maritime counties, instructed Captain Roger Twysden (whose grandson of the same name features later in the Lieutenancy story) to take his horsemen home to the lower division of the lathe of Aylesford, as 'Her Majesty fears that Captain Twysden's horses will take great harme by living here aboute the campe.' And the Earl of Leicester wrote to Kent's Deputy Lieutenants telling them that the soldiers now in camp were to be disbanded for the harvest and replaced with a fresh body of foot from the south and west of the county, although officers were to continue in pay, with men 'planted on the sea coasts of Kent.'

So it was that the rank and file of the ragtag Kentish army that had stood ready to oppose a landing went back to the fields and their trades. A glimpse of the quality of these men as soldiers is given in the comments of a veteran on those, including 2,000 from Kent, sent to the camp at Tilbury:

> …there were regiments of divers shires with divers bands both of demilaunces and lighthorsemen I did see and observe so great disorder and deformitie in their apparrell to arme withal, as I saw but verie fewe of the armie that had anie convenience of apparel and chiefly of doublets to arm upon, whereof it came to pass that most of them did wear their armour verie uncomelie, uneasily… [2]

Yet, rough and amateurish as they looked in their ill-fitting odds and ends of armour and uniforms, they had been ready enough to defend Queen, county, hearth and home.

For the Lord-Lieutenant, now returned from his diplomatic mission, and his hard-working Deputy Lieutenants, there was no time to 'rest on their arms reversed.' Lieutenancy papers for the Armada aftermath are particularly full, reflecting the necessity to keep the county's defences in good order in case of further forays by the Spanish. Orders were issued that the 'shot' of the trained bands should each have two pounds of powder, two of lead and two rolls of match provided at their respective places of rendezvous, and captains of foot were to muster, every officer and soldier to be listed together with his 'furniture' (armour) and type of weapon.

Names of pioneers, owners of carts, and quantities of powder, match and bullet were all to be set down and the muster book was to be sent to the two Justices of the Peace who oversaw arrangements for the general muster of all the county's horse and foot, both trained and untrained men: Sir John Leveson, who was to become Cobham's chief Deputy Lieutenant, and William Lambarde, the county historian and creator of the famous 'Beacon Carde.' Lambarde was a close personal friend of the Lord-Lieutenant and as a magistrate was hearing what were then routine cases, such as bastardy, theft and even witchcraft, with Lord Cobham on a regular basis.

All property owners liable were to be taxed to pay for the county's defence, and constables were to report refusals to pay. Anyone still refusing to pay after being reported to the Deputy Lieutenants would be imprisoned until they *did* pay, and:

> …before his delivery he shall come to the next Quarter Sessions and there answer his contempt tending to the ill of this Her Majesty's service of so great importance.

The following year, at the time of another general muster, Lord Cobham was

TIMELINE

1588
The Armada is defeated and Kent's trained and untrained bands stand down

1591
The Lieutenancy of Kent renews repression of 'obdurate Catholics'

1594
Death of Sir Thomas Scott, the Deputy Lieutenant who led Kent's Armada defenders

1596
Shakespeare is forced by Cobham to change the name of his comic hero to Falstaff

1597
Death of Cobham, whose son Henry succeeds him as 11th Lord Cobham and Lord-Lieutenant of Kent

1599
Further Spanish invasion threat evaporates

1601
Kent Deputy Lieutenant Sir John Leveson defeats the Earl of Essex's revolt

1603
Queen Elizabeth dies and is succeeded by James I; Henry Brooke convicted of treason

ABOVE: Cobham Hall, home to William Brooke, Lord Cobham, whose son Henry lost the family estates on his conviction for treason. The mansion was gifted to Ludovic Stuart, Lord Lennox, who in 1620 was himself appointed Lord-Lieutenant of Kent. It is now an independent school for girls and the former deputy head teacher, Mrs Ann West, is a Deputy Lieutenant of Kent

told that the Queen 'certeintlie knows that the Kinge of Spayne hath all this yeare made grete preparations in building of newe shippes in all his north coast of Spain.' But in Kent the strong feeling was that the most dangerous time was past:

> This was apparent to Lord Cobham himself who, on one occasion in that year, asked (Sir Francis) Walsingham how Kent was to replace lost armour, observing that he saw more unwillingness in the county than inability to pay. He could make the last remark with justification for more than likely he was aware of the returns of the double subsidy in 1589 voted to make provision against further Spanish attack.[3]

Supervising tax collection for the defence of the realm was an unpopular enough task for the Lord-Lieutenant and his Deputies, but there were other – even less palatable – roles. Before the Act of Toleration which guaranteed religious freedom, the Lieutenancies were involved in the suppression of recusants, that is, non-attenders of Church of England services, and this involved seizing their arms and armour to lessen the threat from within in the event of a Catholic invasion from Spain or France.

This had happened during the Armada crisis when a general order went out for 'persons of standing and obdurate in Catholic belief' to be compelled to

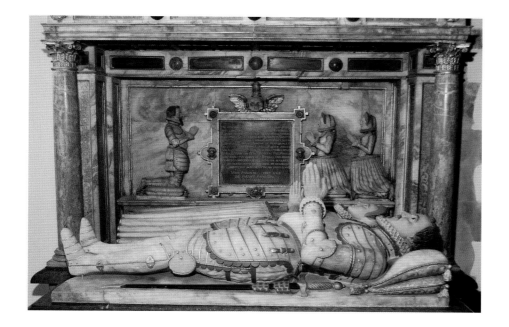

surrender their arms and armour. And now, although the immediate threat of invasion had evaporated, the repression of Catholics continued into the next decade. In December 1591 the Lord-Lieutenant was required to certify which children of recusant gentlemen had gone abroad in the previous seven years – and by whose authority. The Privy Council also ordered Cobham, his Deputy Lieutenants and the Bishops of Dover and Rochester to take action against seminary priests, Jesuits and recusants that:

> …doe harbour in theire howses any person or persons known to be backward in religion.

In the New Year Elizabeth commissioned Lord Cobham, the two bishops, Sir Roger Manwood, Sir John Leveson, William Lambarde and John Boys, were instructed to investigate recusancy in Kent. Suspects were 'not to be pressed on matters of conscience', but on church attendance. If found to be 'willfull recusants' they were to be examined on their loyalty to the Queen and:

> …their devotion to the Pope or to the Kinge of Spaine or upon the maintenance of any Jesuit, Seminarie priest or other person sent from Rome or from any partes beyond the seas, to disswade any subject from their obedience to the Queen's Majestie.[4]

The Lord-Lieutenant and his fellow commissioners were empowered to recruit 'persons loyall in religion' to aid them. Suspected recusant Catholics were duly traced and examined. One, Elizabeth Moninge, questioned on her loyalties, said it was 'a harsh question that never was asked of a woman befour',

COBHAM HALL

Cobham Hall, which is said to have cost Lord Cobham £60,000, was the most palatial Kentish mansion, and its park was 'a place which will feast the spectator's eyes with delightful objects. Fair lawns bedecked with flourishing groves of yew, oak, teal (linden or lime] and hawthorn trees, under which the nimble deer and coneys do sport the time away'

'A female Sovereign there may have been, but there was no hint of emancipation for women'

adding that she was 'a wife and under subjection and therefore of noe abilitie to give ayde' to the commissioners.

A female Sovereign there may have been, but there was no hint of emancipation for women then.

There are indications that at times the Kent Lieutenancy took a soft line with their neighbours who clung to the old religion, as indicated when three of the commissioners, Leveson, Twysden and Lambarde, called 12 suspected recusants to Leveson's house at Halling, telling them that they would be 'used friendly' and not pressed with the full examination 'so long as wee may be holden with any hope of a better mynde in yow'.[5]

The number of commissioners was greatly increased in 1592 and Sir John Leveson was at the centre of administration in disarming and arresting prominent recusants. A new commission was issued by the Privy Council that July and included three other Deputy Lieutenants: Armada defence veterans Sir Thomas Scott, Sir Thomas Fane and Cobham's son Henry.

The Lord-Lieutenant emphasised that the procedures followed in the Armada year were to be adopted again and recusants who did not conform one year after conviction were to be indicted, bound over to good behaviour – and disarmed.

Leveson reported to Lord Cobham how, accompanied by William Lambarde, he searched Thomas Watton's home at Addington and found various items of armour and weapons including a pike, a caliver (an infantry handgun 3½ feet long, fired without a rest) and a case of pistols. These arms, wrote Leveson, were lodged for safekeeping with Richard Clarke, of Offham, one of the Queen's footmen.

Two days later Leveson, accompanied by two fellow commissioners and the Sheriff, searched Henry Bosvile's house at Bradbourne. Here, there were richer pickings in arms and armour – enough to arm a dozen men:

> 6 corslets, 4 almain rivets, 4 swords, 5 daggers, seven bourgonnets with morrions, 5 calivers, 4 flaskes, 4 touchboxes, 3 jacks, and one coat of plate, 11 pikes, and a javelin and one breast of an Almain rivet.[6]

Again, the weapons and armour were confiscated and placed in safekeeping prior to their sale.

Similar searches 'for seminary priests, arms and armour' continued over the next few days, including the home of the Culpeppers at Bedgebury where a considerable stockpile of arms was found. Sir Alexander Culpepper was a well-known Catholic, and his son Anthony claimed that the arms belonged to him, not his father, but to no avail. They were confiscated regardless. Culpepper was among those effectively exiled from their homes, but he was back on his Kentish estate by 1596.

Searches of suspected recusant Catholics' houses were not always fruitful.

Leveson searched Thomas Wilford's house at Lenham and reported: 'we founde not any arms or warlike furniture.'

In December 1593 the Privy Council again ordered Lord Cobham to certify the children of recusant gentlemen who had gone abroad within the past seven years. This was considered of especial importance in Kent, on the main travel route between England and the Continent.

A month after Cobham had received the order his Deputies in each of Kent's lathes had received copies and by the end of January 1594 had submitted their reports. The speed with which this investigation was carried out county-wide indicates a well-run and efficient Lieutenancy administrative and executive machine in an age of relatively unsophisticated and slow communications. In the event, the reports revealed that only a small number of young people had gone abroad. Some suspected recusants travelling abroad were clearly not doing so innocently by Protestant England standards. Returns at Dartford included:

> Greenwich – William Baker is at this present a trumpeter to the French kinge. Crayford – Thomas Macarten, a notorious recusant fledde this realme… but in what countrie or citie he is or is imployed wee knowe not.[7]

Elsewhere, it was reported to Sir Thomas Scott that William Knatchbull of Mersham-le-Hatch had been abroad, 'to noe good purpose.'

Sir Thomas, the Deputy Lieutenant who had made the show of strength on the Kentish cliffs as the Armada passed, died aged 59 and 'much mourned' at the end of 1594, and was buried among his ancestors at Brabourne Church.

SALMON & GLUCKSTEIN LTD.

Falstaff   (Merry Wives of Windsor)

FALSTAFF

Cobham ancestor Sir John
Oldcastle was portrayed
by Shakespeare as a
drunken, lying, gluttonous
lecher, but the playwright
was forced to change his
famous comic character's
name to Falstaff when
the Lord-Lieutenant of
Kent was additionally
appointed Lord Chancellor,
holding power over the
playhouses. Falstaff's comic
image has continued to
be exploited down the
centuries – here on a
cigarette card

Despite his considerable services to nation and county, he had received no recognition from his Sovereign. The Scott family history records that:

> On the application made either by his brother-in-law, Lord Buckhurst, or by his cousin, Lord Robert Dudley, Earl of Leicester, to that monarch in recognition of his public services, that he should be enobled, the Queen petulantly declined, on the ground that Sir Thomas Scott had already more influence in Kent than Majesty herself.[8]

Ironically, for one who had searched suspected recusants' houses, Scott's own monument at Brabourne was totally destroyed by the Parliamentary forces during the Civil War, when Scot's Hall was searched for arms. His scoutmaster Nevynson, who had heard the news of the Armada's defeat from Drake himself, had died four years earlier and the fine memorial brass to him and his wife Anne can still be admired at St Mary's, Eastry.

For Cobham, now permanent Lord-Lieutenant of Kent, Lord Warden of the Cinque Ports and already a Privy Councillor and Knight of the Garter before the Armada crisis, there was further honour. In 1596, following the death of Henry Carey, Lord Hunsdon, he was appointed Lord Chamberlain, a role since described as 'the full-time managing director of the Royal Household.'[9]

Part of his role was supervision of the theatre and this led to a confrontation with William Shakespeare that has intrigued scholars ever since. Cobham was much less sympathetic than his predecessor to the theatrical profession, and was not amused when his ancestor Sir John Oldcastle was portrayed in *King Henry IV Part 1* as a drunken, lying, gluttonous lecher. There was added piquancy to the affair because the great dramatist was a member of the group of players known as the Lord Chamberlain's Men. They had begun a tour of Kent soon after Hunsdon's death and were playing at Faversham's market hall when 'once more they found themselves in an insecure profession.'

The new Lord Chamberlain,

> …had been alerted to the fact that the play's principal comic character was named Sir John Oldcastle, and may well have first seen the play in the presence of the queen at court. He was related to the original Oldcastle, and was not pleased with the farce surrounding the theatrical namesake. The real Oldcastle had been a supporter of the Lollards who had led an abortive insurrection against Henry V; subsequently he had been executed for treason.

> But he was considered by many to have been a proto-Protestant, and thus an early martyr to the cause of Reformation. His descendant did not approve of his presentation as a thief, braggart, coward and drunkard.[10]

Cobham complained to the Master of the Revels and Shakespeare was forced to change the name of the comic character from Oldcastle to Falstaff, in the second part of the play.

> It was in any case changed, and not without a certain humiliation on Shakespeare's part. In an epilogue to the second part of Henry IV he himself came upon the stage and announced that 'for any thing I knowe Fallstaffe shall die of a sweat, unless already a be killed with your harde opinions; for Oldcastle died a Martyre, and this is not the man…' Then he danced, and afterwards knelt for applause.[11]

Shakespeare was forced to appease Cobham, and even the great Bard himself ended up on a 'fag card'

In Kent, renewed fears of invasion by the Spanish in late 1596 brought fresh orders for the sequestration of recusant persons' horse and arms. Yet again, the Deputy Lieutenants were called upon to carry out these orders, but resulting action appears to have been limited and far less severe than before. This may have been attributable to the presence of comparatively few recusant Catholics living in Kent, the fact that the 'usual suspects' were well known to the Deputy Lieutenants and for the most part had already been brought to book at least once – and that as Elizabeth's reign was drawing to a close a more lenient line was being taken.

The 1596 invasion threat came and went. It was taken extremely seriously by the Lord-Lieutenant, who rode the coast himself to view the forts, and at the Privy Council's request 6,000 men were made ready in Kent to march:

> To suche landing places within the county as shall appear to your Lordshipp that the enemye have anie purpose to attempt to land in the same.[12]

The Queen wrote to Cobham commending his work both as Lord-Lieutenant and as Warden of the Cinque Ports and 'mentioned in particular his assiduous care in directing his deputies.'

Cobham's health declined and after suffering a winter 'ague' he died in March 1597, his friends Lambarde and Leveson paying tribute to him as 'the honourable father of our countie…'

Despite his will's rejection of 'vanity' there was a grand funeral procession through north Kent and he was buried at Cobham. He died a wealthy man, with an estimated £5,000 a year – at the time 'one of the greatest aristocratic incomes in England.'[13]

Shakespeare's reaction is unrecorded. But at Cobham's death, George Carey, the new Lord Hunsdon, was appointed Lord Chamberlain and became patron of the Lord Chamberlain's Men,

> The actor's winter under Cobham's rule had been turned to glorious summer with the son of their former patron and supporter.[14]

Henry Brooke, 11th Lord Cobham, succeeded his worthy father as Lord-Lieutenant of Kent, but was 'a worthless mortal', 'but one degree from a fool' and ended up in the Tower for plotting against the Monarch he was supposed to represent in the county

Inscribed on a marble mantle-piece erected by Henry Brooke, Lord Cobham, at Cobham Hall in 1599 was the prophetic Latin motto *Sibi quisque naufragium facit: Each man makes his own shipwreck*. Within four years Cobham fulfilled it, being found guilty of plotting against James I and incarcerated in the Tower of London

With their close connection to the Queen and the powerful Cecils, to whom they were linked through marriage, and with their wealth, power and influence in Kent '…Cobham's family seemed securely positioned . Unfortunately his sons Henry and George Brooke were to throw this away.'[15]

Throughout a long and distinguished career in an age when it was extremely difficult to remain detached from conflicting interests at court, William – although implicated to some extent in the Ridolfi plot in the 1570s – had otherwise managed to tiptoe through the minefield of Tudor politics relatively unscathed.

His son Henry was to prove far from sure-footed. And as Kent's new Lieutenant, although appointed to represent the Sovereign in the county, he was to find himself in conflict with her successor and in danger of losing his head.

Born at Cobham Hall the family seat in 1564, Henry Brooke was the second son of William and his second wife Frances, and is seen in the iconic family group portrait as a chubby toddler. He became his father's heir on the death of his eldest brother Maximilian in France in 1583, and all had promised well. From an immensely wealthy and privileged background, Henry himself travelled to Paris and the Low Countries, was entered at Gray's Inn the following year, and served as Member of Parliament for Kent at the time of the Armada.

He was 32 when he succeeded to the title as the 11th Lord Cobham and to his father's roles not only as Lord-Lieutenant of Kent, but also as Lord Warden. The Cinque Ports appointment caused great friction because the faction led by the Earl of Essex had wanted both offices, which carried with them considerable Parliamentary patronage, to go to the Brookes' Kentish rivals, the Sidneys. Sir Robert Sidney had been told that both offices 'are wished unto you by the gentlemen of Kent', and wrote telling Essex that the Wardenship in particular was 'the place in England that I have the greatest desire unto', adding that in his opinion Henry Brooke was totally unworthy of the honour and 'beloved of never a man in Kent.' But it was all to no avail and Sidney was passed over for both roles.[16]

However, instead of immediately appointing a new Lord-Lieutenant the Queen and Privy Council appointed commissioners for musters, two of whom had been Cobham's Deputy Lieutenants, as 'by the decease of our very good lord, the late Lord Chamberlain to her majestie there is no lieutenant at this present in the countie of Kent…'

The commissioners' immediate task was to have 1,000 men armed and ready in case the Cardinal of Austria's forces attacked Boulogne and posed any threat to England.

When Henry Brooke, the new Lord Cobham, was appointed Lord-Lieutenant and Lord Warden more than six months after his father's death, it was to cause great bitterness between him and the Essex faction.

But he immediately threw himself into his Lieutenancy work, writing from Dover within a day of his appointment:

> I have taken present order for the mustering of the whole forces of the shire of horses and foote. This day Sir Edward Wotton, Sir Thomas Wylford and myself arr going to viewe all the castles on the Downes.[17]

The following July the Privy Council wrote telling him that Spanish ships had made an attempt to land in the West Country and requiring him to report on the readiness of Kent's trained bands. Sir Walter Raleigh also wrote to Cobham about the Spanish move, signing himself off: 'I am yours before all that live.' It was a friendship that was to turn sour in the harsh light of subsequent events.

Instead of a serious Spanish invasion that year attention switched to Ireland where the Earl of Tyrone led a rebellion. Cobham's principal Deputy, Sir John Leveson, recruited and equipped 100 men in Kent for service in Ireland under the Earl of Essex, and others were raised to replace soldiers posted there from the Low Countries.

Yet another Spanish invasion was threatened in July 1599 and Cobham wrote, although ill and 'so feeble that I can write no more' offering such services as his father had performed 11 years earlier, and reporting an assurance that 'the French king would not suffer the Spanish to enter any of his ports.'

Still unwell, Cobham was forced to remain at his Blackfriars house as the Privy Council, attended in his place by Sir John Leveson, taking this latest threat extremely seriously, swung into action and assembled a sizeable army, instructing:

> …the men of Sussex to go to Sittingbourne by the 10th of this month, and those of Kent to assemble at Canterbury; for an army of 12,000 men to be drawn together in Kent, to consist of 6,000 from Kent, 4,000 from Sussex, and all the horse from Surrey, which are to be commanded by Sir Thos. Wilford, in the absence of the lieutenant (Cobham); the horse bands to be put in readiness; 3,000 men of London trained under Sir Thos. Gerard. Letters to be written for the rest of the forces to come near London, and be quartered in fit places, the force to consist of 13,500 to be drawn from London and eight neighbouring counties.[18]

Once again the threat evaporated but, on behalf of Kent, Cobham nevertheless was commended by the Queen via the Privy Council both for its efforts during the crisis and for 'the service of Irelande.' But not everyone shared the Queen's opinion of her Kentish Lieutenant.

The 11th Lord Cobham, Henry Brooke, appears to have held a high and arrogant view of his office as Lord-Lieutenant of the shire. This is evident in one of his letters to his brother-in-law, Sir Robert Cecil, written in April 1602:

Raleigh's friendship with Cobham 'was to turn sour in the harsh light of subsequent events'

By my letters patent I find that a man cannot be levied without her majesty's letter to me to authorise the same, and if by virtue of these warrants I might do it, I am bold to say that it is a mistake to join me with mayors and sheriffs, who have nothing to meddle in this kind, but as inferior officers to receive direction.[19]

Although, health permitting, Henry Brooke had always done his duty as Lord-Lieutenant, he was not the hard-working, dedicated person his father William had been.

He could divert and charm some – the Virgin Queen included – but annoy and antagonise others. Evidence of the Queen's fondness for him was his nomination as a Knight of the Garter on St George's Day 1599. The following year he 'sumptuously entertained the Queen at his London home in Black-friars' and no doubt helped by her affection, 'won the hand of the redoubtable Frances Fitzgerald, dowager countess of Kildare… and daughter of Charles Howard, Earl of Nottingham.' They married in 1601.

The Earl of Essex was first among those definitely *not* captivated. This was hardly surprising since not only had he been thwarted over the Lieutenancy and Wardenship of the Cinque Ports, but he had also been Elizabeth's favourite and no doubt saw Cobham as a rival for favour at Court. He persisted in calling Cobham 'Sir John Falstaff' – a reference to his Oldcastle ancestry and Shakespeare's lampoon.

Essex thought Cobham 'a sycophant', which he undoubtedly was, and bore him a grudge for the remainder of his life. But the loss of the Queen's favour following his messy Irish campaign and the abortive rising the disaffected Essex led in 1601 ended in his execution. Cobham's position at Court was now secure, but only for as long as Elizabeth reigned.

Cobham's principal Deputy Lieutenant Sir John Leveson played a leading role in countering the 1601 revolt. He was asked to command the loyal forces gathered in London, and when they barred the rebels' approach and Essex harangued them, Sir John stood firm. Some blood was spilt, and it was Essex who backed down.

When Henry Brooke succeeded to his father's defence roles the Spanish threat was still real, and the pattern of musters and hounding recusants continued. In 1597, another Armada had been forced to turn back after a severe storm that sank 28 of their ships. This time Kent was not in the firing line as the intention had been to capture the huge sheltered anchorage Falmouth and Pendennis Castle as a base for an invading army.

Kent recusants in arrears with their fines were warned again in 1598, and the following year the last of the Spanish invasion scares threatening England led to the re-arrest and brief internment of prominent recusants, but after that their repression – and what had been an unpleasant and divisive role for the Lieutenancy – assumed less importance and came to a gradual end.

The redoubtable Sir John Leveson, Cobham's principal Deputy Lieutenant

At the end of Elizabeth's reign, there were 38 known recusants in the Canterbury diocese and 18 in the Rochester diocese. They had clung to the old religion during difficult and dangerous times. How great a threat they would have been in the event of an actual invasion aimed at overthrowing the Protestant Sovereign and returning England to Rome can never be calculated. Certainly the Lieutenancy, in compliance with Privy Council instructions, had acted against them with considerable zeal and efficiency.

After the scare of 1599 England was no longer threatened directly, but in late 1601, 4,000 Spaniards landed unopposed in Ireland and the Privy Council ordered 2,000 men to be assembled at Rochester to embark for Ulster.

Cobham, was ordered to provide 200 of them from Kent and he promptly delegated the task of finding the men and overseeing the embarkation to his Deputies, Sir John Leveson and Sir Thomas Walsingham. The Lord-Lieutenant warned of the likely danger from troops sent to Rochester from outside the county:

> ...consideringe how hard a matter it will be to contain them, being strangers, and lodged abroad in the villages from running away and committing of outrages usual with such kind of people.[20]

Leveson took charge of the assembly and embarkation and his efficient arrangements, which included accommodating and feeding all the troops, worked well and minimised trouble. Some companies arrived deficient in numbers and Leveson was ordered to make up strengths by impressing:

> ...idle and vagabond persons in Gravesend... and other places in the county to make upp the nombers compleat in each company.[21]

Nevertheless, the force still sailed short of 88 men, the Kentish levy that sailed in the 500-ton *Warspite* itself being '13 men wanting'. Leveson involved himself closely with the embarkation, bobbing about in barges and longboats on the Medway directing the operation at first hand – not a task that many of today's Deputy Lieutenants would relish. Not surprisingly, having encountered bad weather in transit, on arrival in Ireland the contingent that set sail from Rochester and Queenborough did not inspire confidence and it was reported that 'there be not ten of them can shoot a gun' and half the force had to be rested, lest, it was feared 'most of them would have died before they could have made cabins.' However, the English prevailed in the ensuing campaign.[22]

The Spanish threat had been very real and prolonged – over 15 years, and near beggared the county. In the changed, more tolerant atmosphere, Henry Lord Cobham, sought to further a petition from a Catholic to the Government. According to Sir Thomas Wynne, Henry Brooke was himself to die a Catholic, 'though this statement apparently lacks corroboration.'[27]

Deputy Lieutenants were ordered to impress 'idle and vagabond persons in Gravesend'

Although he was King James I's representative in Kent, Henry, Lord Cobham plotted against his royal master

By early 1603 Elizabeth's life was ebbing away. She had reigned for 45 years. Now, at 69, black-toothed and raddled, she resigned herself to her fate, refusing food and medicine, and died in March.

With her passing the balance of power and influence changed dramatically. Cobham was one of the signatories to James I's proclamation and he was with the party that met the new King on the road to London.

He may have charmed the ageing Queen, who had not seen through his flattery, but James did not take a similar fancy to Henry Brooke and instead gave him 'a dusty reception.' The new King was far from alone in his distaste for Kent's Lord-Lieutenant, and plenty of detractors were to emerge from the woodwork after he became implicated in a treasonous plot, describing him variously as 'but one degree from a fool'[24], and 'a worthless mortal, without friends, credit or reputation.'[25]

'Disenchanted with the dawning Jacobean age,' living beyond his means with debts in excess of £10,000 and quarrelling with his influential brother-in-law Robert Cecil, Cobham's letters 'very sinister in the light of subsequent disclosures' were full of his plans to travel abroad.[26]

Less than three months after the accession of James I, with Cobham not yet formally re-appointed Lord-Lieutenant of Kent, details of a plot against the King began to emerge. The so-called Bye plot aimed at kidnapping James to secure toleration for English Catholics included Henry's younger brother, George Brooke. Suspicion settled on Cobham himself and George admitted that his brother had known about the plot, and what is more had been negotiating for Spanish financial support 'to assiste and furnishe a second action for the surprise of his majesty.'

This became known as the Main plot, aimed at the overthrow and death of the King and replacing him with Arabella Stuart, granddaughter of Bess of Hardwick.

In the last years of Elizabeth's reign, Arabella, sometimes known as Arbella, had been next after James VI of Scotland in succession to the English throne.

Her portrait shows her bejewelled and richly dressed with high, exquisite laced collar, an intricately embroidered dress, with raised shoulder flaps that give it almost an appearance of armour, and a near beehive hairstyle swept up leaving an expanse of forehead that gave her an alien look.

Although she was probably a largely innocent dupe, James eventually sent her to the Tower, where she went out of her mind.

Cobham had been promptly arrested and committed to the Tower where he denounced his former friend Sir Walter Raleigh apparently in an effort to save his own skin.

He later retracted his accusations against Sir Walter, although the damage had been done, but admitted soliciting foreign gold anticipating 'generall discontentment' in England; and furthermore admitted telling his brother he looked forward to the day when 'the kinge and his cubs… were all taken away.'

Arabella Stewart. Kent's Lord-Lieutenant was accused of plotting to put her on the throne

Confined in the Tower, Cobham fell silent and the investigating officer described him as 'verry much distempered, and very penitent.'[27]

Plague in London forced the Bye and Main plot trials to be held at Winchester, but Cobham did not appear. Instead he was brought before his peers where,

> …he made 'such a fasting-dayes peece of worke of it that he discredited the place to which he was called. Never was seene so poore and abject a spirit.'[28]

Plotting against his Sovereign had not been a terribly clever thing to do, particularly as the King's representative in the county.

Found guilty, he was attainted, losing his title and appointments; his achievement as Knight of the Garter taken down and kicked out of St George's Chapel, Windsor. Although his brother George *did* lose his head and Cobham came within a whisker of losing his, a last minute act of clemency by the King spared both him and Raleigh. They were to remain for many a year in the Tower, where the former Lord-Lieutenant of Kent devoted his time to study and writing pathetic appeals to the King.

William Camden wrote of Cobham in his *Britannia* that:

> Because fortune did not answer all his expectations, in the transports of his passion (he) rebelled against his most gracious sovereign, and was condemned to suffer capital punishment, but lives a monument of the royal clemency.

Suffering from ill health, he was allowed to spend the summer of 1617 and again the following year, taking the waters at Bath, and was not then forced to return to the Tower, dying 'in a dingy apartment in the Minories' in January 1619, apparently following a stroke. There is but a fleeting – and pathetic – mention of his passing in State Papers: 'Lord Cobham is dead, and lies unburied for want of money.'[29] His widow was allowed to live in Cobham Hall until her death in 1628. They had no children.

Cobham's arrest had come a week before James I was crowned King of England in July 1603. Ironically it was Cobham's principal Deputy Lieutenant, Sir John Leveson, who was made responsible for security at the coronation. The trust placed in him by the King, who was paranoid about his personal safety, may well have stemmed from Leveson's part in thwarting the Earl of Essex two years earlier.

The Privy Council requested Leveson to:

> …putt in readiness some competent numbers of men armed to serve for the better assurance of peace & quietnes… ageinst anie troublesome or sedicious persons that might move anie disturbance at that time.

Elizabethan hero Sir Walter Raleigh was denounced by his one-time friend Henry Brooke

Castrum Royale Londinense   vulgo   the TOWER.

ABOVE: The Tower of
London as it was when the
disgraced Lord-Lieutenant
of Kent escaped the
executioner and was
incarcerated there

Leveson was to raise this security force in Kent, and against outbreaks of plague:

> …yow are to hauve speciall regard that none of the said men maie be taken out of Kentstreete or anie part of the Countie neere unto London, but out of places… more remote & free from the infeccon of the Plague.[30]

Cobham's fall in 1603 had left the Frontline County without a Lord-Lieutenant and the Cinque Ports without a Lord Warden. What was needed now above all in this vulnerable corner was a safe pair of hands.

~ FIVE ~
MUSTERS AND MULBERRY TREES

t was hardly surprising that Henry Brooke's disgrace and close brush with the executioner's axe led the King's advisers to recommend choosing a safe pair of hands to act for him in the Frontline County, but he did not rush to appoint a successor.

Although from another of Kent's leading gentry families and a cousin and executor of Henry Brooke, Edward Wotton, 1st Baron Wotton, was an altogether different kettle of fish to his predecessor.

When eventually appointed to the Kent Lieutenancy in January 1604 he was 55 and had a distinguished track record which included being Elizabeth I's special ambassador to Scotland where the then James VI took a great liking to him. James wrote to Elizabeth thanking her for sending 'so honourable and so wise a gentleman, so well affected to amity and so well thought of by you, as Edward Wotton, your ambassador.'[1]

Elizabeth knighted him and appointed him a Gentleman of the Privy Chamber and eventually Comptroller of Her Majesty's household, responsible for supplies, food and transport. He was, wrote Camden, the Kent historian:

> …a man remarkable for many and great employments in the State, during her reign, and sent several times Ambassador into foreign nations. After her death, he was by King James made Comptroller of his Household, and called to be of his Privy Council, and by him advanced to be Lord Wotton, Baron of Marley in Kent, and made Lord Lieutenant of that County.

ABOVE: Early 17th Century Kentish Militiamen training – as shown in the remarkable carved frieze at Godington House. It is one of the few surviving depictions of military training at the time and consists of 86 images of men carrying out weapons drills

Edward, Lord Wotton – a safe pair of hands

HOW THE ROLE DEVELOPED

'The office of His or Her Majesty's Lieutenant for a county or counties began as a temporary military post, and the story of its origin and growth might be considered to belong to military history. But it belongs also to the history of local administration. As time progressed those matters with which the Lieutenant and his Deputies were called upon to deal in the service of the Crown demanded at least as much administrative skill as aptitude in the military arts.'[3]

Wotton's years as Lord-Lieutenant are noteworthy not so much for momentous events, but more for the minutiae of a Stuart Lieutenancy's work, as revealed through the survival of a letter book covering his tenure of office that gives a rare detailed picture of the Lieutenancy during that period.

It is remarkable not only for its revelations of the measures taken for the defence of the county but for its insight into the great variety of activities the Lieutenancy undertook on the Sovereign's behalf: from commissioning the surveying and valuation of 'all His Majesty's woods, underwoods, and copses that are in the Co. of Kent', to the encouragement of the planting of mulberry trees to kick-start a silk industry around Maidstone 'to prevente them from idleness (the mother of all vices)' to keeping the peace at Shooters' Hill and finding troops to campaign in Ireland.[2]

His family background was distinguished, the Wottons having long enjoyed close links with the Tudors. The family seat was in Boughton Malherbe, in the centre of the county, and he was fifth in descent from Nicholas Wotton, Lord Mayor of London in Henry V's time. His grandfather, after whom he was named Edward, was Treasurer in Calais in 1540 and an executor of Henry VIII. His staunchly Protestant father, Thomas, was imprisoned under Mary for his beliefs, and the first great county historian William Lambarde dedicated his 1576 *Perambulations of Kent* to him.[4]

Unlike his father, described by Izaak Walton as a man 'of great modesty', Edward Wotton, according to his half brother, *sought* honours and high position. And, most unusually for a Lord-Lieutenant at that time, he was also a closet Roman Catholic.

Born at Boughton Malherbe, he was privately educated and as a result of his Continental travels as a young man – including several years in Naples – became an accomplished linguist in Italian, Spanish and French. His fluency was to serve him well in his career as a diplomat and administrator.

In 1577 he was chosen to accompany soldier poet Philip Sidney to Prague to greet the newly-elected Emperor Rudolf, and called with Elizabeth I's compliments on other Continental rulers. Later that year 'young Mr Wotton and other gentlemen that are languaged' were sent by Elizabeth I's Secretary of State and spymaster Sir Francis Walsingham to escort a high-ranking diplomat from Brussels to England for talks on the Dutch crisis with the Queen.

Sir Philip Sidney, ancestor of the present Lord-Lieutenant, was a good friend of Wotton. In *The Defence of Poesy* Sidney called him 'the right virtuous Edward Wotton' and recalled learning horsemanship with the future Lord-Lieutenant of Kent at Emperor Maximilian II's court in Prague.

They remained friends until Philip's heroic death after being mortally wounded fighting the Spanish at Zutphen in the Low Countries in 1586, and he bequeathed to Wotton 'One fee buck to be taken yearly out of my park at Penshurst, during his life natural'.[5]

A literary genius, Sir Philip was the first commoner accorded a state funeral

– an honour not to be repeated until the death of Nelson, and later for Welling-ton, and Sir Winston Churchill, who had Sidney blood in his veins. In 1579 Wotton was appointed as special envoy to Portugal to present the Queen's compliments to Henrique II on his accession to the throne. While there he appraised the contenders who might succeed Henrique and concluded that Philip II was the most likely.

Tellingly, Wotton had reported that the stumbling blocks to that were the great and deep-rooted hatred between the Portuguese and the Castilians – and the growing disfavour in England, France and Italy of the growth of Spanish power and influence, which was to reach a cataclysmic climax within a decade with the sailing of the Armada.

His skills as a diplomat were to prove equally useful later and in 1608 the French Ambassador in London, Antoine le Fevre de la Boderie, thought highly of him:

> …he is an upright man, among the more courteous here… he speaks French and Italian very well and shows good judgement, but he is thought to be a little Spanish.[6]

This last may well be a hint at Wotton's crypto-Catholicism. Indeed, his eldest son Pickering Wotton had died in Spain after turning Catholic.

In his home county Wotton served as a Knight of the Shire, as a JP, as Sheriff in 1594, and during the various Spanish invasion threats was involved in organising the defence of Kent and of London; while on the national stage he was appointed a member of Elizabeth's Privy Council in addition to his role as Comptroller, winning praise for the latter: 'he put new life into it by his example.'

Within a month of the new King's arrival in London, James I created this 'honourable and so wise a gentleman', who had so impressed him on his diplo-matic mission to Scotland 18 years earlier, Baron Wotton, of Marley.

It was a busy year for the newly-enobled Wotton. He married in September, his wife Margaret more than 30 years younger than him; and in November the King demonstrated complete trust in him by appointing him to the commis-sion presiding in Winchester at the trials of some of those implicated in the Main plot. With such impeccable credentials, small wonder Lord Wotton was chosen as the King's representative in the Frontline County.

His Commission of Lieutenancy exempted the Cinque Ports from his juris-diction, but not the City and County – as it then was – of Canterbury, the City of Rochester 'and all other corporate and privileged places within the limits of the County of Kent'. Perhaps it was considered that too much power had been in the hands of first William and then the unfortunate Henry, Lord Cobham?

Whatever the reason, the office of Lord Warden that William and Henry Brooke had both held in conjunction with the Lieutenancy, was now separated

Heroic soldier poet Sir Philip Sidney was a close friend of Lord Wotton

SIR PHILIP SIDNEY

The 16th Century soldier poet Sir Philip Sidney, who was born at Penshurst, is an ancestor of Kent's present Lord-Lieutenant, Viscount De L'Isle. Mortally wounded on the battlefield at Zutphen in the Netherlands in 1586, Sir Philip famously passed a water bottle to a dying soldier saying: 'Thy necessity is greater than mine.'

Lord Wotton ordered 'a vigilant and strong watche' to be kept at the notorious Shooters Hill

and went not to Wotton but to Henry Howard, later Earl of Nottingham, and then to Lord Zouche.

However, 'the presence of two great officials in the County did not always make for peace, witness the numerous disputes concerning areas of jurisdiction when Lord Zouche was Warden (1615-24) and Wotton Lord-Lieutenant.' Such turf wars were irritants but major confrontations were avoided.

Wotton's commission gave him authority to appoint the muster master and if necessary a provost marshal. It also assigned his Deputy Lieutenants as Sir Peter Manwood, Sir John Scott (son of Sir Thomas who had commanded the camp at Northbourne during the Armada scare), Sir John Leveson, Sir Thomas Walsingham and Sir Thomas Fane the younger.

The year after Wotton became Lord-Lieutenant, the Gunpowder Plot and its grisly aftermath shook the nation. There is no evidence that Wotton had any sympathy for the extreme Catholic plotters who had sought to destroy King and Parliament, and with outside threats no longer dominating, he and his Deputies concentrated on ensuring order within.

Earlier in 1605 the letter book records that Wotton was asking Sir Thomas Walsingham, one of his Deputy Lieutenants, to combat straightforward lawlessness with 'a vigilant and strong watche sett at Sutters (Shooters) Hill because of the late disorders there.'

A month earlier, the Lord-Lieutenant's role in the administration of local justice was touched on in his letter to Sir Oliver Leigh in which he revealed he had been informed of 'various misdemeanours in the West of the County and that these are caused by a lack of justices.'

Wotton reminded Sir Oliver that he had been for a long time in the Commission of the Peace but had not yet taken the oath – and implored him to do so. Later Wotton was again reminding the Commissioners for the watch on Shooters Hill, who included some of his Deputies, to pay the watchmen and to continue the service there. He empowered them to 'levy a charge on the area and if anyone refuse to pay you maie binde them over to appeare before me at suche dates as by you shall be thought fit to answere their contempt.' And the Lord-Lieutenant ended his instructions with the remark that he thought there would be no difficulty about collecting the money since there had been so many robberies there that 'the people will paye a fine for a gain in a greate deale of quietness'. Shooters Hill's reputation as a magnet for highwaymen and footpads clearly has deep roots.

Meanwhile, in this period of peace, the absence of regular musters had impacted on the standards of the trained bands. So the Privy Council had written in June 1605, instructing the Lord-Lieutenant:

> The Bands trained and untrained are to be enrolled and put in a state of readiness… And they are to meet at fit places for the muster master's view.

Arms were to be distributed on one occasion and the cost defrayed by the county.

In passing the instructions on, Wotton urged his Deputy Lieutenants to use all care and diligence in making good defects in men and armour revealed in the musters – and that the places of Captains 'dead or removed' be reported so that action could be taken to fill the vacancies. His letter was directed 'to both parts of the Shire the same day by the Messenger John Stevens.' And in a postscript Wotton added that Captain Brett was his chosen Muster Master, charged to view 'arms, furniture, men etc', 'under you and with your assistance.'

Captain Brett was requested to 'repair to the Deputy Lieutenants and to proceed with their directions to take the view by the 11th September.'

The Lord-Lieutenant separately informed his Deputies that Brett 'maie have the same intertaynment as formerly hath been given to the muster masters to be as liberal as it heretofore hath beene.' This clearly refers to the feeding and accommodation requirements for Brett's cross-county horseback travels for taking the musters. Additionally he was to receive payment from every captain of foot and horse, levied by the constables. All captains were ordered to provide:

> …a perfect muster book signed… with names, numbers of carriages, pioneers, and the weight of powder and bullet to every company belonging. And with the names of rendezvous and the number of Beacons within every division. New captains are to take the oath in the recognised formula.

All this indicates not simply a calling out of bands of amateur soldiers, but the

TIMELINE

1603
Edward, Lord Wotton, appointed Lord-Lieutenant

1604
Treaty of London: peace between Britain and Spain

1605
The Gunpowder Plot

1607
Founding of Jamestown settlement in Virginia

1609
Rebellion in Ireland

1610
Wotton appointed Ambassador extraordinary to France

1611
Publication of Authorised Version of the Bible

1616
Death of Shakespeare; Wotton appointed Treasurer of James I's Household

1620
Pilgrim Fathers land in Massachusetts; Wotton resigns Kent Lieutenancy

Pioneers were labourers mustered to support the fighting men

existence of a relatively complex logistical organisation for the provision and transport of ammunition and victuals, with the 'pioneers' supplying the labouring muscle to make and strike camp, construct basic defences, dig latrines and the like. And the responsibility for ensuring that the organisation of all of this was in place and worked efficiently fell to the Deputy Lieutenants.

By August, Wotton was sending out new commissions, which were in his gift as the Sovereign's representative, for captains – via his Deputies. The captains were 'to call before them at convenient days and places persons of good ability; enrol them and note the defects.' And to make the chain of command absolutely clear, they were told they must follow instruction 'which from time to time they will receive' from the Deputy Lieutenants.

A hiccup in the commissioning process is revealed in a letter from the Lord-Lieutenant to Sir Richard Sandes (elsewhere spelt Sandys) at the end of August 1605 concerning his refusal to command 'the select bands of the 4 hundreds' – this despite having 'asked of that band' when they had met at Greenwich.

Wotton hoped Sandes only meant to defer the command 'to avoid the trouble of mustering in this sommer' – a time of year when the amateur soldiery was required for harvesting. He assured him there was 'noe man within the County of Kent soo fit as yourself, in fact none fit but yourself to my knowledge.' And, after warning Sandes about the bad example he might give by continuing to refuse, ended by sending the commission again.

Clearly the Lord-Lieutenant, as the Sovereign's representative, did not consider further prevarication an option. To reinforce the point, Wotton wrote again a few days later charging Sandes to take his company to the place assigned for the muster.

At the same time Lord Wotton was confiding to Sir Peter Manwood that although no doubt he would have his men in a state of readiness, he did not believe 'there would be any great use of the present service'; presumably a nod towards the absence of a credible and serious external threat at that time.

From Wotton's letter to Sir John Smith in September 1605 appointing him as captain of the men of Ashford, it appears that in William, Lord Cobham's time they had objected to being mustered with the rest of the division. Their reasons are not now clear, but we shall see that some 150 years later men of independent spirit living in the Ashford area caused serious problems for the Lieutenancy

A commission to Sir John Boyes, Mayor, and 12 others of Canterbury, quoted the opening words of Wotton's own commission as Lord-Lieutenant, making it clear that his authority included the City of Canterbury.

He went on:

Whereas Mr Alcocke is by me appointed Captain of the select band within the liberties of the said city and Mr Charles Wheatnall Capt. Of the

General Bands that you bee from tyme to tyme ayding and assisting them and allowing them to meete in the assigned places and for a training in armes and furniture.

However, Wotton's commission specifically excluded the Cinque Ports from his authority to arrange musters.

Another commission went to 'my loving cousin and friend' Sir William Twysden, of East Peckham, renewing his captaincy of the Light Horse in the Lath of Aylesford. Twysden was given a list of 10 instructions, worth repeating as they indicate the detailed nature of the Lieutenancy's work at that time:

1. He is to take the musters and make enrolment with the names of the persons chargeable; to note defects, and make certificate to the Lord Lieutenant.
2. He details the armour for horse and rider.
3. Nobleman's servants that do not want to be enrolled and trained with the general bands are to be enrolled and trained with the calivers; and if any yeoman finding horse be of ability of body then he shall likewise be enrolled and trained.
4. That the said persons, your soldiers, do receive the oath of a soldier which I sent unto you.
5. None of the said persons, your soldiers, are to go out of the lath to be enrolled elsewhere, without giving notice first to you.
6. That his band contain, a lieutenant, a trumpet, a cornet, an armourer, a surgeon, a blacksmith (to sharpen the daggers) and a sadler.
7. When his band is not complete he is to confer with the nearest Deputy Lieutenant and to deliver the names of all such as are wanting to me.
8. The rendezvous for the horsemen is to be Pendenham [sic] Heath, that on the firing of the beacons or other warning they must meet him there.
9. East Malling is to be the place of training as heretofor it hath been.
10. Besides the general muster day that there be some other days appointed to exercise the men in the management of their horses and in the use of their weapons.

In May 1608 a Privy Council letter to 'our right trustie and right well-beloved councillor the Lord Wotton, the Lieutenant of Kent' asked him to make arrangements so that 50 men might be sent from the county to serve in Ireland, where rebellion was festering.

The recruited men were to set off in 'suche tyme that they faile not to be at Chester by the 14th June next.' Interestingly, Wotton, as a Privy Councillor, was one of the signatories of the letter – to himself.

The cost of arms and armour for the service in Ireland was to be met by a levy on the counties. Wotton copied the letter to his Deputy Lieutenants

Sir William Twysden

ordering them to consider how many days would be required for the journey to Chester – and to pay 'coat and conduct money', a reference to uniform coats and subsistence allowance. And he reminded his Deputies to be careful in their choice of men, apparel and armour. As a Privy Councillor he could not be seen to provide the sweepings of the streets and farmyards for the Irish service. Kentish pride was at stake.

As the deadline for Kent's 50 men for the Irish service to rendezvous at Chester came and went, the Privy Council again communicated with Lord Wotton pointing out that it had been a long time since there had been a general view of arms, men and, in a phrase that resonates with military men in any age, that:

> …in this happy tyme of peace… there is commonly in men an improvident forgetfulness of sicknes so long as they find themselves in good health, because peace is best continued when there is readie and sufficient provision for warre… His Majesty in his wisdom has given order for a general view to be made and a certificate of the said forces… invasion not imminent this tyme.

As a necessary gesture to Kent's landowners and farming community, the Privy Council added:

> So as to avoid interruptions of necessary labour the view and training is to take place betwixt the harvest and seed time next coming.

Again, the Privy Council's detailed instructions for the review give a comprehensive picture of the minutiae and complexity involved in gathering large numbers of men in an age when physical and verbal communication within the county relied on foot and horsepower alone. And they emphasise that the role of the Lord-Lieutenant and his Deputies was no sinecure.

Enrolments of all the trained and untrained officers were to be made and vacancies filled. All arms, weapons and (horse) furniture were to be cleaned and repaired. Care was to be taken about exemptions of those claiming to be part of the King's household, or of any nobleman, and even the clergy were included in the summons:

> Youre Lordshippe is to take expresse order that noe suche persons bee exempted in that case except only those that are known to be His Majesty's ordinarie servants in Courte and meniall and household servants unto noblemen… the rest are to be charged and rated at the musters and other public services. The J.P.s are not to spare themselves in finding horse for a better example to be given others, they will do it of their own accord readily and willinglie.

'Peace is best continued when there is readie and sufficient provision for warre'

Passing these instructions to his Deputy Lieutenants, Wotton acknowledged that no doubt the bands of horse were badly broken up and that in the past many had been backward in finding arms and furniture – saddles and tack. Those who refused to cooperate for this review were to be bound over to appear before the Court of the Council. He informed the Deputies that he had again appointed Captain Brett as Muster Master to conduct the review and that he was to receive the customary 'entertainment'.

To avoid the same arms and armour appearing over and over again at different locations – a prevalent abuse employed by soldiers facing kit inspections down the ages – the Privy Council reminded the Lord-Lieutenant that the musters were to be taken in all divisions on the same day. However, Captain Brett could not be in several places at once, and in such a large county common-sense forced Wotton to countermand this order, explaining to his Deputies:

> I see not how it can bee well performed unless the muster master had an ubiquitie of bodie and therefore I will that the muster bee taken on severall daies in the severall divisions…

But to avoid the abuse of parading with borrowed arms, Captain Brett was to use some means of marking them 'or otherwise as he shall thincke good for the preventing of the said abuse.'

Powder and bullet were to be provided and carriages to be kept in readiness, and the Privy Council ordered:

> Perfect and orderlie certificate is to be made unto us by the laste of November next with numbers of both horse and foote and all the kines of supplies made.

Wotton certainly gave the impression of being a very conscientious Lord-Lieutenant. At this time he begged Robert Cecil, James I's most influential minister, to excuse his absence from the Court, 'till the musters are dispatched' adding that he would then 'fly to Court.' In a letter of September 1608 to Sir Ralph Bosseville, Lord Wotton agreed that there were good grounds for complaint about levying too many taxes on the county, but asked him to rate, charge and supply a band's defects and fit them out with coats in the first place, and then 'You shall find me ready to doe what is fitting.'

The following week the Lord-Lieutenant was dealing with an appeal by a Mr Turke apparently to do with muster-related taxes, but 'since considering how neare he is to Dover I began to doubte whether he will be within the [Cinque] Ports or not.' If so, Wotton asked that Turke be informed that he is outside his jurisdiction and should correspond with the Lord Warden.

A totally different side to the Lord-Lieutenant's role is revealed in a commission Wotton received in March 1607 – in Latin – for a survey to be taken of His Majesty's woods and copses. He promptly wrote to three Justices of the Peace requiring them to ensure that 'this survey maie bee exactly taken'. And he told the chosen valuers, William Hyden of Woodchurch and Richard Hardres of Barswell:

> Informed of your skill in surveinge and valuing of lands and woods I have made choice of you to make a survey and valuation of all His Majesty's woods, underwoods and copses that are in the Co. Of Kent.

They were to be well paid, at 7/6d (37½p but worth far more today) a day, as were the 'Measurers': Thomas Pope of Hucking and Thomas Yates of Broad, Marston. The Commissioners for this woodland survey were given precise instructions. They were to:

- Make note of and value all growing timbers and mark them with a J & K [presumably standing for King James]
- Note all rotten trees and set down a reasonable value on whatever good timber they may have
- Note all timber on copses, deer parks, lands and manors of His Majesty's since the beginning of his reign
- Survey and value all underwoods and certify what may be made yearly of them to be sold at reasonable prices.
- Certify the acreage of copper [coppice?] woods and new places apt and fit for planting new woods and to make an estimate of what the annual charge of maintenance would be
- Survey timbers only on his Majesty's lands
- Take information without administering an oath
- Enquire into all waste in timber since the beginning of the reign
- Do all other things necessary for the better execution of His Majesty's Service

Lord Wotton was commissioned to survey all the King's woodlands in Kent

Warnings from the King in November 1608 about 'the dangers of idleness and the ills of poverty that result', together with instructions for the making of silk, set Wotton on one of the most unusual tasks of his Lieutenancy.

In pursuit of 'the honour that honest labour brings to a country' he was to have mulberry trees planted to encourage the silk industry around Maidstone. The plants were to be sold in the fair at six shillings (30p) per hundred and would be chargeable on a levy within the county.

Wotton immediately sent a letter of encouragement, echoing the King's words, to his Deputy Lieutenants:

Kent's Deputy Lieutenants were urged to buy mulberry plants to kick-start the silk industry in Maidstone

> …to set the common people on worke to prevent them from idleness (the mother of all vices) and also to bringe generall profit and gain to them.'
> The Deputies were instructed to debate at the next Quarter Sessions how to implement His Majesty's directions. And Wotton desired them to buy mulberry plants themselves to give a good example – (myselfe intending to invest in one thousand plantes).

The Weald of Kent was already an important centre for broadcloth production, and the immigrant colonies in Maidstone, Canterbury and Sandwich pioneered the manufacture of various fabrics. Despite Wotton's mulberry-planting initiative, it was Canterbury that led the way with silk-weaving which was to flourish there towards the end of the century.

In his military role, the Lord-Lieutenant was drawn into a plea by Sir Nicholas Gilborne who, on the strength of being Scoutmaster between Lydd and Dover, argued that he should be exempted from finding – that is providing – arms within the shire.

Wotton wrote to a Deputy, Sir Peter Manwood, that he did not remember ever seeing a commission or other testimony of Gilborne's employment in that service, although he had in fact been commissioned as Scoutmaster back in 1587 when he succeeded Thomas Nevynson, the man who had heard first news of the defeat of the Armada from Drake on board *Revenge* at Margate.

Notwithstanding the implied doubt about Gilborne's appointment, Wotton concluded that being within the Cinque Ports he was outside the Lord-Lieutenant's jurisdiction, but ought to find such arms as were fitting for a man of his rank.

There is a somewhat intriguing, quaintly-worded and slightly sinister reference in the Wotton Lieutenancy letter book in a communication to Sir Richard Hoddard:

> I will and command you to repaire unto me at my chamber at Court upon Wednesday the xxth of December by nine of the clocke in the fornoon for some special occasion concerning H.M Service. Faile ye not.

'To set the common people on worke to prevente them from idleness (the mother of all vices) and also to bringe generall profit and gain to them'

'Tax avoidance is clearly nothing new'

Sadly there are no further clues to this, although its appearance in the letter book indicates that it concerned Lieutenancy business.

Once again, in January, 1609, Wotton was concerning himself with the watch at Shooters Hill. Having been informed that some people were backward in paying the watchmen, he ordered that the constables were to impose an equal rate on the wealthier inhabitants.

Another 'view of arms' was called for by the Lord-Lieutenant in the Spring of 1609 and the resulting low turn-out and poor contributions from those eligible to pay for arms, led Wotton to reprimand his Deputies as the returns were 'much below the other of the late queen's tyme.' He commented on the meanness of the contributions considering that 'in this countie thear bee so many knights.' Tax avoidance is clearly nothing new.

There follows a gap in Wotton's Lieutenancy letter book, perhaps explained by his appointment as Ambassador extraordinary to France in 1610 on the accession of Louis XIII – and the fact that later his attention was diverted elsewhere when he became Treasurer of the Household for King James I in 1616.

Perceived Catholic threats from the Continent caused the Privy Council to up defensive activity once again but the muster scheduled for Autumn 1614 was carried out unsatisfactorily in Kent and ordered to be held again the following year. Wotton once again passed on detailed instructions and warned his Deputies:

> I am fully resolved to a severe course for the punishing of suche neglecte therein before I have done.

In April 1616 the Privy Council, complaining of 'the many and grete defects' reflected in many county returns, again called for Wotton to arrange another general view of men and arms, repeating earlier detailed instructions. And that August Wotton, from his home at Boughton Malherbe, sent a commission for the scoutmaster Sir Thomas Harfleete, his area of jurisdiction being in the lath of St Augustine, and for better performance of the service he was to have a staff of three. As scoutmaster he was to have authority to order the various constables to repair or build up beacons and watch-houses and to cause them to provide all watchmen with arms.

The scoutmaster was to see to it that all persons living near beacons 'forbear making fires, or that there be any extraordinary ringing of bells'. And he was authorised to have offenders punished. Finally, he was 'to be ready on all occasions to attend or inform the Lord-Lieutenant or one of his Deputies, for anything necessary for the better service of His Majesty.'

Musters were again called for by the Privy Council in a letter to Wotton in January 1619 – sparked by the outbreak of the Thirty Years War – and this time Kent won praise for its efforts.

Passing on the instructions to his Deputies in the usual way, albeit after a delay of several months, the Lord-Lieutenant wrote emphasising that defaulters not dealt with since the last muster must answer for their neglect at the Council table. Curiously, his letter is signed: 'From the ruins neere Cant. This last of June 1619'.

This was the last of Lord Wotton's correspondence recorded in the letter book. 'It would appear that the last decade of his life from 1618 until his death aged 80 in 1628 was spent in retirement and little is known of it'.

He resigned his Lieutenancy in May 1620 but continued to attend Privy Council as needed, to serve as a JP – and even to appoint to certain beneficiaries in the established church. This, although he was himself 'a Catholic in private.' 'Growing weary of waiting at court', his partial retirement at 70 – resigning his office as Treasurer for a £5,000 golden handshake – 'enabled him to follow certain other Catholic gentry who sheltered at time itinerant priests in their manor houses in Kent.'

In retirement he was doubtless freer to practise his faith than he had been in office, but when he died, aged 80, at his home at Boughton Malherbe he was buried there in the Anglican church he had avoided for 12 years through pleading ill health.

Five years after his death, his widow Margaret was fined the then considerable sum of £500 for having an inscription placed on his tomb:

> To her beloved husband, Lord Edward Wotton, Baron of Marley, a Catholic. His grieving wife, Lady Margaret Wotton, daughter of Lord Wharton of Wharton, a Catholic.[7]

The Anglican church of St Nicholas at Boughton Malherbe where Wotton was buried – despite being revealed as a Catholic

~ SIX ~
'THE UNSETTLED STATE OF CHRISTENDOM'

hen Lord Wotton resigned his Lieutenancy in May 1620 it was at the request of that flamboyant, arrogant and sometimes outrageous royal favourite George Villiers, Marquess of Buckingham. Born in 1592, second son of minor Leicestershire gentry, Villiers was reputed to be 'the handsomest-bodied man in all of England.' At the age of 22 he had come to the notice of James I, who took a fancy to him, and he rocketed from being 'a threadbare hanger-on at court' to *the* most powerful man in the country – and one of the wealthiest.[1]

In rapid succession James knighted him, raised him to the peerage, first as a viscount, earl, then marquess – and eventually made him a duke.

At 70 and tiring of the demands of office, Wotton put up no resistance to the then Marquess of Buckingham's request and on 31 May 1620 (OS) the King's favourite, who already held the Lieutenancy of his namesake county, Buckinghamshire, was additionally appointed Lord-Lieutenant of Kent.

Yet a mere nine days later, with the ink scarcely dry on his commission, Buckingham himself resigned the office in favour of the King's Scottish cousin Ludovic Stuart, 2nd Duke of Lennox. There was a close relationship between the two, with shared business interests in the New World:

> At this time a fresh patent was granted, to the Duke of Lenox [sic] and Marquis of Buckingham, of the whole of the Country of Virginia lying between the latitudes of 40 to 48 north, which was called New England.[2]

Why Buckingham first sought the office and then so soon gave it up is something of a mystery, the most likely explanation being that he was power-broking. This is borne out by the claim that 'he wished to give it the Kent Lieutenancy to Ludovick Stuart'[3], and a letter from Dover Member of Parliament Richard Younge: 'Buckinghan has resigned the lieutenancy of Kent to the Duke (of Lennox), and has hope of the Cinque Ports.'[4]

Edward, Lord Zouch, had been Lord Warden since 1615 and in 1620 it was reported that he was resigning his place to the Duke of Lennox. It can be conjectured that Buckingham had used his great influence to secure the Lieutenancy of Kent from Wotton although he had really wanted the Wardenship, and handed it over to Lennox who had been earmarked as Lord Warden. However, in the event Zouch retained the Cinque Ports and there was a wait of four years before Buckingham, by then Lord Admiral and a duke, 'bought the Wardenship of Lord Zouch…' in 1624.[5]

George Villiers' rise from 'threadbare hanger-on at Court' to a Dukedom was meteoric. He held the Lieutenancy of Kent for a mere nine days

Buckingham whose machinations were usually at the very least suspect and more often downright ill-advised. Before the old King died, Buckingham had involved himself in seeking an alternative bride for the heir to the throne, and it was he who negotiated the marriage with the daughter of Henri IV and Louis XIII's sister, Henrietta Maria, to cement an alliance with France.

Within three months of his father's death, Charles I, who was 24, married the 15-year-old Henrietta Maria at St Augustine's Church, Canterbury. They were not happy at first, thanks in part to her dislike of his close friend Buckingham, and the new King clashed with her large French retinue which included 30 priests and more than 400 other attendants, who were soon sent packing back across the Channel.

As for that other royal marriage irritant, Buckingham, that one-time, albeit short-term, Lord-Lieutenant of Kent, had become politically dangerous and due to him the new King found himself at war first with Spain, and then – despite his French bride – with France, where the royal favourite wanted to help the Huguenots.

First, Buckingham lost credibility over the abortive expedition to Cadiz and then the failed foray to the island of Re, off La Rochelle, and was assassinated in 1628 – stabbed by one of his discontented veterans of that fiasco.

It had been Buckingham's unpopularity with Parliament that caused members to refuse to grant Charles money for the wars against Spain and France and sowed one of the seeds of confrontation that led to eventual civil war. The King's cavalier attitude incensed MPs, who petitioned to control his excesses, and in March 1629 he adjourned Parliament so that he could rule with absolute authority.

On Buckingham's death, Kent's new Lord-Lieutenant also took over the Duke's Buckinghamshire Lieutenancy, and in addition to those two counties was appointed to the Lieutenancies of Cornwall, Somerset and Wiltshire from 1630-42. 'The association of two or more counties in the commissions of Lieutenancy was a common feature of the period.'[15]

No one man could possibly give close attention to counties from the far east of England to the far west and Philip Herbert was too fully occupied on the national stage – and with hunting – to bother much with Kent, although he was somewhat more connected to the county than his predecessor had been, through his mother Mary, nee Sidney, of Penshurst, and was named after his uncle – soldier poet Sir Philip Sidney.

Herbert, who was 40 when appointed to the Kent Lieutenancy and succeeded as 4th Earl of Pembroke in 1630, had been, like Buckingham and Lennox, one of James I's favourite favourites. The Earl of Clarendon wrote that he:

> …had the good fortune, by the comeliness of his person, his skill, and indefatigable industry in hunting, to be the first who drew the King's eyes towards him with affection… He pretended to no other qualifications than

Philip Herbert, 1st Earl Montgomery

Beacons were once more repaired, 'ready to blaze forth their warning in time of danger'

to understand horses and dogs very well, which his master loved him the better for.

And the diarist John Aubrey noted:

His Lordship's chiefe delight was in hunting and hawking, both of which he had to the greatest perfection of any peer in the realm.[16]

Royal favour brought a shower of honours, but there was another side to the courtier who loved nothing better than participating in tournaments and masques, gambling and hunting. He was foul-mouthed, had 'incorrigibly rough manners' and a nasty temper which erupted at times into violent assaults. Like most bullies:

Fear, which was the passion always predominant in him above all his choler and rage, prevailed…[17]

While Pembroke strutted his stuff at Court and in the hunting field it was left to his Deputy Lieutenants to do all the work involved in organising the county's forces and to supervise the increasingly unpopular raising of taxes.

Their authority was sometimes questioned, as in 1636 orders were also issued through the Deputy Lieutenants that the Justices of the Peace were to ensure that the beacons were once more to be repaired and manned, 'ready to blaze forth their warning in time of danger.'

Some of the justices were doubtful about the propriety of their taking orders from the Deputy Lieutenants, but Sir Roger Twysden, a senior magistrate and future Deputy Lieutenant, of whom we will hear much more, was able to quote precedents from his grandfather's papers. These showed that it had been done before (though then the Deputy Lieutenants had only *prayed* the justices, whereas now they *prayed and required* them) and the justices then agreed to pass on the instructions to the Constables.'[18] However, when war came it began in the north.

Charles believed that he, as Monarch, had the divine right to be not only infallible ruler of his kingdom but to be spiritual head of the church. But this was especially staunchly resisted by the Scots. They had been happy to be loyal to the Stuarts, but they could not, and would not, stomach the King's interference with their forms of worship.

His introduction of the Book of Common Prayer to Scotland in 1637 provoked fury and, when he declared that opposition to the new liturgy would amount to treason, the die was cast. In droves they signed the National Covenant of 1638 rejecting royal interference with the affairs of the Presbyterian Church of Scotland, and over winter assembled large forces, apparently ready to invade England's northern counties.

All this meant little to the people of southern counties, that is, until Charles decided to raise an army consisting of the 'old regiments' of his small standing forces backed up by members of the trained bands to deal with the Covenanters. The King wrote to Pembroke in February 1639 directing the immediate selection of men from the Kentish Trained Bands. Naturally, his letter gives his own somewhat biased view of the developing situation:

> The great forces lately raised in Scotland without order from us by the instigation of some factious persons, ill affected to monarchical government, who seek to cloak their too apparent rebellious designs under pretence of religion, (albeit we have often given them good assurance of our resolution constantly to maintain the religion established), has moved us to take care to provide for the safety of our Kingdom of England, which is in apparent danger to be invaded. Wherefore we have resolved to repair in person to the northern parts with our army. And this being for the defence of this Kingdom, unto which all our subjects are obliged, we have appointed that a select number of foot shall be presently taken out of our trained bands and brought to York, or to such other rendezvous as the General of our Army shall appoint, there to attend our person and standard, of which number we require that you cause to be forthwith selected out of the trained bands of your county 1,200 men, whom you are to cause to be put in readiness, and to be weekly exercised so that they may be ready to march to their rendezvous, whither they are to be brought at the charge of that county, as soon as you or the deputy lieutenants shall receive order from the General.[19]

At a time when most people seldom ventured further than the next village or town, a campaign hundreds of miles from home must have been a daunting prospect. But there was a get-out clause for the reluctant, provided they could find and afford a substitute:

> …where any trained soldier desirous to stay at home shall offer any other as able to serve with his arms in his place, we leave it to your deputies to entertain and enlist the person offered.

Authority was also given to the Deputy Lieutenants to impress a replacement at the charge of anyone excused as unfit.

In order to avoid the possibility of the levies themselves causing trouble en route to the rendezvous, the King warned Pembroke:

> It is left to you and your deputy lieutenants to give order to those in charge of bringing the said men to the said rendezvous to take care so as to govern and order them in their march thither as that they do not take anything but what they pay for, nor commit any insolences or disorders on the way.

TIMELINE

1620
Buckingham holds the Kent Lieutenancy briefly and is succeeded by Lennox

1624
Lennox (now Duke of Richmond) dies and is succeeded by Philip Herbert, Earl of Montgomery

1625
James I dies; Charles I marries French Princess Henrietta Maria in Canterbury

1627
England declares war on France

1628
Buckingham murdered

1634
Charles I introduces unpopular Ship Money tax on maritime counties

1639
Kentish Trained Bands sent to fight the Scottish Covenanters

1642
Kentish Petition and start of the Civil War

A third of the Kentish soldiers sent to Scotland were pikemen

The Lord-Lieutenant was further ordered to ensure that the men of Kent's Trained Bands selected for service against the Covenanters were provided with knapsacks paid for by the county.

A month later the King wrote again to the Lord-Lieutenant to report that 'those factious and rebellious spirits in Scotland continue still their warlike preparations' and now ordered Pembroke to select 1,000 of 'ye most able' from the 1,200 already earmarked and assemble them with their arms at Gravesend a fortnight later. Two-thirds were to be musketeers, one-third pikemen, and there were to be 20 sergeants armed with halberds, and 20 drummers.

At Gravesend the King's gunsmith, Henry Rowland, gauged the Kentish soldiers' muskets and took moulds to determine the bore of the ammunition required, and their weapons were inspected and counted for an inventory. Powder, match, shot and lead were to be forwarded to the ships waiting to convey the troops north.

Sir Thomas Morton, a professional soldier, took command of the Kentish force, and under him each lath had its own contingent commanded by a Deputy Lieutenant. They were designated Colonels of the Kentish Regiments of Foot (Trained Bands), although the largest of these units were only 230 strong. The Deputy Lieutenants involved were: 'Sir George Sondes (Lath of St Augustines), Sir Humfrey [sic] Tufton (Shepway), Sir Edward Hales (Scray), Sir Francis Barnham (Aylesford) and Sir Thomas Walsingham (Sutton at Hoane) [sic].'

Everyone tried to avoid sending men or arms for this far-away conflict, and on arrival at Gravesend the Deputy Lieutenants immediately complained of 'divers defects in the arms and persons of the men,' many of whom were not trained at all, but inefficient substitutes, hired at between £8 and £12 each. Some owners of Kent property whose duty it was to supply arms sent the worst they could find:

> Many of the muskets having no touch-holes, and some having them so large as one might turn one's thumbs in them, and the pikes were so rotten as they were shaken many of them all to pieces.

One of the captains spotted a musket better than the rest remarked that he wished all had been as good, whereupon the musketeer replied:

> Nay, my master sought to have found a worse musket, but he could find none in all the town; if he could, I should have had it!

The reluctance of those who had to fork out for the expedition was not blamed on the Deputy Lieutenants and it was recorded that:

> These deficiencies were against the will and instructions of the Deputy

Lieutenants, whose care and zeal is especially remarked, and through whose exertions the deficiencies in men and arms were made good.

Just before the force sailed north in a mixed fleet of King's ships and colliers, a bundle of spear-like weapons known as partisans and carried by officers as a symbol of rank arrived on board so that 'poor Sir Thomas was spared the mortification of seeing his Lieutenants sail without them.'

Delayed by severe gales and hit by smallpox, the Kentish force at last arrived in the Firth of Forth, occupied the island of Inchcolm, and eventually linked up with the King's main army encamped at Birkhill, near Berwick. One of the Kentish officers who took troops north – 60 of them, he said, worthy to be generals – was Sir Thomas Wilsford of Ileden, near Kingston. He told the King he was come out of Kent and said, 'I pray God send us well to do in this business, but I like not the beginning…' Nor did it end well. There was some minor skirmishing against the Covenanters, but on 18 June a peace treaty advantageous to the Scots was signed and the Kentish force made its way home.

Kent's Deputy Lieutenants complained bitterly of their 'sufferings in this troublesome and unfortunate service…' and it appears to have been the first and last time that that they accompanied the county's forces on campaign so far from home.

In their turn they, themselves, were complained about. In Parliament John Pym drew attention to:

> Millitary charges and impositions upon counties by letters only from the counsel table, whereby coates and conduct money for souldiers are to be paid at the countries charge and horse provided alsoe, without ground of laws, many things in this kinde being done by deputie lieutenants of their owne accord.

There was further resentment because:

> Southern coastal counties like Kent, England's first line of defence against invasion from the Continent, questioned the policy of borrowing their trained band arms for the Scottish campaign. Sometimes the weapons were not returned, thereby undermining shire military preparedness.[20]

As an example, in November 1639 the Crown reimbursed the Kentish Trained Bands for lost weapons, including 137 muskets, plus pikes, swords, and belts, for a combined cost in excess of £150.[21] Another contingent was raised in Kent in 1640; but at the rendezvous some of the men would not:

> …go beyond their colours, others will not go into Scotland, all are yeoman and farmers who say they must be as assuredly undone by going as by

Partisans, carried by officers as a symbol of rank

A Kentish Militiaman of 1640

'Additional taxes imposed by the King racheted up the level of discontent'

refusing... they have thrust out their rugged resolutions in this language: take one and take all; and then forsaking rank and file they fell into disorder, not to be reduced by the command of their officers.[22]

Billeting of troops from other counties was also extremely unpopular and the inhabitants of Rochester complained: 'The Sussex men are especially ungovernable.'[23]

Kent's Lord-Lieutenant, Pembroke had strongly favoured peace and was involved in negotiations then and again the following year, urging Charles to accept the Scots' terms, 'whereupon the King ordered him to return to London and to raise £200,000 towards the costs of the campaign. Thereafter Pembroke became rapidly more alienated from the court.'[24]

Raising money to run the country and especially to meet the ever-increasing costs of defence and military campaigns such as these forays was becoming ever more difficult for Charles. Early in his reign he had called on his loving subjects to grant him a 'loan', Kent's share being more than £7,000.

Far greater resentment was stirred up nationwide – and especially in the inland counties – in 1635 by his general demand for 'ship money,' a tax levied on landowners to finance a bigger and better Royal Navy. From then on Kent was required to pay large sums, not all of which was spent on the navy, and additional taxes, such as one for replenishing the county's magazines with powder, match and bullet, imposed by the King ratcheted up the level of discontent.

Meanwhile, the King twice recalled Parliament in an attempt to raise money for the campaigns, but, having been stood down for 11 long years, MPs were understandably reluctant to kowtow to his demands and pressure for change grew.

Among them, elected as a Knight of the Shire for Kent, was the remarkable Sir Roger Twysden, who has been called England's first constitutional historian – a notable scholar in regular correspondence with a number of 17th Century thinkers and antiquaries; a magistrate, a landowning Lord of the Manor, stubborn defender of his rights – and a future Deputy Lieutenant.

The so-called Short Parliament, which met on 13 April and was dissolved on 5 May, turned into a discussion of the subjects' grievances rather than the voting of supplies – the only matter for which Charles had convened it.[25]

After the King's unsuccessful campaigns of 1639 and 1640 against the Covenanters, the north was temporarily quiet, but almost immediately yet another maritime invasion scare threatened in the south. The beacons had had to be watched, day and night in July 1636, in November 1638, September 1639, and again in September 1640, at 'great expense to the hundreds they were in.'

On this last occasion the Privy Council wrote to Pembroke, the Lord-Lieutenant of Kent:

His Majesty understanding that a great fleet of the King of Spain's ships carrying aboard a great proportion of land soldiers, is now in the Downs, out of his care as well as for the safety of his coast and subjects, as for the maintenance and defence of his interest and prerogative in his seas, has commanded us hereby to require you to take order that the trained bands of your county be forthwith put into such readiness that they may be fit for service whensoever and wheresoever they shall be summoned to meet, and that you take order that all beacons and seaguards of that county be kept and watched with all safety and diligence.[26]

But, yet again, it came to nought. The next big threat to the King's rule was to come from within.

It was not only what was seen as unfair taxation that fanned smouldering discontent. Charles was deemed sympathetic to Archbishop Laud's moves to reform the Church on Catholic principles, and Kent was the main source of protest.[27] This came in the first of a series of what have become known as the Kentish Petitions, some protesting against the Archbishop's reforms and his persecution of Puritans, and others concerned also with taxation. When the Long Parliament met in November 1640 members set about ending royal abuses and punishing the 'evil counsellors' who had encouraged them. The Commons had two of the King's most powerful and ruthless supporters, the Earl of Strafford and Archbishop Laud, sent to the Tower accused of high treason and later beheaded.

Kent's Lord-Lieutenant, Pembroke, hated by the Queen, had earlier been dismissed as Lord Chamberlain when his temper flared at a meeting in the Lords and he twice struck a fellow peer with his staff, and he further offended the King by supporting action against Strafford.

> Pembroke's subsequent allegiance to parliament was probably grounded on a mixture of personal alienation from the court and an underlying attachment to godly Protestantism.[28]

Royalist sentiment had appeared strong in Kent in February as crowds turned out to see Charles I accompany his Queen on her way to Dover where she was to take ship for Holland and attempt to sell the Crown jewels to buy arms and drum up Catholic support for his cause against Parliament. But it was no doubt the opportunity to see famous personages rather than loyalty that attracted the crowds. Like everywhere else in the kingdom, the county was increasingly becoming sharply divided.

Kent became heavily involved in the worsening situation with petition following petition. One, signed by 2,500 Puritans, attacked the Bishops, demanding 'root and branch' reform. But the most significant of all was the Kentish Petition drawn up by county leaders who met at Maidstone's Star Inn for the

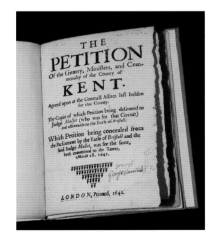

The Kentish Petition of March 1642

Richard Lovelace

Stone walls do not a prison make

Nor iron bars a cage;

Minds innocent and quiet take

That for a hermitage

Richard Lovelace,
written while imprisoned
by Parliament

Assizes in March 1642. One of the petition's triggers was the expulsion from the Commons of the enlightened antiquarian, religious reformer and leading Kentish justice and moderate Sir Edward Dering, of Surrenden Dering, by his Puritan enemies. His expulsion further alienated Kent's moderates and it was he who was appointed chairman of the Grand Jury which drew up the petition.

It urged King and Parliament 'to come to a good understanding,' calling for county autonomy, moderate reformation of the church, repair of sea-forts, renewal of magazines and regulation of the Militia 'so that the subjects may know how at once to obey both His Majesty and the Houses of Parliament.' It 'provided moderate opponents of the parliament everywhere with a clear manifesto' and other counties followed Kent's lead.[29]

Reasonable though the petition was, as soon as Parliament heard of it the arrest of the prominent instigators was ordered, including Dering and his cousin Sir Roger Twysden. When it was delivered by Richard Lovelace he, too, was arrested and imprisoned in the House of Commons Gatehouse, where it is claimed he wrote his poem beginning, memorably, with the words 'Stone walls do not a prison make, nor iron bars a cage…'

Kent's strategic importance as the Frontline County bordering the capital was sufficiently important for Parliament to send a party of its supporters to sit, without lawful warrant, at the next Maidstone Assizes to help administer justice, but in reality to act as 'Big Brothers' ensuring that Kent's Grand Jury did not draw up any more petitions.

The King's relationship with Parliament had reached rock bottom in January 1642 when he tried to arrest members of rebellious factions in the House itself, and then left London. MPs reacted by passing a Bill to transfer control of the armed forces from King to Parliament – the Militia Ordinance. This called for commissioning of county Lieutenants by Parliament rather than the Sovereign, with power to muster and train local forces and 'nominate and appoint such persons of quality as to them shall seem meet to be their Deputy Lieutenants, to be approved by both Houses of Parliament.' The Deputies would have power to appoint officers, and to lead these forces 'for the suppression of all rebellions, insurrections and invasions.' Charles denounced the Ordinance vehemently, and in demanding that he should surrender control of the military Parliament forced the issue which inevitably led to the outbreak of civil strife.

The new county Lieutenants were tasked to raise levies for the Parliamentary army and the King countered by turning back the clock and attempting to gather *his* forces through granting Commissions of Array to his supporters. All hopes of a peaceful solution were now dashed.

No wimps these – the struggle for power between King and Parliament was to bring turmoil and bloodshed to Kent. Here, members of the Sealed Knot re-enact the Battle of Maidstone 360 years on outside the Gabriel's Hill Wimpy restaurant

~ SEVEN ~
CIVIL WAR COMES TO KENT

As Civil War clouds gathered, the Frontline County's loyalties hung in the balance – none more so than those of Kent's new Parliamentary-nominated Lord-Lieutenant – and the crunch issue put him and his counterparts nationwide at the epicentre of the rapidly-approaching storm.

What amounted to the last straw that made conflict inevitable: the *Ordinance of the Lords and Commons in Parliament, for the safety and Defence of the Kingdom of England, and Dominium of Wales* passed in March 1642 in effect transferred command of armed forces from the Monarch to Parliament, 'and so seized control of the lieutenancy from the crown.'[1]

The Ordinance was not an Act of Parliament because the King did not consent to it. It was merely a resolution, and although not law it was put into effect as if it were. Importantly, where it concerned raising forces, Parliament had got in first.

The King, who had lost the goodwill of the county Lieutenancies through neglect and unpopular revenue-raising, had no standing army. He countered the Ordinance by reverting to the ancient procedure of issuing Commissions of Array to raise forces – and this move did not help his cause.

In effect, he had allowed the Lieutenancy system to be hijacked by Parliament, giving it some semblance of authority, and rather than helping the King's cause the Commissions of Array caused confusion on the ground, with

'Kentishmen are a people that are sooner drawn by gentle means than any way enforced; their affection must flow uncompelled'

many perplexed as to which of the contradictory signals and orders to obey concerning recruiting.

In Kent there had been a last-ditch move to have a dual Lieutenancy, with joint Royal and Parliamentary Lieutenants. But it could not have worked and the idea was soon abandoned. This was no typical county. A key point underestimated by both King and Parliament was the strength of local loyalty between kinsmen and neighbours – stronger in Kent than loyalty to either of the contending factions.

The people of Kent were used to managing their estates and affairs away from Court and Parliament. They were moderate in politics and religion, there was no single dominant family, few noblemen and the 30 or 40 gentry families could trace their independence back to the freeholders of the 14th Century. In Kent these factors were to lead to the County Committee system that in effect replaced the Lieutenancy becoming more like local parliaments with their own agendas.

On the whole there was more sympathy at the outset for the King's cause than Parliament's, but,

> …because of its isolation from other royalist shires, it never succeeded in escaping from the vice-like grip of parliamentary control. The grip was vice-like because of the strategic situation of the county, and because Parliament simply could not afford to countenance rebellion so close at hand: more than once in past centuries – under men like Cade and Wat Tyler – the men of Kent had made the city of London tremble.[2]

At the outset of the Civil War,

> …two small cliques of genuine royalists and ultra-parliamentarians emerged on either wing of the Kentish community, which at heart wanted to remain neutral…[3]

Instead of being appointed by the King, it was the Ordinance, which had predictably failed to gain royal assent, that named Robert Sidney, 2nd Earl of Leicester, as Lieutenant of the County of Kent and the City and County of Canterbury. His predecessor and kinsman, Pembroke, was now appointed as Lieutenant of Southampton and the Isle of Wight, and two Welsh counties.

Choosing sides at this climactic hour was difficult for all and especially for those like Pembroke and Sidney who had long been close to the King and Court, yet leaned towards support for Parliament's stand. Not least among their concerns was the future of their great estates. Both were charged to commission Deputy Lieutenants but neither was to do much about it – not least because new appointees would be putting their own estates at risk of sequestration.

Robert Sidney, 2nd Earl of Leicester, was a reluctant Lord-Lieutenant firmly caught on the horns of a dilemma

The foul-mouthed but '*godly Protestant*' Earl of Pembroke had on Parliament's behalf been involved in negotiations with the King right up until the last and was a moderate Parliamentarian, but backed what he believed would be the winning side, largely, it has been alleged, in order not to risk losing the family seat at Wilton in Wiltshire.[4]

Leicester, nephew of soldier poet Sir Philip Sidney, had similar concerns for the family's great Penshurst estate in West Kent, which had already been their seat since 1552 and remains so today, now the home of the present Lord-Lieutenant, Viscount De L'Isle. Pembroke and Leicester were related through marriage and in the early 17th Century 'seem to have been operating as a unified family and political grouping both at court and in London metropolitan life.'

Leicester was born in the Pembrokes' house at Baynard's Castle, in the City of London, and the two families often frequented each other's residences.[5]

A Knight of the Garter, he had served as Member of Parliament, first for Wilton, then Kent, and finally Monmouthshire – and became a Privy Councillor. He had seen military service in the Low Countries during his father's governorship of Flushing, and succeeded to the title at the age of 31 in 1626.

A talented linguist, he was English ambassador to Denmark and later to Paris, and was prominent at Court. The King had recalled him to England in 1641 and appointed him Lord-Lieutenant of Ireland to deal with a Catholic rebellion, but he never managed to get there, caught between King and Parliament in their dispute about command of the army sent to crush the Irish rebels. 'Rather a speculative than a practical man,' he was in a near impossible position but nevertheless managed to retain the confidence of the Lords, even acting as temporary speaker of the House – and then being additionally appointed Parliament's Lord-Lieutenant of Kent.

As Civil War loomed Leicester, 'by nature indecisive,' found it difficult to choose sides and tried to satisfy both by inaction. Both his Irish and Kentish Lieutenancies placed him firmly on the horns of a dilemma.

> He repeatedly refused to grant commissions to his deputy lieutenants under the militia ordinance, stymieing efforts to raise Kent for Parliament until he was replaced in mid-August 1642.

He complained:

> I am environed by such contradictions, as I can neither get from them, nor reconcile them. The Parliament bids me go [to Ireland] presently; the King commands me to stay till he dispatch me. The supplyes of the one, and the authority of the other, are equally necessary. I know not how to obtain them both, and am more likely to have neither; for now they are at such extremes, as to please the one is scarce possible, unless the other be opposed... I am suspected and distrusted of either side.[6]

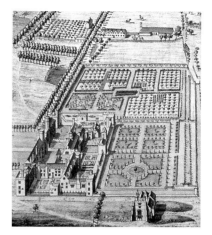

Penshurst Place – from a Kip engraving of 1623

'Leicester was damned if he did – and damned if he didn't'

In his eyes he was damned if he did – and damned if he didn't. As Lord-Lieutenant of Kent, the earl avoided granting Deputy Lieutenant commissions,

> …because some [of the gentry] have refused them and others, principal gentlemen of that county think it not a fit time now to execute the Militia [Ordinance] there, by reason the country is now distempered…'

Kent was wavering and:

> The Lord-Lieutenant's hesitancy was symptomatic of that of the county as a whole. Many of his own deputy lieutenants, such as the Honeywoods of Evington and Scotts of Scot's Hall, who later supported the County Committee, were no more eager to execute the Ordinance without royal sanction than the earl himself. [7]

The county was not unique in dithering. Many of the new Lieutenants appointed under the Ordinance, and especially Deputy Lieutenants, showed a reluctance to fight a civil war. As in other counties, 'lieutenants were slow to name deputies, deputies were slow to appoint officers, and everyone was reluctant to muster.'[8]

Both Houses of Parliament pressed Lieutenants to act and in Kent and elsewhere the crunch point came when Parliament commanded them to execute the Militia Ordinance forthwith, whereupon Leicester preferred to 'deliver up his commission of Lieutenancy and be excused.'[9] His resignation was accepted and now Parliament turned once more to the Earl of Pembroke, who was re-appointed Lord-Lieutenant of Kent in August, just 12 days before the King raised his standard at Nottingham, effectively signalling the start of the Civil War. Now it was a straight choice – either the Commission of Array or the Militia Ordinance: King or Parliament.

It appears that Pembroke's appointment was merely nominal, as he was more than occupied elsewhere and in any event had never interested himself greatly in Kentish affairs: 'a fact which further weakened parliamentarian influence.'[10]

Royalists initiated the King's Commission of Array in Kent before the Parliamentarian Militia Ordinance began to take effect, and ultimately the county was one of the last to declare for Parliament, a decision forced upon it from outside.

Even before the King raised his standard, Parliamentarian troops were taking arms and armour from the houses of known Royalist supporters in Kent – and indulging in some looting on the side. On the eve of the King's gesture at Nottingham, Dover Castle fell to Parliament without resistance and Walmer, Deal and Sandown Castles were taken equally easily.

Shiploads of horses and men were arriving at Dover from the Continent and a packet of Royalist correspondence that fell into Parliamentary hands revealed the imminence of a Cavalier coup to be led by Sir John Sackville of

Knole. Immediately Parliament despatched Colonel Edwyn Sandys, a Kentish Puritan from Northbourne and 'a noted rebel', to thwart the threat with troops raised in London. They captured Sackville while he was at church, ransacked Knole and took away five wagon-loads of arms.[11]

The following week Sandys was back in Kent at the head of 500 horse and dragoons with a commission to disarm all malignants and secure all castles, forts and arms, calling first at Cobham Hall, seat of two previous Lord-Lieutenants, where the Duchess of Richmond, fearful of depredations, quickly sent word that the contents of the magazine would be delivered up to them.

In Rochester, Sandys' troops captured Lord Teynham and others who were there on the King's behalf to execute the Commission of Array. Chatham Dockyard and 300 pieces of ordnance about to be delivered to the King fell into their hands, ships in the Medway were taken and Upnor Castle was seized without resistance while the garrison was out harvesting and their captain – no Drake he – was playing bowls.

Rochester Cathedral was targeted during a service and soldiers destroyed altar rails and other furniture they considered ungodly. Sir William Boteler's servants were treated cruelly at Barham Court, Teston, the 'malignant town' of Maidstone was secured and en route to Canterbury the Parliamentarians plundered other family seats, finding ammunition, 'pikes, armour, head-pieces, swords, gunpowder, bullets and match' at the Earl of Thanet's Hothfield house.

> Outrages such as those… were of course not calculated to endear the cause of the Parliament to the gentry of Kent, but it was the series of wanton affronts offered to Religion which was so powerful a factor in the transformation of the people of the county from being generally the most loyal of Parliamentarians to the opposite extreme of ultra-royalism.[12]

The greatest depredations were at Canterbury, where Sandys' troops,

> …giant-like began a fight with God Himself, overthrew the communion table… violated the monuments of the dead, brake down the ancient rails and seats with the brazen eagle that did support the bible… mangled all our service books and books of common prayer, bestrowing the whole pavement with leaves thereof; a miserable spectacle to all good eyes…[13]

The Cathedral was to suffer again later at the hands of the infamous Puritan zealot Richard Culmer who wrought great destruction on anything he considered idolatrous. Dover, Thanet, Romney Marsh and the Weald suffered next before Sandys' men returned to London, collecting their prisoners from Upnor Castle on the way. A few Royalists who had escaped their attention now left to join the King, taking with them troops raised from their tenants and labourers.

Sandys, 'well known for his depredations and insolent cruelties to the loyal-

Kentish Puritan Colonel Edwyn Sandys 'well known for his depredations and insolent cruelties to the loyalists'

At Canterbury Cathedral Sandys' troops 'giant-like began a fight with God Himself'

'It is some comfort to reflect that Colonel Sandys, the brutal author of these outrages, did not long survive his looting expedition through Kent'[15]

ists' soon met his comeuppance.[14] He was severely wounded in a skirmish at Powick Bridge near Worcester in September 1642, the first significant engagement of the Civil War, and taken prisoner. The Royalists put out propaganda claiming that on his deathbed he had repented his disloyalty to the King. But Sandys was still alive and before he died 'ranting in pain' wrote rejecting this 'most scandalous aspersion of late raised and cast upon me.'[16] He would certainly not have been mourned by those affected by his depredations in Kent.

Moderate Parliamentarians like the Scotts of Scot's Hall, descendants of the Sir Thomas of Armada fame, and the Honeywoods of Evington, now agreed to accept commissions from the new Lord-Lieutenant, the Earl of Pembroke. Their orders were to counter the King's Commission of Array, execute the Militia Ordinance forthwith, fortify strategic places, search suspicious persons and places, seize horses and arms, bring in money and plate and protect Parliament from 'false aspersions.'

Within 48 hours they were able to report that officers had been appointed, musters organised, summonses for subscriptions sent out, and work on repairing beacons had been started.

Kent was now firmly under Parliamentary control, although the many moderates strove to remain as neutral as possible, tip-toeing through the political minefield just as their ancestors had in Tudor times. As time went on their dissatisfaction with the King was modified by the realisation that they were no better off under Parliament and wanted to go back to what it was like before, but for now that was not to be.

The county may have had Parliament's foot on its throat, but Sandys' depredations had left many with 'angry hearts' and a legacy of bitterness and hatred that would long fester in private and eventually erupt into open rebellion. For now though, the scene of conflict switched elsewhere. The first major engagement at Edgehill, in the Midlands, in October ended in what amounted to stalemate and the minor clashes that followed were equally indecisive.

At Christmas 1642 the King summoned the Earl of Leicester to Oxford where he,

> ...passed the next year in the royalist headquarters in a tortured state, declining to take any part in the King's affairs. Penshurst was sequestered by the Kent county committee on the grounds that Leicester had flown to an enemy garrison, but the countess, probably with the help of [her brother] Northumberland, persuaded the parliament to lift the sequestration.

Leicester's wife, the former Lady Dorothy Percy, who bore him 15 children, was a formidable person and 'efficiently ran her husband's finances and the Penshurst estate, supervising the education, introduction to court and marriages of their children.'[17] Their second son Algernon, a republican sympathiser, was to lose his head for his alleged complicity in the 1683 Rye House plot.

Civil War powder flask

After the King induced Leicester to resign as Lord-Lieutenant of Ireland in favour of Lord Ormond whose loyalty he did not doubt, the Earl retired to private life at Penshurst and his London mansion on the site of the modern Leicester Square, concerning himself with his estates and academic pursuits. Clarendon described him as 'very conversant in books, and much addicted to mathematics. He could write interchangeably in five languages, English, Latin, French, Spanish and Italian.' After Charles I's execution Leicester and his wife were entrusted by Parliament with the care of two of the Royal children, Henry Duke of Gloucester and Princess Elizabeth, who resided for a short time at Penshurst.

Having faded from the scene at the start of the Civil War, Leicester was to make a brief come-back at the Restoration, taking his seat in the Lords and serving Charles II for five months in 1660 as a Privy Councillor, before pleading ill health and retiring once more to Penshurst where 'he went on to enjoy a further 18 years of ill health' before dying there in 1677.[18]

By reverting to Commissions of Array in opposition to Parliament's Militia Ordinance, the Crown had effectively given notice that it had abandoned the county Lieutenancies, which had been half-hearted in their support for his Scottish campaigns, as instruments of government. After that,

> …Charles made no serious move to rescue the lieutenancy from the clutches of a rebellious Parliament… it lived on under parliamentary control… and was largely responsible for raising the army fielded against the King in 1642. The irony of the lieutenancy's collapse and rebirth from 1640 to 1642 is that an institution established to guard against rebellion, its primary duty "enemies and rebels and traitors to fight, and them to invade resist repress subdue slay kill and put to execution of death by all ways and means", became the organiser of rebellion… Although the institution continued to exist, the civil wars reduced the lieutenancy to irrelevance… abandoned by a king who no longer trusted it. The result was oblivion – at least temporarily.[19]

Counties like Kent that fell under Parliamentary control were now governed by committees of local gentry, notably Deputy Lieutenants, with powers of martial law, assessment of taxes and sequestration of Royalist estates. The County Committee's origin lay in the commission of Deputy Lieutenancy, and its members' authority 'derived from the authority of Pembroke, the Lord-Lieutenant, but he never entered the county nor attempted to influence its politics.'[20]

'Till the end of the war those appointed to the Committee were also appointed DLs.'[21] Initially Sir Edward Hales was chairman, but had strong Royalist sympathies and was soon expelled, subsequently supporting the 1643 rebellion.

'Counties like Kent that fell under Parliamentary control were now governed by committees of local gentry, notably Deputy Lieutenants'

TIMELINE

1642
Robert Sidney, Earl of Leicester, appointed to Kent Lieutenancy, resigns and is replaced by the Earl of Pembroke; Charles I raises his standard; Parliamentarian troops target Kent Royalists

1643
Parliament creates County Committee system; Kentish rebellion defeated at Tonbridge

1645
Further Kentish rebellion put down

1647
Plum Pudding riots at Canterbury

1648
Battle of Maidstone

The Committee and its title developed gradually. State Papers mark the evolution from 'deputy lieutenants' to 'deputy lieutenants and committees' to 'committees' and finally 'Committee of Kent,' although in both Parliament and locally they were often called the Committee of Deputy Lieutenants.[22]

Using various headquarters – including Knole, sequestered from the Sackvilles, yet destined in the following century to be home to three succeeding Sackville Lord-Lieutenants, the first three Dukes of Dorset – and with a secretariat, the main committee and its offshoots in the lathes was to act as an embryonic civil service, developing a role already pioneered by Deputy Lieutenants and Justices of the Peace.

In Shepway, Scot's Hall was used as the local headquarters and Pepys called this division 'Sir Edward's Lathe,' a recognition of the rule Sir Edward Scott exercised over it until 1648.

Committee work was no sinecure. It was extremely difficult, demanding and labour-intensive, and during peak periods members of the Central Committee and Sutton at Hone Upper lathe were sending out an astonishing 20,000 letters and packages a year. In dealing with local disputes such as the suppression of supernumerary alehouses, two committeemen might be sitting as Deputy Lieutenants or JPs, or both.

There had for some years been only around six Deputy Lieutenants in Kent, but total membership of the Committee and its offshoots grew from 24 in 1643 to near 90 in the late 1650s, and the structure was complicated, inefficient and developed *ad hoc*.

It also changed in composition, having few peers or members of gentry families, and was pro-Parliament, at least in the beginning.

General Committee duties and powers spelt out in the original commission of Deputy Lieutenancy were widened by the ordinance of 30 May 1643 and its 'Instructions to the Lord-Lieutenant and Deputy Lieutenants.' They were to raise and provision the armed forces, monitor Catholics, disarm and imprison opponents – in such places as Leeds Castle and Knole – create ammunition storage magazines, administer 'such Covenant and protestation… as shall be agreed [by Parliament],' and inform the county that Parliament 'do not, nor never did intend any evill against His Majesty's person, His Crown or Dignity.' This must have been somewhat hard for Royalists and moderates alike to swallow at a time when Parliament and Monarch were on opposing sides in what was shaping up into a bitter civil war.

A clause in the instructions required the Deputy Lieutenants to convene once a month in some convenient place in the county 'during the time of these publique distractions, so that all orders and ordinances of parliament may be better divulged and intelligence given and received to and from parliament.'[23]

Overall Chairman of the Committee of Kent following Hales' expulsion, and in the absence of the Lord-Lieutenant, effectively the Parliamentarian leader of the county, was Sir Anthony Weldon, of Swanscombe, both a Deputy Lieutenant and JP, and an able administrator devoted to Kentish interests, but an embittered, uncompromising 'personally detestable' man whose 'violence, spleen, and dictatorial methods gradually antagonised almost everyone in the county.' Back in 1617, while accompanying James I to Scotland, he most unwisely wrote an inflammatory paper complaining:

> The aire might be wholesome but for the stinking people that inhabit it. The ground might be fruitful had they wit to manure it. Their beasts be generally small, women only excepted, of which sort there are none greater in the whole world.[24]

The Scots-born King was not amused and dismissed him, a slight which later provoked Weldon into dubbing James himself a fool, and Charles I a villain. Weldon was not sparing with his venom. He spread it around politicians, bishops, and anyone, including neighbours, who crossed him.

One of those to suffer his persecution was that future Deputy Lieutenant, Sir Roger Twysden, who as a constitutional scholar believed 'popular stirs many times, if not most, set up the worser sort of the people, the fiercest, cruellest, fullest of fraud.'[25]

There can be little doubt that the chief personality he had in mind was Weldon, with whom he had jousted in a lawsuit, and – in hindsight perhaps unwisely – had worsted.

Although he had only been trying to avoid a trial of strength between King and Parliament, Twysden, a stubborn defender of his rights, had got into great difficulties over the Kentish Petition and suffered the first of several arrests and sequestration of his family seat at Roydon Hall, East Peckham. At the behest of the County Committee, troopers were soon searching his home and making off with a few personal weapons, a box of his wife's silver and even the nurse's laced handkerchief.

When Twysden, disguised with a wig, tried to slip away to France he was recognised, apprehended and humiliated by Committee-men including the

Deputy Lieutenant Sir Anthony Weldon, who as Chairman of the Committee of Kent 'gradually antagonised almost everyone in the county'

'If the prisoner was *not* Sir Roger Twysden then he was a rogue and must be whipped as such'

prickly Weldon, who sardonically remarked that if the prisoner was *not* Sir Roger Twysden then he was a rogue and must be whipped as such.

The exactions and at times despotic rule of the County Committee and its myriad offshoots increasingly alienated the Kentish moderates, and in his journal Twysden complained, justifiably in own his case at least, that they 'sit judges of men's liberties, estates, fortunes; admitting not the law for their rule, but their own arbitrary, ambiguous, revocable, disputable ordinances and orders.'

Such power led some Deputy Lieutenants to bully their neighbours. In East Kent Weldon's henchmen John Boys of Wingham and Edwin Boys of Goodnestone persecuted their innocent neighbour Sir Thomas Peyton of Knowlton Court. In 1644 he wrote to John Boys' aged father, Edward, of Betteshanger, that 'I desire not in anything herein to asperse the legitimate power derived to your son as deputy lieutenant by any ordinance of parliament; but find fault with that that studied and contemplated opposition from him to whatsoever favour I may be admitted…'[26]

Relations between the County Committee and the Central Committee in London were often strained, as when the latter tried to assess Kentish Deputy Lieutenants for payments in 1644. The County Committee reacted angrily: 'You well know that the service of deputy lieutenants draws on a charge sufficient to free from further payment… we beg that no tickets may be granted against any deputy lieutenant…'[27]

As ever, the Cinque Ports, under a royalist Lord Warden, the Duke of Richmond, and with their expensive commitment to watch the coast, were jealous of their privileges and declared that it was 'contrary to the liberties, customs and freedoms of the Ports and their members' for the Deputy Lieutenants to attempt to boss them around. But, with the proposal to form a South Eastern Association of counties with a unified command, even the 'senior port and ringleader, boastful Sandwich' was reined in, and by early 1645 the Ports were reckoned as a hundred of St Augustine's Lathe.

The Deputy Lieutenants spelt out the reason for their need to levy soldiers from the ports:

> Wee shall bee forced to presse from the ploughes handle the most of them, which in this tyme of the countrymans beinge cast much behind hand in their seasons (which must be both yours and our livelihoods) by reason of the longe and tedious frost: wee are Enforced to desire your Ayde.[28]

At times from then on there are references to 'the Committee of Kent and the Cinque Ports.' Canterbury was at that time still a county in its own right, although the Militia Ordinance had specifically placed it under the Lord-Lieutenant, and in December 1644 Kent's Deputy Lieutenants reinforced this by seeking power to act also as Lieutenants of Canterbury.[29]

Rochester, where the castle was owned by Committee of Kent Chairman Weldon himself, had already similarly been brought under the Committee's control. But it was Parliament's attempt to administer the Covenant, which demanded assistance to 'the forces raised and continued by both houses of Parliament against the forces raised by the king without their consent,' that sparked the Kentish Rebellion of 1643.

Nationally the war had raged on, fluctuating this way and that until July when the Royalists won a major victory at the Battle of Roundway Down, followed a fortnight later by Prince Rupert's storming and capture of Bristol, the greatest Parliamentary stronghold in the west.

Between these two Royalist successes, trouble was again brewing in Kent. The Rector of Ightham refused to accept the Covenant and parishioners armed themselves to protect him from arrest by Parliamentary troops. Within days the countryside around was ignited and rebels gathered at Sevenoaks, strategically placed across the approaches to the county from London and the King's headquarters at Oxford. Others gathered at Aylesford and on the Downs south of Faversham. There was a forlorn expectancy among many that the King's cousin, the Duke of Richmond, would return to his native county and lead the rising, and for a while London trembled, as it had when threatened in times past by Men of Kent and Kentish Men led by Wat Tyler, Jack Cade and Sir Thomas Wyatt.

The Committee-men were torn, and various Deputy Lieutenants played safe neither appearing nor assisting one side or the other. One, Captain Thomas Blount, declared that 'by his commission, he alone, without another deputy lieutenant, could not act anything.' Eventually a group of Committee-men managed to open negotiations with the rebels and agreed to send a petition to Parliament, provided both sides stuck to 'a cessation of arms.' Thomas Stanley, leader of the moderate faction, entreated his fellow-rebels:

> …to send me a letter by this bearer which may testify your consent to avoid all sorts of hostility and plundering… that I may give an account unto the deputy lieutenants.

But there was no response and when the petition reached Parliament the members promptly denounced what they regarded as this unofficial attempt at mediation and rebel hotheads were soon facing a three-pronged Parliamentarian advance into the county.

By the time Colonel Richard Browne's troops reached Sevenoaks all but 500 or 600 of the rebels gathered there had slipped away and those remaining were driven back by cavalry to Tonbridge. There they broke down the bridge over Hilden Brook and turned to face the Parliamentarians. Browne reported 'a most gallant charge' that reached the bridge which his men crossed using planks and again charged the rebels.

'Within days the countryside around was ignited and rebels gathered at Sevenoaks'

A stained glass window at Maidstone Museum commemorating the Civil War

After three hours and a half very hot fight, with the loss of five or six men… and 30 or 40 wounded… we entered the town by force. We found about 12 of their men dead in the town and believe there are many more in hop-gardens and hedges… beside many wounded.[30]

Thereafter the rebellion melted away and the odious County Committee Chairman and Deputy Lieutenant Sir Anthony Weldon reported to the Commons:

God of His infinite mercy, and by the care and endeavours of the honourable parliament, hath quenched this great flame even ready to consume the whole county.[31]

However, despite Weldon's protests, punishment of the leading rebels was relatively light.

Many considered this a time to keep a low profile, and some of the Deputy Lieutenants were accused of 'working their own ends by appearing most zealous,' and it was alleged that they 'diligently meet and talk much that nothing may be concluded.' Before the end of the year Parliament won the First Battle of Newbury, but in Kent discontent festered and early in 1644 Parliamentary troops gathered at Sevenoaks ready to march west angrily protested against leaving their county to support the South-Eastern Association at the siege of Arundel Castle. Weldon reported to Parliament that some:

…did not only in a mutinous manner refuse to follow their colours, but secretly whisper into the ears of all the other to mutiny with them… Some of them offered to draw upon their officers, and the deputy lieutenants understanding thereof, riding up to them, were not without danger of their lives.[32]

One sergeant 'as it were in scorn of the deputy lieutenants, captains and officers…' even attempted to seize the magazine before the County Committee ordered the execution of two ring-leaders, restoring order 'through fear and shame.' The defection of Sir Edward Dering from the King further boosted the Committee's grip on Kent, although Royalist plotting and scheming was ever present in the county, including a plan based on recapturing Dover Castle that was betrayed to the Committee-men.

At Marston Moor in June the largest single battle of the Civil War resulted in a major victory for the Parliamentarians, but one from which the Royalists were able to recover sufficiently to draw the Second Battle of Newbury in October. But the formation of the New Model Army under Sir Thomas Fairfax and Oliver Cromwell was to prove more decisive.

In April 1645 Royalists rose again in Kent, this time planning a surprise

A trooper of the New Model Army

attack on the Committee itself, then based at Aylesford Friary. Weldon promptly called out the trained bands and a party of Parliamentary horse was brought into the county. A brief and messy campaign ended in the defeat of this latest Kentish Rebellion and with it the King's last real hope of entering this most strategically important county.

Weldon, the Committee Chairman and leading Deputy Lieutenant, whose own home had been plundered by the rebels, told the House of Commons:

> We are now past our third rebellion. The two first have yet passed without the punishment of any, except imprisonment only. If this pass so, we must expect monthly rebellions, if not hourly, when undoing well-affected men is held but a recreation. We shall therefore humbly desire that you will be pleased to let some of these be made speedy examples of your justice, who have already so surfeited upon your mercy that they grow wanton and insolent.[33]

Lobster pot helmet as worn by the New Model Army

This time Parliament heeded and authorised the Committee of Kent to punish the rebels with a new round of property sequestrations.

The Committee of Kent was among those given quotas to raise men for the New Model Army in 1645 but there was a reluctance to join for what would inevitably mean service out of the county and 'Even when raised it was a problem to prevent them from promptly deserting. The Kent contingent… mutinied so purposefully that a regular military operation was needed to bring it to heel.'[34]

Nevertheless, within months the Battle of Naseby saw the first full use of what had rapidly become the highly disciplined, psalm-singing New Model Army with its formidable cavalry, dubbed Ironsides, winning a decisive victory – and effectively the war.

After that, there was nothing but retreat for the King and in May 1646 he gave himself up to the Scots and six weeks later his stronghold at Oxford surrendered.

By creating the New Model Army, Parliament had centralised the military and from then on effectively abandoned the county Lieutenancies, although Weldon and his fellow Deputy Lieutenant Committee-men retained their grip on Kent for a further two years. Kent may have been pacified, but the Committee's harsh and often unfair rule rankled, religious divides between Puritans and Anglicans festered, and in the county that had remained unconquered by William the Norman many longed for the restoration of their ancient liberties.

When trouble broke out again at the end of 1647 with the so-called Plum Pudding Riots at Canterbury it was triggered by the County Committee's move to enforce the puritanical Parliamentary ordinance by publishing a county-wide order requiring strict observance of the injunction proscribing

Protestors chanted: 'For God, King Charles, and Kent'

the Christmas festival. This involved attempting to prevent divine service and forcing traders to open their shops. Church doors were defended by armed protestors so that ministers were able preach sermons according to Church of England rites and most shopkeepers disobeyed the mayor's order to hold a market and refused to trade. Those who did open for business had their stock thrown down and a riot involving 'great numbers of rude persons' ensued.

Rioting continued over the weekend. Protesters surged through the city chanting 'For God, King Charles, and Kent' and the Mayor, Sheriff and others including Committee members and the Cathedral defacer Richard Culmer were attacked and abused.

Rioters seized the city magazine and defences, armed 1,000 men and mounted guard on the gates to deny access to Deputy Lieutenant Committee-men approaching with trained bands.

The uprising was further fuelled by rumours that the King, who had been handed over to Parliament by the Scots at the beginning of the year and was now at Carisbrooke Castle on the Isle of Wight, was expected to make his way to Kent. The situation was defused by a compromise declaration calling for the King to be restored to his rights, coupled with the preservation of Parliament and its privileges, and rather than face a siege the rebels accepted a promise of indemnity from Committee-men and laid down their arms.

Weldon and his henchmen now sought retribution. The city gates were burned, sections of wall pulled down and command of the local Militia placed in 'trusty hands.' By now the make-up of the Committee had changed and virtually everyone outside Weldon's immediate circle was against what was increasingly seen as Parliamentarian tyranny. Originally,

> In every county a certain number of Deputy Lieutenants, known to be warm partisans of the Parliament, reigned supreme. In Kent, it appears that at last none but the most determined adherents to the Parliament remained to do business. And their business appears to have been to do entirely what they pleased, provided the interests of the Parliament were furthered at all hazards.[35]

There had been a significant change in the balance of power in the county and:

> By this date, none of Weldon's supporters came from the old landed families of the shire: all were relative nouveaux-riches of legal or mercantile origin...[36]

Far from drawing a line under the riots the subsequent trial of alleged ring-leaders was conducted in an atmosphere of menacing confusion and served only to unite Kent's Cavaliers, moderates and neutrals, sparking yet another county petition framed by:

TIMELINE

1649
Execution of Charles I

1650
Pembroke dies

1651
Charles II defeated at Worcester, escapes to France

1653
Cromwell appointed Lord Protector

1658
Death of Cromwell who is succeeded by his son Richard

1659
Richard Cromwell abdicates as Lord Protector

…the knights, gentlemen, and franklins of the County of Kent, the most free people of this late flourishing nation by the wisdom and valour of our ancestors, delivered from the laws of a conqueror…

The petitioners, clearly not shy of trading on Kent's handling of William the Norman, called for a treaty to settle both the King's and Parliament's rights; disbandment of the standing army; government by established laws; and – most popular demand of all – that 'our property may not be invaded by any taxes or impositions whatsoever.' It was a petition,

> …worthy of unconquered Kent, and of a people whose ancestors always claimed the right to march in the van of the English army. Thus did they place themselves in the van of those who struggled for their King and his just rights, and demanded to be governed and judged by the known and established laws of the kingdom, and not otherwise.[37]

Committee-men loyal to Weldon retreated to Maidstone, declared the petition seditious and sent more troops to suppress it. But their actions had the opposite effect, boosting the petitioners' cause such that soon only Weldon and a few of his henchmen remained opposed to it. He wrote despairingly:

> Never was the fair face of such a faithful county turned of a sudden to so much deformity and ugliness.

Everywhere men signed, troops were raised, magazines seized, castles delivered up, ships' crews declared themselves 'For Kent and the King', and Cavaliers from elsewhere flocked to the county. Remnants of the Parliamentarian County Committee, backed by 800 foot, managed to arrange a brief armistice in Maidstone, but the troops mutinied and negotiations collapsed.

The Earl of Thanet, until then a Royalist supporter, acted on an approach by 'divers gentlemen' who told him that if they were allowed to petition Parliament and 'have indemnity for what is passed' they would be satisfied. Such a compromise, if universally backed, could have avoided bloodshed, and:

> With this message Thanet called upon his cousin the Earl of Pembroke in London, and he, as the absentee Lord-Lieutenant, pleaded the cause of Kent and of Thanet in the House of Lords.[38]

Indemnity was duly offered and many petitioners happily accepted, but hardliners refused to disarm while the despised rump of the Committee of Kent remained in power. Royalist insurgents sent to the Continent for arms, men marched towards a proposed gathering at Blackheath, but the petitioner's Council was divided and everywhere there was order, counter-order, disorder.

'It was a petition, worthy of unconquered Kent'

Stumpwork featuring Charles II and Queen Catherine

A portrait of Fairfax, victor of the Battle of Maidstone, at Leeds Castle

A plaque outside Maidstone Town Hall commemorates the Battle of Maidstone

At this critical moment the staunch Royalist Earl of Norwich, who was related through marriage to both Lord Abergavenny of Birling and the Scotts of Scot's Hall, appeared in Kent, reconciled the rebels' fractured leadership and was appointed their general. Alarmed, Parliament ratcheted up the crisis by ordering its Commander in Chief, Fairfax himself, to advance into the county where his New Model Army was charged with 'managing the business of Kent.'[39]

On the very day appointed for the petitioners' gathering, Fairfax occupied their proposed rendezvous at Blackheath. Moderates now willing to accept Parliament's terms laid down their arms, but the hardcore rebels remained defiant and as Fairfax manoeuvred his well-trained force, skirmishing began.

Astute generalship kept the rebel leadership completely in the dark regarding his movements until the evening of 31 May when his army was found to be just four miles west of Maidstone.

Improvised defences were hurriedly erected, but Fairfax fooled the rebels with a feint towards Aylesford, instead crossing the Medway with his main force at East Farleigh. The following evening, to the Royalists' horror, Fairfax appeared on their flank and as the defenders chanted 'For God, King Charles and Kent' his men stormed the town in a torrential downpour. Every step was fiercely disputed and afterwards Fairfax declared it the most desperate fight he had experienced.

Before rebel reinforcements could arrive the New Model Army's superior command structure, numbers and training made the result inevitable and Maidstone fell. More than 300 rebels had been killed and hundreds more captured, together with a large quantity of arms and horses. Among those imprisoned in the Cathedral-sized All Saints' Church was the erstwhile Deputy Lieutenant and Committee-man Edward Scott.

At a stroke the rebellion was crushed and mopping up operations commenced. The rebel commander Lord Norwich and 500 of his followers crossed from Greenwich to Essex. For the rest it was every man for himself; capture or creeping home and keeping a low profile if they were lucky.

Although the Duke of York landed in Thanet with Dutch soldiers at the beginning of July, they were quickly routed. All was lost. The hated Deputy Lieutenant and Committee of Kent Chairman Sir Anthony Weldon, who had tried so hard to promote what he saw as the county's interests yet had done so much to sour it, died three months later 'a broken-hearted man.'

Meanwhile, Pembroke, the 'absentee Lord-Lieutenant', who had been voted a dukedom by Parliament, was appointed as Constable of Windsor Castle – 'in effect the Charles I's gaoler' – and six months after the collapse of the Kentish Rebellion the King was executed and England was declared a 'Commonwealth and free state', with the House of Commons as supreme authority. Pembroke took little further part in the divided nation's affairs and died in January 1650.[40]

The Rump Parliament ruled for the next four years during which Cromwell campaigned cruelly in Ireland and then defeated supporters of the exiled Charles II at Worcester. He dismissed the Rump, replaced it with the short-lived Barebones Parliament and was himself appointed Lord Protector in 1653.

Kent's geographical situation en route to the exiled Court of Charles II made it a natural magnet for conspiracy and intrigue throughout the Inter-regnum, but periodic Royalist plots and schemes came to nought.

The Parliamentary Lieutenancies had long been subsumed into the laby-rinthine County Committee system, its republican counterpart and then the Council of State itself.

Two years into the uneasy term of the Protectorate the country was divided into military districts, each commanded by one of Cromwell's major generals. Effectively the 'severe but just' Thomas Kelsey, who had long been Governor of Dover Castle and virtual governor of the county, was now the ruler of Kent and Surrey with greater powers than those of a Lord-Lieutenant.

The County Committee structure had been haphazard and involved unpopular activities, though not as unpopular as the short-lived rule of the Major Generals.

For now, the county Lieutenancies were dead, but all was to change with the death of Cromwell, the unseating of his son Richard who succeeded him, and the growing clamour for the return of the Monarchy.

ABOVE: The Battle of Maidstone was one of the hardest-fought of the Civil War

BELOW: Commonwealth and Cromwell's seals

RIGHT: The Earl of Winchilsea was with General Monck to welcome Charles II when he returned to Dover – as depicted in a stained glass window at the Maison Dieu

~ EIGHT ~

THE AMOROUS PEER AND RETURN OF THE KING

un salutes echoed around the White Cliffs as the exiled Monarch Charles II came ashore at Dover. Somewhat theatrically he marked the triumphant moment by kneeling on the beach to thank God for his safe return – and in thanking the Mayor for the symbolic gift of a handsome, gold-embossed Bible, claimed that he treasured it 'above all other things in the world.'

The King's sense of occasion was clearly not shared by one of his favourite dogs. Diarist Samuel Pepys, who was present, reported that it 'dirtied the boat, which made us laugh and me think that a king and all that belong to him are but just as others are.' A less polite version reports that the dog 'shit in the boat.'

Among the vast crowds there to welcome Charles was General George Monck, the one-time Parliamentarian architect of the restoration, and staunch Royalist Heneage Finch, the 3rd Earl of Winchilsea, who had risked all and almost bankrupted himself by borrowing heavily to send supplies to the exiled Court. A fortnight earlier, as the recently-appointed Governor of the castle and town of Dover, Winchilsea had the honour of leading the ceremonial proclamation heralding the return of the King.

Of that demonstration of loyalty Dover's town clerk recorded that:

The king's Most Excellent Majesty Charles the Second, by the grace of God King of England, Scotland, France and Ireland… was proclaimed in this town and port of Dover King… by the mayor and jurats… accompanied with the Right Honourable Heneage earl of Winchilsea, Governor of the Castle and Town of Dover, and divers other knights, gentlemen, and others of his Lordship's troops, with their naked swords in their hands held up… all persons present being bare and uncovered.

The excited town clerk of course meant that all were hatless. He added: 'And there was [sic] great acclamations of joy and rejoicing for his Majesty, and crying out, God Save the king!'[1] That same day Winchilsea had sent a message to the ships in the Downs declaring 'nothing is now wanting… to bring a most glorious prince unto his most dutiful subjects.'

The King's spaniel was unaware of the historic significance of the occasion and 'dirtied the boat'

The austere government of the 11-year interregnum since Charles I's execution was at an end and with the Monarchy restored Dover was aflame with colour and romance. Amid scenes of great rejoicing, the King, his brothers the Dukes of York and Gloucester, and their entourage – including the incontinent dog – came ashore in triumph on Saturday 26 May 1660 and set out by coach along Watling Street to the ancient Kentish rallying point at Barham Downs.

There 'were drawn up divers gallant troops of horse, consisting of the nobility, knights, and gentlemen of note, clad in very rich apparel' – including Lord Winchilsea who commanded a troop composed mainly of the gentry of Kent. Several Kentish foot regiments and multitudes of spectators cheered loudly as the King, now on horseback, rode to the head of each troop. Standing three deep, they bowed to him 'kissed the hilts of their swords, and then flourished them above their heads, with no less acclamations; the trumpets, in the meantime, also echoing the like to them.'[2]

Impressed at the enthusiastic display of loyalty orchestrated by Winchilsea, and as a reward for his support during the dark days of exile, the King knighted him next day although he was already a peer, and further honours including a baronetcy were soon to come his way.

The King arrived at Canterbury to an equally ecstatic welcome and on Sunday worshipped at the dilapidated Cathedral, which had suffered much from puritanical depradations, and where now 'the people seemed glad to hear the Common Prayer again.'[3]

At Rochester garlands were strung across the streets, the King received a loyal address from the Kentish regiments, and left 'betwixt four and five in the morning , the Militia forces of Kent lining the ways, and maidens strowing herbs and flowers and the several towns hanging out white sheets.' At Blackheath he reviewed more troops and, accompanied by Winchilsea and other

The stone commemorating Charles II's return to Dover

The day the King re-entered London was designated Oak Apple Day and long thereafter the anniversary was marked by wearing an oak sprig as a reminder of when he escaped capture by hiding in an oak tree after his defeat at the Battle of Worcester. In Kent, the oak symbol harked back to the days of William the Norman

trusty supporters, entered London to great rejoicing amid 'great pomp and triumph.'

Within six weeks Charles additionally appointed the faithful Winchilsea as Lord-Lieutenant of Kent. The country's revived Lieutenancy appointments all went to staunch Royalists like him, men who had proved their loyalty by opposing Parliament and in many cases had suffered for it through sequestration and imprisonment.

The ascendancy of Parliamentary-appointed Major Generals was over for ever and in appointing his trusted supporters like Winchilsea to the county Lieutenancies the King was re-establishing direct control of the shires – and their Militias.

As a reward for loyalty and as a sign of royal favour, Deputy appointments reverted to the older gentry, men with a vested property interest in their county, whereas during the later days of the County Committee they had gone to lowlier men. In Kent two thirds of the new Deputy Lieutenants were from old families such as the Twysdens, Derings, and Knatchbulls, and most of the remainder had been established in Kent for at least a century. The Lieutenancies would now again be the Monarch's eyes and ears in the counties.

Winchilsea himself had impeccable credentials for the Lieutenancy appointment:

> As a peer and head of the influential Finch clan he was a natural leader of the close-knit group of royalists in his part of Kent, and in the abortive rising of 1655 was to have seized first Dover and Rochester, then Colchester for the King.

When that dream came to naught he wisely left England to travel on the Continent and formed a lifelong love of Italy and its antiquities.[4]

With the mood in England warming to a return of the King, Winchilsea was home again in April 1660 and chaired the election meeting in the County Chamber of the Star Inn at Maidstone which returned Kentish Royalist sympathisers to the Convention Parliament, and was appointed by Monck as Governor of the castle and town of Dover. Frequently described for reasons which will become clear as 'the amorous young peer,' Winchilsea, then 32, was on the second of his three marriages and was to father in all 27 legitimate children, eleven of whom were stillborn or died in infancy.

With the Restoration, acts were passed placing the Militia firmly under Royal rather than Parliamentary control, and on a more definite footing. Along with Winchilsea's Lieutenancy went control of Kent's re-formed armed forces.

Each county's Militia, horse and foot, were to be provided by the owners of property who would also have to pay the costs of a fortnight's annual muster and exercise, and in the event of a calling out – or embodiment – of the force, were to advance a month's pay. The Militia were only liable to serve out of their county in the event of 'insurrection, rebellion or invasion,' and the Crown did not have the power to compel them to send them outside the kingdom.

Among Winchilsea's newly-appointed Deputy Lieutenants was his cousin, the redoubtable Sir Roger Twysden, of East Peckham, the constitutional historian, magistrate, and leading Kentish moderate who had suffered greatly for his principles during the Civil War. In his commission, for which Sir Roger had to pay a fee of £5, the new Lord-Lieutenant referred to his 'wisdome, valour and dilligence' – words worthy of a man who had always put the rule of law above political expediency and been imprisoned and had his estates sequestered for his pains.

The redoubtable Sir Roger Twysden, Deputy Lieutenant and a stickler for principle

Winchilsea barely had time to take up his Lieutenancy before he was off to Turkey. In an attempt to repair his family fortunes which had suffered so much owing to his financial support for the exiled Court, he volunteered to go to Constantinople as ambassador on a five-year contract with the Levant Company for a large salary and expenses.

It was with considerable regret that he sailed in October 1660, taking his wife and latest baby but leaving his other children behind, and 'to exchange my native country… to live amongst barbarians.' Despite his motto 'neither elated nor cast down,' he wrote that it was necessary 'to make my selfe miserable that I might make my posterity happy.'[5]

His ship was twice almost lost in storms, but once he arrived the earl, 'a jolly Lord… having a goodly Person and Mustachios, with a World of Talk, and that all (as his Way was) of mighty Wonders, the Vizier delighted in his Company' was well received and lived in some splendour. A man of strong passions, he threw himself into his ambassadorial role representing English interests to the Ottoman empire with considerable success – and reinforced his 'amorous' reputation.[6]

There was little Winchilsea could do from his post abroad to carry out his duties in Kent, and so in his absence his second wife's brother-in-law, Thomas Wriothesley, Earl of Southampton, was appointed with him in the Lieutenancy with effect from July 1662. This suited Winchilsea who, although far away, revealed in his letters concern for the well-being of the Kentish Militia.

Southampton, 'a man of great and exemplary virtue and piety', had been appointed a Privy Councillor and created a Knight of the Garter on Charles II's arrival at Canterbury, and shortly afterwards was appointed Lord Treasurer, devoting himself to ensuring that the restored Monarchy was financially secure and not dependent on Parliament.[7] Already the Lord-Lieutenant of Hampshire, Wiltshire, Norfolk, and shortly of Worcestershire, his acceptance of the Kent Lieutenancy was in the nature of keeping it warm for his kinsman Winchilsea. Nevertheless, he took his duties seriously and three weeks after his appointment he sent instructions to his Kentish Deputy Lieutenants, Lord Culpepper, Lord Buckhurst, Sir Edward Hales, Sir Thomas Peyton, Sir George Sands, Sir Oliver Boteler, Sir John Tufton, Sir Edward Dering, Sir Anthony

Thomas Wriothesley, Earl of Southampton, was appointed joint Lord-Lieutenant

Aucher, Sir Norton Knatchbull, Sir Roger Twysden, Sir William Swan and Robert Barnham, assuring them:

> I shall trouble you with no more than to desire your vigilancie and care in this great businesse. And that the particular powers in the Act of Parliament, his Majesties Comission and Instructions be observed and forthwith put in Execution, that in these crazie times that exact from all that are in trust their uttermost endeavours, Your preparedness and diligence may prevent and withstand that ill spirit that of late hath… much distracted this Nation.[8]

The detailed instructions required them to meet frequently until the Militia should be put 'in a good posture', make returns of the values of peers' estates for tax assessment, secure all places of strength in the event of risings or disorders, apprehend and punish 'vagrants and idle persons' spreading false and seditious rumours, encourage and thank those demonstrating affection to the King, watch and if necessary arrest disaffected republicans.

Regarding the Militia, the Deputy Lieutenants were instructed to fine anyone eligible to provide horses, men, arms and armour for refusing or neglecting to do so. This last was to have awkward repercussions for that stickler for principle and newly-appointed Deputy Lieutenant, Sir Roger Twysden.

The studious Twysden made his own painstaking analysis to master the complex Militia Act of 1662, which represented the restored Monarch's stamp of authority on the conduct of the Lieutenancies in exerting total control of the county forces. He produced a detailed summary that became his bible for his work as a Deputy Lieutenant. It covered the taking of oaths of allegiance and supremacy; the amounts anyone could receive annually before being charged with providing horse or foot soldiers; the powers of the Lord-Lieutenant in calling out, arming, and forming men into units; granting commissions to officers; and appointing treasurers and clerks to receive and pay monies levied by the Act.

It laid down the criteria for searching the house of a peer; for commandeering carts and horses in the event of invasion, insurrection or rebellion; and Deputies' powers for training and exercising the Militia, and for punishing any who 'imbezill their armes' or failed to appear 'compleatly furnished at beat of Drummes.' The penalty for failing to appear was imprisonment for five days or a fine of 20 shillings (£1) for a horseman and 10 shillings (50p) for a foot soldier.

Other clauses covered searching the homes of suspected persons judged a potential danger to peace, examining witnesses, making assessments and penalising 'refusers or neglectors' – a section that would later place Twysden himself in conflict with his own Lord-Lieutenant.

Twysden made detailed notes of the arming of Militia soldiers: the horsemen were to have 'pistoll proof' breast and back plates and pot (helmet) and carry

Deputy Lieutenants were instructed to apprehend and punish 'vagrants and idle persons' spreading false and seditious rumours, and encourage and thank those demonstrating affection to the King

pistols with at least 14 inch barrels and swords. 'Musquetiers' were to be armed with muskets, with barrels not under three feet long, and swords; while pikemen were to have 16 foot ash pikes, also carry swords, and be protected by back, breast and headpiece.

His complete mastery of the Act meant that when problems arose, Twysden knew it so well that he was able to guide the discussions with his fellow Deputy Lieutenants. But 'his interest was in the logistics of the Militia, not in its training as a military force; he was no soldier, and by now was an old man.'[9]

Southampton's onerous duties as Lord Treasurer and efforts to curb the growing excesses of Charles II's profligate Court meant that he had little if any time to devote to his various county Lieutenancies, and in Kent little progress was made in putting the Militia in the 'good posture' he had required of his Deputies.

There were meetings of the Deputy Lieutenants at Rochester in January and Maidstone in February 1663 to fix the amount of tax to be levied under the Act and discuss tricky questions such as whether or not the clergy should be taxed and the payment of substitutes found by those unwilling to serve in the Militia themselves.

Twysden asked himself if the temporal – churchmen – were taxable by the lay, and wrote asking his Lord-Lieutenant – the Lord Treasurer – for a ruling. The reply indicated that the clergy could be assessed for tax by Deputy Lieutenants, but as a stickler for the letter of the law Twysden still had his doubts, especially when it came to assessing bishops whom he deemed peers and as such should be assessed by the Lord-Lieutenant himself.

Twysden's fellow Deputy Lieutenant and Justice of the Peace, Sir Norton Knatchbull, a person 'of known worth, wisdom and loyalty' joined him in 'proportioning of men to find horse, to know men's estates…'

Sir Norton's warrant book shows that his duties were by no means confined to recruitment and defence, and he undertook everything from supervising tax collection to removing 'one big of a bastard child to the place where she was last legally settled,' ordering the whipping of 'wandering rogues' and taking 'net, dog and other engines from such as are suspected to destroy game.'[10]

Owing to the Dutch threat the Militia were embodied for a week in January 1664, but it was still far from being in a 'good posture' and in October 'a great meeting was at Maydstone of Deputy Lieutenants for receiving an accompt what had been done' to fulfil the instructions of the King and the Lord-Lieutenant. Twysden was there and reported:

> Sir Thomas Peyton with great reason spake of the generall negligence in our parts for mustering the hors, which had not been done at all in this Lath since the King's coming and heer incidentally mentioned their having two voluntary Troops in East Kent where we had none and desired us to styr up our neighbours to raise one.[11]

Sir Norton Knatchbull, a busy Deputy Lieutenant 'of known worth, wisdom and loyalty'

This, Twysden and other West Kent Deputies resisted, arguing that such recruitment should be based on law, not volunteering, and to raise troops of horse as Peyton suggested would cast an aspersion on those who declined to volunteer. The proposal fell. This apparent lack of resolve on the part of some Deputy Lieutenants to put the Militia, and especially the horse, in good order was to have serious repercussions in the coming conflicts with the Dutch.

In August 1665 the Lord-Lieutenant was instructed to have 'particular care that ye captains and officers of ye Militia bee ready when they shall bee called upon to doe their duties and provided with powder, match and Bullets', there being at that time many Dutch prisoners interned at Canterbury, Rochester and Maidstone following the Duke of York's defeat of their fleet off Lowestoft.

Meanwhile, the Great Plague had broken out in London creating such terror that many deserted the capital for healthier Kent, which was less affected, although because of it Kent's Deputy Lieutenants postponed their meeting planned for October.

When the Kent Deputies did meet in mid-December, Twysden's fixation with following the exact letter of the law provoked conflict with some of the others. Sir John Tufton asked him to sign a warrant fining a man who had failed to serve the full period of mustering, 'but he neither told Twysden who the man was nor summoned him before them to give the culprit a chance of making his defence.'

Predictably Twysden refused to sign the warrant, angering Tufton and the man's captain, although other Deputies supported his stand.

It was not until January, when France declared war on Britain, that Kent's Deputies received a letter direct from the King requiring them to deploy the Militia near ports and elsewhere along the coast, and repair and watch beacons constantly.

The Militia regiments were ordered to muster in February under their colonels, including the Deputy Lieutenants Lord Buckhurst, Sir Anthony Aucher, Sir Oliver Boteler, Sir William Swan and Sir John Tufton, and in June with the threat to Britain's shores escalating, the Earl of Middleton was appointed Lieutenant General of all the Militia in Kent.

The Lord-Lieutenant, Lord Southampton, increasingly disillusioned with the spendthrift King, fell gravely ill towards the end of the year and was to take no further part in either national or Kentish affairs.

Meanwhile, the capital, already reeling from the plague, was ravaged by the Great Fire of London in September and the Kent Militia, along with those of neighbouring counties, were summoned to assist in maintaining order.

The Kent Regiments were to rendezvous at Southwark, , and about 200 of the foot were told off as a working party, with food for 48 hours, and carts laden with pickaxes and ropes, buckets etc to prevent further spreading of the fire. The Militia were likewise to assist in facilitating the bringing in of provisions, especially bread and cheese to the city. When the fire was over they were permitted to return to their homes, the King expressing his thanks for their ready concurrence in the measures ordered as above.[12]

After bearing a painful illness with great bravery, Southampton died at his London home on 16 May 1667, and for a year, with Winchilsea still in Turkey, Kent was without a sitting Lord-Lieutenant at a time of great crisis. For, following the Great Plague and the Fire of London, a third disaster was taking shape and once again Kent was in the frontline.

Since shaking off the Spanish yoke, the emergence of the United Provinces of the Low Countries – the Netherlands – had made them rivals with Britain for trade and command of the sea and led to a series of wars, mainly fought at sea. But in the summer of 1667 the Dutch saw an opportunity to strike a crippling blow against the Royal Navy's capability, already weakened owing to shortage of money, corruption and inefficiency.

In the escalating crisis it was the Scottish Earl of Middleton who was given command of the Kentish Militia

Two weeks after Southampton's death there were reports that the Dutch were embarking troops and the Earl of Arlington, Secretary of State responsible for foreign relations, was instructed to write to the Lord-Lieutenants of maritime counties – in Kent's case for action by the Deputies:

> His Majesty understanding that the Dutch are ready in a few days to put to sea with their fleet, and believing they will not fail to appear before the coast, to give the alarm to the country, and possibly, if they find the occasion easy, make an attempt to land, with design at least to spoil, burn and sackage what part they can of the country, his Majesty, out of his gracious care for the safety and quiet of his subjects, hath commanded me to give you this notice of it, and to signify to you his pleasure that, forthwith upon receipt hereof, you give order that the militia of that county be in such a readiness that, upon the shortest warning, they may assemble and be in arms for the defence of the coast, in case of any attempt or appearance of the enemy's fleet; taking care in the meantime that the several beacons upon and near the coast be duly watched, by the respective hundreds, in which they are, for the preventing any surprise or sudden descent of the enemy. And his Majesty commands me particularly to mind you that, in all places where you shall be obliged to make head or appear to the enemy, you make the greatest show you can in numbers, and more especially of horse, even though it be of such as are otherwise wholly unfit and improper for nearer service, horse being the force that will most discourage the enemy from landing, for any such attempt.[13]

Beacons and making a show of apparent strength on the coast had been an Armada tactic. Now, in Arlington's letter there was a tacit admission that all was not well with the 'horse'. Making a show, however poor in quality, was all.

On 5 June the 80-strong Dutch fleet under Admiral de Ruyter reached the English coast a few miles off the North Foreland, but was temporarily scattered by a gale. Ashore, Kent's Deputy Lieutenants met on Sunday 9 June to discuss assembling the county's forces, but because there was no clear indication of where the Dutch would attack they decided to await instructions from Lord Middleton, who had been given command of the Kentish Militia, and next day he ordered the Deputy Lieutenants to march forthwith 'with such forces as they could get… the rest following' to rendezvous at Rainham.

The Earl of Middleton was not without military experience. A Scotsman, he had enlisted as a pikeman in 1632 for service in France, fought for Parliament in the Civil War and was promoted Lieutenant General of Horse. But now he had become one of Charles II's trusted military commanders.

Dutch warships were sighted off Sheerness preparing to mount an attack on the uncompleted fort, and Sir Edward Spragge, a veteran Irishman who was in command of the ships lying in the Medway, ordered that the 66-gun *Monmouth* should place herself above the chain which stretched across the river from below Gillingham to Hoo marshes and when raised theoretically prevented ships from sailing up-river.

Spragge asked the Earl of Middleton, effectively the acting Lord-Lieutenant of Kent following the death of Southampton and in the absence of the Earl of Winchilsea, who was still in Constantinople, to send men of the Scottish regiment – the First of Foot, later known as the Royal Scots, nicknamed 'Pontius Pilate's Bodyguard' who were stationed at Margate – to Sheerness.

They embarked, only to be ordered ashore again. Only one company reached Spragge – and in the confusion and disarray vessels carrying sailors from the *Monmouth* for the defence of Sheerness ran aground at night and many of them 'took to their heels.'

A trained band company which had marched from Sittingbourne was diverted to the island to join the regulars and some seamen and gunners – altogether some 250 men – to defend the fort. But the quality of the Kentish troops 'was so poor, and their morale so low', that Edward Gregory, Clerk of the Check at Chatham Dockyard, later told Pepys, somewhat diplomatically, 'that upon the major's courage and his men's resolution he would undertake to make no comment.' Small wonder that a fierce bombardment followed by a landing of 800 Dutchmen quickly forced the defenders to abandon the Sheerness fort and soon the Dutch flag was fluttering above it.

Meanwhile the majority of the Kentish Militia under Lord Middleton concentrated around Chatham, where only a handful of dockyard men remained, hardly surprising since they had not been paid for 15 months, and began constructing makeshift batteries at each end of the chain.

The appearance of the Dutch in the Medway/Thames estuary provoked panic and ashore there was nothing but indecision and inaction. Pepys wrote in his diary on 10 June:

'Soon the Dutch flag was fluttering above it'

> Down to Gravesend, where I find the Duke of Albermarle just come, with a great many idle lords and gentlemen, with their pistols and fooleries.

As the situation worsened 'they tended to give orders independently of one another' causing 'confusion, not to say chaos' – further weakening the morale of seamen and dockyard-men alike. One of the few sensible decisions given by Albermarle – the former General Monck – was to command Sir Edward Scott with his company to strengthen Upnor Castle, and put him in charge of it.

But despite the valiant efforts of a few, the Dutch sent in fireships to break the chain and when their cannonade proved too hot, the troops manning the hastily-constructed defensive batteries had to be withdrawn. Now only a miracle could stop the enemy from taking or destroying the English ships wallowing helplessly up-river.

The tide ebbed, delaying the advance of the Dutch ships and Kentish Militiamen were set to work throwing up new batteries near Upnor Castle and over the river at Chatham. The new batteries, along with Sir Edward Scott's men in the Castle, opened up on the enemy as they resumed their progress, but nothing could now prevent the destruction of the *Loyal London*, *Royal Oak* and *Royal James*, and the capture of the English flagship *Royal Charles* 'with a boat of nine men.'

Eventually the Dutch withdrew on the ebbing tide, taking with them the *Royal Charles* and the frigate *Unity*. They ran the gauntlet as detachments of Kentish horse and foot gathered and fired on them whenever they could. But this was little more than a futile gesture. The *London Gazette* report was classic early spin. While admitting that the Dutch had 'made themselves masters of Sheerness' the official mouthpiece painted a picture of 'stout resistance' and

Diarist Samuel Pepys, eyewitness to the return of the King to Dover – and the Dutch raid on the Medway

'considerable loss to the enemy' as the chain was contested. And it spoke of the Dutch suffering:

> …very much Dammage [sic]… and by some Prisoners we have taken we finde that the loss we have received has been hitherto so fully returned upon them, that they can have but little reason to Brag of their Success, and less encouragement to make any farther Attempts on these parts.

It was a transparent attempt to play down the disaster, for such it most certainly was for the British. The Dutch had won complete mastery of the Medway and Thames estuary, spreading panic in London and the home counties, as revealed by Pepys' diary note recording 'the beating of drums this night for the train-bands upon pain of death, to appear in arms tomorrow morning…'

A letter sent from Chatham to the Navy Board summed it up: 'So heavy is the hand of God now upon this place that we fear it is as well the hand of man now apparently fights against us.' The following day a correspondent writing from Deal said that when the news of the Dutch victory in the Medway reached the town:

> …the common people and almost all others ran mad, some crying out we were sold, others that there were traitors in the Council… and truly, had not the news suddenly changed, they would undoubtedly have rose and attempted strange things… As it is at and near Deal, it is all the country over.[14]

The diarist John Evelyn, who had at the Restoration been offered, but declined, a captain's commission in Kent's Horse Militia, saw the Dutch ships at anchor and rightly called it 'a Dreadful Spectacle as ever an Englishman saw, and a dishonour never to be wiped off.'

A provisional peace agreement was drawn up at Breda at the end of June, but until it was fully confirmed the Dutch continued their blockade of London and eventually it was scurvy that sent them home at the beginning of October, so ending one of the most embarrassing, shambolic, humiliating and dishonourable episodes in the county's and nation's maritime history.

But this was a raid designed to damage the Royal Navy's capability, not an invasion. So Kent, although violated, could still claim to remain unconquered.

Commendable aggression may well have been displayed by individuals such as Sir Edward Scott at Upnor, but the Lieutenancy as a whole had come out of the debacle with little merit or honour. A combination of factors including the death of Southampton just before the crisis exacerbated by poor leadership and training of the Kentish Militia by his Deputies, had spelt disaster when coupled with the even worse neglect of the Navy by Charles II, whose personal excesses and apparent lack of concern is summed up by Pepys diary note:

'A Dreadful Spectacle as ever an Englishman saw, and a dishonour never to be wiped off'

...the court is as mad as ever; and that night the Dutch burned our ships the King did sup with my Lady Castlemaine, at the Duchess of Monmouth's, and there were all mad in hunting of a poor moth...

Only some 80 years earlier the Lieutenancy had reacted efficiently, swiftly and with great determination to face the Armada threat. Now there was only weakness and vacillation, with the Kentish Militia laid as low as the ebbing tide that bore the victorious Hollanders down-river.

Ironically, only a decade later William of Orange was to sail from Holland, landing in the West Country and ride unopposed to London to accept the English Crown and reign jointly with his wife Mary, daughter of James II.

But for now, in the aftermath of the disaster and with Winchilsea still in Turkey, Kent needed a new Lord-Lieutenant and in May 1668 Charles Stuart, 3rd Duke of Richmond, was appointed to hold the office jointly with him and with power to act alone in his absence.

The joint appointment of Richmond did not please the absent Winchilsea, who in letters home had complained:

> ...to have a partner in the office of lieutenancy suites not well where the government is monarchical... I looke on this modest demand of the Duke to bee the first step to crowd mee out and assume the whole power to himself.[15]

He also wrote to the Deputy Lieutenants revealing his anxiety about Kentish Militia appointments, reminding them that when he left for Turkey he had urged them to make the Kentish Militia an 'example to other counties,' but was sorry to hear of so much omission in their musters, internal divisions and 'underhand dealing.'

He referred to Richmond as 'that insatiable petitioner of favours from the crown' and urged friends to persuade Kent's Deputy Lieutenants 'to an unity, that the common business may not through private piques receive any interruption.'

Whether Winchilsea liked it or not, Richmond was now in the driving seat. Of a staunchly Cavalier family, his father had been mortally wounded fighting for Charles I at the Civil War battle of Edgehill and his mother imprisoned for smuggling Royalist correspondence.

The London-born Duke, had taken part in an abortive Royalist rising against the Cromwellian regime, was punished through sequestration of his estates, which included his Kentish seat at Cobham Hall, and from exile returned with Charles II at the Restoration, attending the King on his triumphant progress through Kent.[16]

Rewarded with a clutch of Scottish offices and titles that nodded to his family's roots, he was also appointed Lord-Lieutenant of Dorset, a Gentlemen

No King will heed our warnings,

No Court will pay our claims –

Our King and Court for their disport

Do sell the very Thames!

For now De Ruyter's topsails

Off naked Chatham show,

We dare not meet them with our fleet

And this the Dutchmen know!

Rudyard Kipling

Charles Stuart, 3rd Duke of Richmond

of the Bedchamber and Knight of the Garter – all evidence of royal favour – but later his political affinities earned him the mistrust of the King.

In 1665, the already twice-married Richmond fought a duel over the honour of a lady of the Court, for which he and his adversary were sent to cool their heels in the Tower for three weeks, yet nevertheless was given command of a regiment of horse known as 'the Select Militia' the following year.

Shortly after the death of his second wife he eloped with Frances Stuart to Cobham Hall, granted to his family after the attainder of Henry Brooke. She was described as 'the prettiest girl in the world' – although her beauty was later tarnished by smallpox – and was reputed to be mistress of the King, who certainly fancied her, although some commentators claim that she 'defended her honour against a prolonged royal siege before suddenly eloping with Richmond.'[17]

At the height of her beauty Frances achieved a kind of immortality as the model for the image of Britannia on England's copper coinage. Charles was furious at their elopement but even so commissioned Richmond as Lord-Lieutenant of Kent.[18]

From its lowest point, the Militia's only way was up, although the divisions that so concerned Winchilsea showed themselves at the treat which Richmond gave to his Deputies at Rochester a week after being appointed.

Through the pernickety Sir Roger Twysden's copious records we can gain a remarkable insight into the political machinations of his turbulent times, and particularly into his relationship with the Lieutenancy which at times became embarrassing to the point of farce.

At the new Lord-Lieutenant's Rochester meeting he found himself in conflict with some of his colleagues when the question arose as to whether a man who owned estates in several parts of the county – as Twysden himself did – was to be assessed to pay for the Militia for every estate or only for the division in which he lived. Twysden argued for the second interpretation, more out of respect for the letter of the law rather than self-interest, but Richmond decided otherwise.

The Duke also instructed that Kent's Militiamen were to wear uniform, his own men in yellow coats, the rest in red, and he called on his Deputies to compel those under obligation to send horsemen or footmen to dress them accordingly. Twysden had studied the legislation carefully, knew this was not a requirement, and would not agree.

The Lord-Lieutenant was not to be a man to be crossed lightly. A fortnight after the argument at Rochester, Twysden was asleep in bed when a messenger arrived:

His lordship the Duke of Richmond sent me eight warrants to subscribe for charging the trained bands with coats, by a Post who blowed hys horn, making us somewhat amazed to hear a Post-horn at that tyme of night.

Richmond's wife Frances as Britannia

Twysden refused to sign the warrants and repeated that he would not be a party to a practice which, without the authority of Act of Parliament, imposed a charge upon the subject.[19]

A late-night posthorn alarmed the Twysden household

His Deputy's disobedience incensed Richmond who cancelled Twysden's Deputy Lieutenancy with immediate effect.

More trouble was brewing. The trained bands of the Hundred of Littlefield were ordered to muster at Penenden Heath in August, and Twysden and his son were called upon to provide two horses and two men.

Affronted, he wrote complaining that neither his father, nor his grandfather nor his great-grandfather had ever supplied more than one. What is more, he recalled, as a former Deputy Lieutenant, that there were letters from the Privy Council in 1663 and from the King himself in1665, requiring that the county should not be burdened with mustering in time of harvest. As far as he was concerned, unless these orders had since been countermanded, the Deputies were exceeding their authority.

The muster was a failure and a further gathering was ordered. Again Twysden and his son were required to provide two horses and two riders, but sent only one horse and one man armed with a carbine, which 'the Duke tooke very ille and the Muster Master pycking a fault in the Karabine (carbine) broke it, upon which I arrested him and he confest a judgment.'[25]

Twysden, who, as his brother said, was 'not to be awed by greatness,' awaited a summons to answer for his actions before the Privy Council, but it never came. His motivation had been his deep respect for the letter of the law. Technically he was right in this case, and perhaps wiser heads in the Council knew it and preferred to let the matter drop quietly.[20]

He was perhaps lucky that he did not cross the Lord-Lieutenant further, for three years later Richmond and fellow peers, in drink, drew their swords against parish constables in a disreputable area of London and killed one. Charged with murder, they were saved only by the intervention of the King, who declared a general amnesty.

In December 1672, as ambassador to Denmark, Richmond went on board an English frigate off the coast of Elsinore, drank at least two bottles of wine and on leaving, 'being a little merry' fell between ship and boat into the freezing water – and although briefly resuscitated, went into violent convulsions and died. The Kent Lieutenancy was once again the sole province of the 'amorous', but absent, Earl of Winchilsea.

RIGHT: A heavily romanticised re-creation as used in the educational publication *Look and Learn* of the scene when the Earl of Winchilsea went to the aid of the disguised James II, held by 'rude Kentish fishermen' at Faversham when trying to flee the country

~ NINE ~

THE KING AND THE RUDE KENTISH FISHERMEN

ent's absentee Lord-Lieutenant, that 'amorous peer' the Earl of Winchilsea, had left his ambassadorial post in March 1669 to sail for home, stopping briefly in Sicily to see the lava flow from Mount Etna following an eruption. While in Turkey he 'had many women... and built little houses for them,' and on his return to England Charles II remarked to him: 'My Lord, you have not only built a town, but peopled it too' – with his illegitimate children.[1]

The eyewitness account of the eruption he sent to the King from Naples was published in London later that year as *'A True and Exact Relation of the Late Prodigious Earthquake and Eruption of Mount Aetna.'* A century later when visiting Etna the ambassador and scholar Sir William Hamilton, sadly now best remembered as the cuckolded husband of Nelson's mistress Emma, attached a copy of this now-rare publication to his own descriptive report to the Royal Society.[2]

Understandably Winchilsea chose not to venture into print regarding his amorous adventures while in Turkey, although he appears to have acknowledged his natural offspring happily – in addition to his 27 legitimate children.

By the time Winchilsea arrived back at Dover in July 1669 his hated rival and co-Lieutenant, Richmond, had in effect severed his Kentish ties, first visiting France, touting unsuccessfully for an ambassadorial post in Poland and for the prestigious appointment of Lord Chamberlain before his arrest for murder and his death in Denmark the year after. So, Winchilsea had a free hand and by the autumn he was back in Kent issuing orders as Lord-Lieutenant.

There was but a short period of peace before Charles II declared war on the Dutch once more in March 1672, thereby fulfilling the undertaking he had given in the secret Treaty of Dover two years earlier. The alliance had been sought by Louis XIV to bolster his campaign in the Spanish Netherlands, but the Prince of Orange frustrated his plans and the United Provinces were saved.

By early 1674 most of the territory invaded by the French was won back and the redoubtable Dutch admirals, de Ruyter, of Medway fame, and Cornelis Tromp did not allow the English to achieve dominance at sea. Charles II had no option but to make peace, bringing the third and final Anglo-Dutch War to an end.

Meanwhile, with the death of Richmond, Winchilsea had become sole Lord-Lieutenant – and Vice-Admiral – of Kent and was to serve as such for the next 15 years. For all the concern he had shown for the Kentish Militia while abroad, on his return Winchilsea does not appear to have thrown himself at the task of sorting out its woes. Rather, he was active elsewhere, additionally holding the Lieutenancy of Somerset during the minority of the 6th Duke of Somerset and, 'clearly regarded as a safe pair of hands' was active in mobilizing support for the King during the so-called Exclusion Crisis of 1679-81, when successive Parliaments tried to keep his Catholic brother James from the succession.[3]

These struggles came to a head in 1681 when Charles dissolved Parliament, forcing the county Lieutenants, some of whom were regarded by the House of Commons as undesirables, and by now more important for their political influence and for promoting loyal propaganda than for controlling their Militias, into the dispute.[4]

Around the country traditional suspects – religious dissenters – continued to undergo harassment: 'the Kentish deputies closed conventicles, threatened to burn down meetinghouses, and roughed up insolent Quakers in Canterbury.'[5]

Despite politics, plots and battles with the Covenanters in the north, this was a relatively peaceful period in the south-east – as indicated by the scant surviving records of Kentish Militia activities. That excellent Militia historian Colonel John Bonhote recorded:

> 'For the next 20 years (1668-87) I find but few notes relating to the Kent Militia, and only just sufficient mention to show that they were in existence…'[6]

Relative stability elsewhere in the country was brought to an end with the death in February 1685 of Charles II, who in his own words took 'an unconscionable time dying' following a stroke and was at last formally received into

'Kentish deputies closed conventicles, threatened to burn down meeting houses, and roughed up insolent Quakers'

The French-born Louis de Duras, 2nd Earl of Feversham, victor of Sedgemoor, was rewarded with the Lieutenancy of Kent

the Church of Rome on his deathbed. No sooner had James II succeeded than his brother's illegitimate Protestant son, the Duke of Monmouth, landed at Lyme in Dorset, raised insurrection in the West Country and proclaimed himself King.

Many of those who flocked to join Monmouth 'the Protestant Duke' were dissenters from areas that had been staunchly for Parliament in the Civil War, and a goodly number of them had fought in the New Model Army. They detested a Monarchy they regarded as being infested with Papists and 'marched to combat the spread of Popery.'[7]

Across the country Deputy Lieutenants and JPs were employed to gather intelligence and disarm 'all dangerous and suspected persons,' although this was hardly necessary in Kent as the insurrection was confined to the south west, where the disaffected and the gullible were swayed into following the 'glamorous, handsome, youthful, royal' Monmouth.

At first the King appointed Lord John Churchill (later to become the victorious Duke of Marlborough) to command his forces in the west, but next day changed his mind and instead appointed Louis de Duras, 2nd Earl of Feversham, over him. Ironically, Duras had earlier served in Flanders as second-in-command to Monmouth.

Churchill sulked and complained privately: 'My Lord Feversham has sole command here, so that I know nothing but what it is his pleasure to tell me… I see plainly that the trouble is mine, and the honour will be another's.' The honours for Feversham were to include the Garter and the Lieutenancy of Kent.[8]

Lord Feversham was a naturalised French Huguenot, a nephew of the great Marshal Turenne, a military tactician greatly admired by James, and was happy to serve under a Catholic king who had himself held high rank in the French army. Feversham had come close to death in 1679 when timber fell on him during the construction of a firebreak in London, but was trepanned – and recovered. As an Extra Gentleman of the Bedchamber he was one of only two Protestants at Charles II's deathbed when the King was received into the Catholic Church.

The Royal Army, including foot guards and cavalry, was to be supported by the West Country Militias, but in the event many of the part-timers melted away, a good number joining the rebels, and although the largely loyal Devon Militia could field 4,000 men they were poorly trained for a few days a year 'and then only attended the muster, (were) counted, had a few drinks and went home.'

It is for conjecture whether or not the Kentish Militia would have done better. However, the Gloucestershire and Wiltshire Militias did prove useful on the royal army's flanks and the rebellion died a sudden and bloody death at the Battle of Sedgemoor, with its even bloodier aftermath in which Monmouth lost his head and many of his followers were hanged or sold into slavery.

The Roper arms in St Peter and St Paul's Church, Lynsted

The drama had taken place far from Kent, but the Kentish Militia had been called out as a precautionary measure, ready to defend the capital if necessary, and in July 1685 diarist John Evelyn recorded that he and his son had provided two horsemen for service in the county and that the 'troops were now come home after a month's being out to our great charge.'

Following Sedgemoor and in their campaign for a regular standing army, the King's supporters poked fun at the Militias – as shown by the poet John Dryden's probably fairly accurate satirical lines.

With his position temporarily strengthened following the crushing of the rebellion, James was able to revoke the Test Act which favoured the Anglican Church and excluded Catholics, non-conformists and non-Christians from office by issuing a Declaration of Liberty of Conscience allowing freedom of worship to other churches.

Lord-Lieutenants were ordered to question their Deputies and JPs to see if they would support the King in ensuring the election of a Parliament willing to pass the necessary legislation. The Lieutenants were told that if they lacked enthusiasm for the move the King 'thought fit to dispose otherwise of your lieutenancies so that you are to act no more in that capacity.'

The Earl of Winchilsea, a staunch Church of England man, was one of those who refused to countenance such an inquisition and he was among those purged by James from the county Lieutenancies. Twenty counties lost their Lieutenants in the purges of 1687/88, causing considerable resentment that was to fester and weaken the King's authority in the coming threat to his rule. In Kent, there followed what could be described as a game of musical chairs, with the Lieutenancy changing hands four times in little over 18 months.

Having ousted Winchilsea from the Kent Lieutenancy and installed in his place Christopher Roper, 5th Baron Teynham, James was soon to have need of the man he had slighted.

Teynham, from an old-established Roman Catholic family, the Ropers of Lynsted, was appointed on 16 January 1688 and it was now down to him to put the questions to the Kent Deputies and JPs: would they agree to repeal of the Acts if elected to Parliament; would they support the candidacy of anyone who did promise repeal; and would they live peaceably with non-Anglican neighbours if a declaration of indulgence was made?

Most could happily agree to the third question, but the first two troubled consciences. When questioned, Sir John Knatchbull, a long-term Deputy Lieutenant, told Teynham, two of whose daughters were nuns:

> He could not make any commitments about what he might do in the House of Commons before he had heard all the arguments both for and against repeal.[9]

The result was a purge of Deputies, Knatchbull included. At a stroke James

The country rings around with loud alarms,

Raw in fields the rude militia swarms;

Mouths without hands, maintained at vast expense,

In peace a charge, in war a weak defence.

Stout once a month they march, a blustering band,

And ever, but in time of need, at hand.

This was the morn when, issuing on the guard,

Drawn up in file and rank, they stood prepared

Of seeming arms to make a short assay,

Then hasten to be drunk, the business of the day

John Dryden

had alienated all his Royalist Anglican support, replacing effective Lieutenants and Deputies and in many counties ending up with less competent men who were now in office because they were Catholics, Dissenters or merely yes-men. One serious effect was that around the country the Militias were now neglected to the extent that they virtually went into hibernation.

The King had lost the support of the great majority of his subjects and by the spring of 1688 there was a growing hunger for change. Monmouth being out of the running, the King's eldest daughter Mary, wife of William of Orange, was the only possible claimant for the throne – and by the autumn invasion threatened.

Now was no time to have placemen without military experience – especially in the Frontline County – and after a mere ten months as Lord-Lieutenant virtually in name only, the King removed Teynham and brought in a professional soldier: the Earl of Feversham, victor of Sedgemoor. Teynham had not long to live anyway, dying as an exile in Brussels in 1689.

Feversham was reputed by his critics to be 'lazy and a glutton,' yet others thought him 'an honest, brave, and good-natured man, but weak to a degree not easily to be conceived.' He had married Mary, eldest daughter and co-heir of Sir George Sondes, of Lees Court, who had been created Earl of Feversham, and on the death of his father-in-law the title had descended to him. He was Master of the Horse and later Lord Chamberlain to Queen Catherine and when James came to the throne was appointed a Privy Councillor.

Although said to be a commander of modest abilities, according to Winston Churchill he and a fellow-Huguenot general were 'immune from the passions which shook England. The King could count on their fidelity however his own subjects might behave.'[10]

He had seen at first hand the frailties of the West Country Militia, their suspect loyalty and tendency to flee when faced with a determined enemy, and could be expected to take these lessons learned during the Monmouth Rebellion with him and ginger up the Kentish Militia. But when he assumed the Lieutenancy of Kent he encountered great opposition.

'Feversham's appointment was obviously a move to guarantee the military security of a strategic county,' but it was a mere ten days before the Prince of Orange landed and he found that none of the old Deputy Lieutenants he wanted to restore to office would serve under him, despite his declaration that 'he would admit no papist, and that if the gentlemen would accept of him they should govern him in everything.'[11]

Although a Protestant, he was clearly too close to the unpopular King and Court for the Men of Kent and Kentish Men to stomach at this decisive moment.

Among those he approached was the former Deputy Lieutenant Sir John Knatchbull. Attempting to curry favour, Feversham asked Sir John if he would again take a Deputy Lieutenancy with its attendant duties in connection with

Sir John Knatchbull declined Feversham's offer of a Deputy Lieutenancy

the Militia and encourage others to do likewise. But the influential Knatchbull declined, confiding in his diary:

> I told him it was a very hazardous part for me to be my Lord's Solicitor in this business, because if the gentlemen of the County should not agree with me, it would ruin my interest in the County.[12]

With William of Orange about to land his army this was no time to show support for James II's representative in the county.

In the event William's armada did not land as expected on the usual invasion coast, but at Torbay in Devon on 5 November, now marked as the anniversary of the Gunpowder Plot that had aimed at getting rid of James I. This attempt to oust James II was to succeed brilliantly – and with little bloodshed.

Disarray among the Lieutenancies and weakened Militias meant that concerted opposition would almost certainly have been ineffective, even if the will to resist had been there – and it was not. Two decades earlier the Dutch had breached the Medway with shot and flame, but now they came by invitation.

As William's army began its slow march eastward, Feversham, commanding the main body of the King's troops, was ordered to march west to meet the threat amid confusion and suspicion as first a trickle and then a flood of defections haemorrhaged support from James to his Dutch son-in-law. Feversham argued for withdrawal nearer London and his force did so 'the easier to defend it.' But desertions, including Churchill, continued and his army quickly began to disintegrate.

With William's army growing daily, the appalling weather he had marched through abated and his march became a triumphal progress. When emissaries engaged in negotiation these came to naught and the end was in sight for James, who now decided to flee. Before doing so he wrote to the faithful Feversham blaming the disaffection of his forces for his plight.

By the time Kent's Lord-Lieutenant read the letter the King had made his bid to escape and was already a prisoner – in Kent – and Feversham took steps to disband the rapidly disintegrating Royal Army.

Accompanying the King on his flight was Catholic convert Sir Edward Hales, Kentish Deputy Lieutenant, JP and Lieutenant-Governor of Dover Castle, who brought James the coach in which they made their early morning get-away, allegedly dropping the Great Seal in the Thames before travelling to Elmley Ferry, near Sheerness, where a hoy was awaiting them.

News of the King's flight had spread quickly 'and the rude fishermen of the Kentish coast viewed the hoy with suspicion and cupidity. Fifty or 60 boatmen, animated at once by hatred of Popery and by love of plunder, boarded the hoy just as she was about to make sail.' The local men had struck lucky, although at first the King was not recognised. They stole his watch and money, but failed to find his coronation ring, other valuable trinkets – and were 'so ignorant of

Kentish Deputy Lieutenant Sir Edward Hales, who accompanied the King on his flight

'The rude fishermen of the Kentish coast viewed the hoy with suspicion' jewellery that they took his diamond buckles for bits of glass.'[17] It was the beginning of an extraordinary stand-off between James and disaffected Men of Kent.

The King, disguised with a plain habit and black wig, was wrongly identified as Father Petre, a 'hatchet-faced old Jesuit,' but Hales, whose park was nearby, *was* recognised. He was hated locally and 'at that very moment a band of rioters was employed in pillaging his house and shooting the deer.' Suspicious of his companion, their captors made a more thorough search of James down to his breeches but still failed to find his ring.

Roughly handled by the local men, the prisoners were taken to the Queen's Arms in Faversham and:

> …on going upstairs, the King, perceiving that he was recognised in spite of his disguise, took no further pains to conceal himself, and, being informed that Lord Winchilsea and other gentlemen of the county were assembled at Canterbury, he sent word for them to come to him.[13]

It is for speculation whether or not James spared a thought at this moment for his folly in ousting the faithful Winchilsea from the Kent Lieutenancy and replacing him first with the ineffective Catholic Lord Teynham and then with Feversham, whose hand was for the moment fully occupied elsewhere as commander of the rapidly disintegrating Royal Army.

Soon there was a large mob besieging the pub while the King's captors, the boatmen, kept him under close watch. Next came a body of East Kent gentlemen who proceeded to add insult to injury by reading the Prince of Orange's Declaration blaming James's 'Evill Councellors' for attacking the nation's civil liberties, stating that the intention now was 'but to have a true and lawful parliament assembled, as soon as is possible,' and inviting all to rally to his army of liberation.

Lord Winchilsea, despite having been replaced as Lord-Lieutenant by his ungrateful King, nevertheless arrived that evening to aid him. He forced his way through the baying mob and managed to get James away to the Mayor's house, which was more comfortable, but the seamen went along too, keeping close watch on their prisoner, albeit now acting more as bodyguards than captors.

Next day Sir Basil Dixwell and Sir James Oxenden came to Faversham with their two Militia troops, 'under pretence of securing the King from the rabble, but indeed to secure him to themselves, and to make a merit of it to the Prince of Orange, as contributing to hinder his escape.'[14]

Hearing that the King was detained at Faversham, the Lords called for his return to London and ordered Lord Feversham to cease all further hostile acts against the Prince of Orange and, as Lord-Lieutenant, to go down to Kent with detachments of Lifeguards and Grenadiers to escort James back.

James II was held for three days here in Faversham's Court Street, now the office of Deputy Lieutenant Jonathan Neame, Chief Executive of Shepherd Neame, Britain's oldest brewer

On reaching Faversham the Lord-Lieutenant 'acquainted the King that he had left the Guards at Sittinburn, upon which the King took his leave of the Rabble, and dismissed them, and order'd the two Militia troops to attend upon him to Sittinburn, where meeting his Guards he dismiss'd them.'[15]

Feversham accompanied the King to Rochester and was then sent to rendezvous with the Prince of Orange to propose a summit meeting. But William was annoyed that Feversham had disbanded the English army, which he had hoped to acquire intact to use against the French and Irish, and imprisoned him 'miserable and confused' in Windsor Castle. However, out of respect for the Queen Dowager, Catherine of Braganza, William's aunt, Feversham was released to continue his role as her Chamberlain.

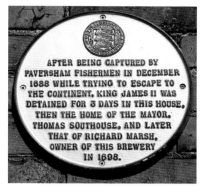

The plaque recording James II's enforced sojourn at what is now the Shepherd Neame offices

The Prince of Orange ruled out further negotiations. Dutch Guardsmen took up post in London and the King was allowed to leave, once again via Kent, travelling by river to Gravesend where coaches and some Kentish Militia awaited to take him on to Rochester to take ship for the Continent. Loyal Feversham, his short period as Lord-Lieutenant of Kent – and his military career – now over, declined to join James in exile and died a wealthy man, aged 70, in 1709.

In February 1689 Parliament formally offered the Crown to William and Mary and in April they became joint Sovereigns of Great Britain. The following month they restored the Earl of Winchilsea to the Lieutenancy of Kent – no doubt because he had been sacked as an Anglican during James II's purge rather than for his efforts to aid him after his first escape attempt. Remarkably it was the fourth time that he had been so appointed, either singly or jointly – a record that has not been equalled before or since. He had improved his Protestant credentials by voting in the Convention Parliament that the throne was vacant and should be offered to William and Mary.

That August William ordered Winchilsea a pension of £500 a year for life, but he was already ill, died that month and was buried in the family vault at St Mary's Church, Eastwell. Sadly, he died 'so heavily in debt that his widow and daughter-in-law fell out over the sparse furnishings of his house; and it required arbitration to prevent his marriage bed from being sawn in two.'[16]

The natural choice to succeed him as Lord-Lieutenant and *Custos Rotulorum* of Kent was Henry Sidney (sometimes spelt Sydney), 1st Viscount, who was subsequently created Earl of Romney, and is an ancestor of the present Lord-Lieutenant, Viscount De L'Isle. Fourth and youngest son of Robert Sidney, 2nd Earl of Leicester, he was born in Paris in 1641, where his father was Charles I's ambassador to the French Court. He was the younger brother of Algernon Sidney the renowned republican.

Henry Sidney, 1st Viscount, who was subsequently created Earl of Romney

Henry Sidney had travelled in France and Europe before returning to the English Court. In 1665 he was appointed Groom of the Bedchamber to James, Duke of York, later James II, and a few months later Master of Horse to the Duchess of York. It was noted he was 'the handsomest man of his

TIMELINE

1669
Winchilsea return from Turkey

1670
Richmond dies

1672
3rd Dutch War beings

1683
Rye House Plot

1685
Charles II dies; James II succeeds; Monmouth is defeated at Sedgemoor

1688
5th Baron Teynham is appointed Lord Lieutenant, is succeeded by 2nd Lord Feversham; James II held at Faversham trying to flee

1689
3rd Earl of Winchilsea again appointed Lord-Lieutenant, dies and is succeeded by Henry Sidney, 1st Viscount Sidney (later 1st Earl of Romney); William and Mary become joint Sovereigns; War with France

times' and 'a terror to husbands,' and in 1666 he was the cause of a serious estrangement between the Duke and Duchess, which was followed by his abrupt dismissal.

However, King Charles II, himself a profligate womaniser, appears to have borne him no ill will and gave him Captaincy of the Holland Regiment, from which the present Princess of Wales's Royal Regiment has a line of descent.[17]

Elected to Parliament, Sidney's arrival in the House had been at the height of the Exclusion Bill debates, by which Parliament sought to prevent the Duke of York from succeeding to the throne as he had converted to Roman Catholicism.

Sent as envoy to The Hague, Sidney succeeded in gaining the Prince of Orange's complete confidence and was perhaps the first Englishman to realise fully the probability of the Prince eventually attaining the English throne. In accordance with the Prince of Orange's wish Charles II made him General of the British Regiments in Holland, a post he held until a few months after James II's accession in February 1685.

Following Monmouth's Rebellion, James II sent Sidney on another mission to The Hague, after which – with the King pushing for more rights for Roman Catholics and stirring up dislike of Popery – he wisely kept himself out of harm's way by travelling in Italy. Back in England in 1688, when an heir was born to James, apparently dashing the hopes of his daughter Mary and her husband William succeeding to the throne, Sidney had renewed his long-standing intrigue and it was said: 'the whole design of the invitation to the Prince of Orange was chiefly deposited with him.'

He obtained permission to leave England, on condition of not visiting the Prince at the end of August 1688. Disregarding his pledge he went almost directly to The Hague; carrying with him a duplicate copy of the invitation and declaration of adherence to William; signed by the members of the association which he had formed.

Possibly most importantly he carried the secret assurances of Marlborough that the Army would not oppose his landing. The fruition of their efforts was to bring about the democratic monarchy Britain enjoys today and finally end the Divine Right of the Sovereign.

Sidney accompanied William's expedition to Torbay and on the day after the proclamation of William and Mary as joint Monarchs he was appointed a Privy Councillor, and went on to serve two tours as Lord-Lieutenant of Kent, first being appointed on 3 October 1689.

War with the French was soon to give him and his fellow-Lieutenants on the invasion coast concern and when the Anglo-Dutch fleet was severely mauled off Beachy Head in July 1690 'an attempt at landing was considered not improbable.' Orders were given on Sidney's behalf for the Militia of Kent 'to be in arms.' The French, finding the invasion coasts too well guarded against Jacobite invasion, retired to Brest, and in the first week of August Queen Mary herself came to Blackheath to view the regiments recently come from Flanders and Militiamen from Kent.

Meanwhile Sidney was present with William in Ireland when he defeated his father-in-law at the decisive Battle of the Boyne in 1690 and during 1691-92 he served briefly as Secretary of State. By February 1692 Louis XIV and James II were planning an invasion, gathering a fleet at Brest and a 30,000-strong army in Normandy. Yet again Kent was vulnerable and, King William having gone to Flanders, in early April the Queen ordered Sidney and the Lieutenants of neighbouring maritime counties to have the Militias ready 'on all occasions.'

Invasion fears bordering on panic led to supposed supporters of James II being targeted:

> Sir Robert Guilford's house in Kent is pulled down by the mob, on resistance made in searching his house for arms; one of the Militia being shot by the butler.[18]

But the invasion scare ended with the destruction of the French fleet off La Hogue in May and a week later the Kentish Militia were recalled from the coast and ordered home.

From 1692-95 Sidney served additionally as Lord-Lieutenant – effectively Viceroy – of Ireland and to help with his duties in Kent one of his Deputy Lieutenants there, Vere Fane, of Mereworth, was made joint Lord-Lieutenant of the county from April 1692 to cover for his absences.

Fane, who had succeeded as 4th Earl of Westmorland the previous year, had first been appointed a Deputy Lieutenant at the Restoration in 1668 but lost office during the 1682 Exclusion crisis because he objected to the address from the Kentish Militia promising loyalty to the King and his heirs 'in the right line.' However, he was reappointed after the Glorious Revolution and was seen as a trusty joint Lieutenant during Sidney's frequent absences on his demanding official duties elsewhere.

From an old Kentish family, Fane had been a Member of Parliament for the county, a JP and Commissioner for Assessment as well as being Warden of Rochester Bridge Trust. According to his son he was 'a very good-natured man, but affected popularity too much, living in Kent where he was greatly beloved, far beyond the compass of his estate would allow...' He was to serve but a short time as joint Lieutenant, making little impact of note, dying in December 1693 aged 48 and being buried at Mereworth.

Meanwhile, during 1693 Sidney was additionally given the lucrative post of Master General of the Ordnance and in May 1694 the title of Earl of Romney was conferred upon him. In discharging his duties to prevent theft, he instructed that all warlike stores be marked with the broad arrow, from the Sidney family's Coat of Arms, a practice which continues to this day.

The broad arrow from the arms of the Sidney family was introduced by Henry Sidney to mark warlike stores when he was Master General of the Ordnance, and is still used today

1690
Battle of the Boyne

1692
Vere Fane, 4th Earl of Westmorland is appointed joint Lord-Lieutenant

1693
Westmorland dies

1694
Queen Mary dies

1701
James II dies in France

1702
William III dies; Queen Anne succeeds

1704
Sidney dies and Charles Finch, 4th Earl of Winchilsea is appointed Lord-Lieutenant

1705
4th Earl of Winchilsea resigns; Lewis Watson, 3rd Baron (later 1st Earl) Rockingham succeeds

Shortly after his elevation, the Earl visited Rochester where he was met at the water-side by the Mayor and Aldermen and by a great number of the gentry of the county, one of the Militia Regiments of Foot being drawn up on each side of the street. In the afternoon the Mayor and Alderman waited on his Lordship at his lodgings and presented him with the freedom of the City.[19] In 1695, Romney moved to a new house in St James's Square where in November of that year he welcomed William back to London after his country progress with a display of pyrotechnics such had never been seen before, applauded by the King in person, who appeared at a window of Romney's house.

Philip Sidney, the 2nd Baron De L'Isle & Dudley, in his *The Sidneys of Penshurt*, records:

> Romney reaped the harvest of wild oats he had sown in the gay days of the Merry Monarch. Some of his lady friends, as they grew older and less lovely, became inimical to him. With one, a Mrs Grace Wortley, he experienced great trouble, and complaint against him was even laid by her at the foot of the throne. Unmarried… he was much attached to a lady of a humble walk of life.[20]

Queen Mary died in 1694 and there was one more scare before the century ended: in February 1696 a plot to assassinate the King and invite a simultaneous French invasion was discovered and the Militia were raised – in Kent to guard possible landing places – but the threat came to naught. William served on alone until his own death in 1702 when he was succeeded by his sister-in-law Anne.

Upon Queen Anne's accession in 1702 Romney lost some of his appointments, although he retained the Lieutenancy until he died of smallpox in 1704.

The Queen, long estranged from her late sister Mary, was like her a Protestant so her reign did not force the nation into yet another religious divide – and in fact under her the 1707 Act of Union finally united the kingdoms of England and Scotland.

When titles are created they are attached to a specific family, for example Henry Sidney had been created Earl of Romney. But on his death, there being no legitimate male heir, the title was extinguished and – as we shall see – was subsequently taken up as a new creation for the Marsham family, who provided a later Lord-Lieutenant of Kent.

On the death of Romney, Queen Anne appointed Charles Finch, 4th Earl of Winchilsea as Lord-Lieutenant of Kent. He was the uncle of the 'amorous peer', the 3rd Earl, who had held the appointment on and off for three decades through from 1660 to 1689. Charles Finch was to hold it but briefly – for a mere eleven months.[21]

The 4th Earl, a former ambassador extraordinary to Hanover who went on to become First Lord of Trade, took up the appointment in May 1704 but resigned from the Lieutenancy and as Vice-Admiral of Kent the following April, apparently for political reasons, without being called upon to perform any significant Lieutenancy duties.

In his place the Queen appointed Lewis Watson, 3rd Baron Rockingham. Born in 1655, he married a daughter of the 1st Earl of Feversham, so was a brother-in-law of Louis Duras, Lord-Lieutenant in 1688.

Rockingham was Whig MP for Canterbury before inheriting his father's barony and in addition to the Lieutenancy he held the appointment of *Custos Rotulorum* as well being Vice Admiral of Kent and Deputy Warden of the Cinque Ports from 1705-8.

The appointment of *Custos*, or Keeper of the Rolls, had begun to be coupled with some county Lieutenancies during the 17th Century, and this was increasingly the case from the time of William and Mary. A judicial appointment, its chief responsibility was to recommend to the Lord Chancellor names of those the Lord-Lieutenant considered suitable to serve as Justices of the Peace, make sure that they performed their duties efficiently and – when necessary – to remove them.

This gave Lieutenants considerable added influence since the right to sit as a magistrate, doling out local justice and involvement in local government including licensing, regulation of prices and wages, administration of the Poor Laws, maintenance of the highways and so on, was considered by the county gentry to be of considerable importance and prestige. Deputy Lieutenants were not involved in the role of the *Custos*, but more often than not were themselves JPs.

'The Lieutenants thus presided over a system of local government which continued till the late 19th Century reforms.'[22] The appointment of *Custos Rotulorum* continues to be held by today's Lord-Lieutenant.

During Rockingham's time as Lord-Lieutenant the military focus shifted to the Continent, where Marlborough was pursuing his successful campaigns, while the Royal Navy was increasingly dominant at sea. The Treaty of Utrecht established peace with France in 1712.

Queen Anne died in August 1714 and Prince George, Elector of Brunswick-Lunenburg, was proclaimed King George I, with Rockingham among the signatories to the loyal proclamation.

The following month the *London Gazette* reported: 'His Majesty has been pleased to direct Letters Patent to pass the Great Seal of Great Britain for creating: Lewis Lord Rockingham, Baron of Throwley in the County of Kent, Viscount Sondes of Lees-Court in the same County, and Earl of Rockingham.'[23]

It was a time of further decline of the Militia and the scant surviving records for this period indicate that although it was called upon during times of threat, notably the various Jacobite scares, its performance was poor to the extent that it 'always looked ridiculous whenever it took the field.'[24]

TIMELINE

1707
Act of Union

1714
Queen Anne dies; George I succeeds

1715
Jacobite rising fails

1720
South Sea Bubble bursts

1724
Rockingham dies and John Sidney, 6th Earl of Leicester is appointed Lord-Lieutenant

1727
George I dies; George II succeeds

1737
Leicester dies and is succeeded by 2nd Earl of Rockingham

1739
War of Jenkins' Ear

1745
Rockingham dies

John Sidney, 6th Earl of Leicester

An Act of 1715 modernised its equipment and empowered the Lieutenancies to 'draw out any part of the Militia with a month's pay, which was to be repaid within six months by a rate levied in the same manner as the Land Tax.'[25]

That year the Jacobite Rising – the '15 – was confined to Scotland and the north, with no need for the Kentish Lieutenancy to do other than take coast watch precautions that proved unnecessary. Once again, Rockingham's chief activity at this time appears to have been presenting loyal addresses from the people of Kent congratulating the King on suppressing 'the late Rebellion.'[26] Rockingham, who was 50 when appointed, went on to serve until his death in March 1724.

The well-connected John Sidney, 6th Earl of Leicester, replaced him. A former Member of Parliament and Lieutenant Colonel of the 1st Foot Guards, he had succeeded to the peerage in his early 20s and was the ceremonial cup bearer at the coronation of George I in 1714. He was subsequently chosen as one of the Lords of the Bedchamber, an indication of his favoured position at Court, and, more importantly, was appointed Lord Warden of the Cinque Ports in 1717.

His selection as Lord-Lieutenant of Kent in 1724 once again brought the two offices together in one man. Further honours and high offices were showered on the Earl who became a Knight of the Bath and Captain of the Yeomen of the Guard the following year, Constable of the Tower of London and a Privy Counsellor in 1731.

His years in office were relatively uneventful. Britain was at war with Spain over Gibraltar when George I died in 1727 and George II succeeded him, but as with other far-off conflicts including the War of the Austrian Succession and the War of Jenkin's Ear, hostilities did not greatly affect the Kentish Lieutenancy and Militia, which were confined largely to an occasional coast-watching role. Leicester died unmarried in 1737 aged 57 and was buried at Penshurst.

He was succeeded by Lewis Watson, 2nd Earl of Rockingham, whose grandfather of the same name had held the Kent Lieutenancy earlier, and he, too, served during a relatively quiet period, dying childless of consumption in 1745. Obituaries described him as 'a true patriot who on all occasions displayed a noble zeal for the real interest of Great Britain.'

For some years the Lieutenancy and the Militia had remained largely ineffective and under-used, but Kent's defences were soon to be threatened yet again as the Stuarts vied one last time for the British crown.

~ TEN ~

THE THREE DUKES OF DORSET

Decades of relative inactivity for both the Lieutenancy and the near-moribund Militia came to an abrupt end with the Stuarts' final – and most dangerous – tilt at the throne. The opening moves came early in 1743, France and Spain again being at war with Britain, with Charles, son of the Pretender, reportedly arriving in Paris ready to take advantage of any events that might favour his cause. Once more Kent was vulnerable to invasion.

A French squadron sailed up-Channel from Brest and ships left Portsmouth and Chatham to counter it; forts on the Thames and Medway were hastily placed at readiness and the Kentish Militia were called out. But by June, George III's defeat of the French at Dettingham – the last time a British monarch commanded an army on a field of battle – meant that the immediate threat was over.

However, the Stuarts were still in the game and in July 1745 the Young Pretender landed – not in the south but in Scotland, raising his father's standard in the Highlands. Nevertheless, following the earlier defeat of the British Army under the Duke of Cumberland by the French at Fontenoy, no chances could be taken and the Militia of Kent and of many other counties were called

Like his grandfather and namesake, Lewis Watson, 2nd Earl of Rockingham, had an uneventful Lieutenancy, dying just as the Stuarts made a new bid for the throne

out in August to face possible invasion from across the Channel as were as the growing Jacobite threat from the north.

Throughout the rest of the year the Militia were raised and stood down several times and at this critical moment the county lost its Lord-Lieutenant with the death of the 2nd Earl of Rockingham in December. The Deputy Lieutenants immediately issued the following proclamation:

> Whereas the deputy lieutenants (the Lord-Lieutenant being dead) of the County of Kent and city of Canterbury and county of the same have lately received from the Lords of his Majesty's most honourable privy council the following order:

> Whereas the unnatural rebellion which broke out in North Britain, and was carried on there for some time, hath extended itself to this Kingdom of England, and is now carrying on in favour of a popish and abjured pretender; and there is the greatest reason to apprehend that those wicked attempts have been encouraged and may be supported by a foreign force; and whereas we think it necessary at this time, that the county of Kent should be put in the best condition of defence; we do therefore, in his Majesty's name, and by his express command, hereby pray and require you to cause the whole Militia of the said county to be put in a readiness for immediate service. And so not doubting of your ready compliance herewith, we bid you heartily farewell.[1]

The Deputy Lieutenants promptly directed and required all persons whose estates were chargeable to the Militia immediately to provide arms:

> …every person chargeable to the horse to provide a broadsword, case of pistols, the barrels thereof to be ten inches long, a carbine with belt and bucket, a great saddle or pad with burs and straps, and a bit and bridle, with pectoral and crupper. And every person chargeable to the foot to provide a musket, the barrel whereof to be not under three foot six inches, and the gage of the bore for bullets of fourteen to the pound, with a bayonet to fix on the muzzle thereof, cartouch-box, waistbelt and sword.[2]

The people of the City and County of Canterbury were likewise directed to provide arms 'for the usual number of foot soldiers found by them in times past.' A Royal Proclamation was issued ordering that the Lord Warden of the Cinque Ports and all Lieutenants and Deputy Lieutenants were 'to cause the Coasts to be carefully watched, and upon the first Approach of the Enemy, immediately to cause all Horses, Oxen and Cattle which may be fit for Draught or Burden, and not actually employ'd in our Service, or in the Defence of the Country, and also (as far as may be practicable) all other

Cattle and Provisions to be driven and removed Twenty Miles at least from the Place where the Enemy shall attempt or appear to land, and to secure the same, so as they may not fall into the Hands or Power of any of our Enemies...'[3]

This time the threat was very real, as a report from Admiral Vernon, commanding the British fleet in the Downs, warned that French and Irish troops were: 'preparing for a descent from the ports of Calais and Boulogne, and which I suspect may be attempted at Dungeness...'[4]

Vernon, who has gone down in naval history for having watered-down 'grog' served to sailors instead of neat spirits, went on to ask that the Mayor of Deal and neighbouring towns should 'have advice for assembling for their common defence' and be informed that his ships' signals on discovering the approach of the enemy would be their jack flags flying at the top-masthead and the firing of a gun every half hour.

This alarming letter sparked the Deputy Lieutenants into publishing it with the invitation attached:

> Everybody who reads the above letter, willing and ready to stand up for the defence of their king and country, their liberties and lives, are desired to assemble on Sunday morning next, 22nd inst, as soon as possible, on horseback, with such arms and ammunition as they have, and to bring two day provision of victuals along with them. The place of rendezvous, or assembling, is Swinfield [Swingfield] Minnis. It is to be hoped all the parishes and towns within twenty miles of the sea coast anyway will not fail to be there with all the able-bodied men they have. The parishes near to the Minnis are desired to bring some pickaxes, shovels and axes, along with them besides their arms.[5]

Despite the short notice some 2,000 well-armed men rallied to the then-unenclosed common at Swingfield, atop the North Downs some three miles from Dover, but the threatened invasion failed to materialise.

This episode has been painted as evidence of the Militia's ineffectiveness, citing that the appeal had to be made to anyone willing to fight rather than marshalling the at least part-trained men, and claiming:

> The Militia had really lost the advantage that could be set against its military inefficiency – namely, that it was a force always in being.[6]

Certainly the revival and reorganisation of the Militia, and in a sense the county Lieutenancies themselves, was long overdue.

In 1746, three months after Bonnie Prince Charlie's bid to restore the Stuarts to the British throne came to a bloody end at Culloden, Lionel Sackville, 1st Duke of Dorset, was appointed Lord-Lieutenant of Kent and for the

TIMELINE

1745
Young Pretender lands in Scotland; 2nd Earl of Rockingham dies

1746
Bonnie Prince Charlie is defeated at Culloden; Lionel Sackville, 1st Duke of Dorset, is appointed Lord-Lieutenant of Kent

1757
Militia Act; 1st Duke additionally appointed Lord Warden of the Cinque Ports

1759
Enforcement of Militia Act provokes riots in Kent

1765
1st Duke dies and his son Charles succeeds him as Lord-Lieutenant

Lionel Sackville, 1st Duke of Dorset, the first of his family to be appointed Lord-Lieutenant of Kent.

ensuing half century the office was dominated by three generations of this extraordinary dynasty from their magnificent seat at Knole, Sevenoaks.

The Duke, previously Earl of Dorset and Middlesex, 'preserved to the last the good breeding, decency of manners, and dignity of exterior deportment of Queen Anne's time, never departing from his style of gravity and ceremony.'[7]

Vita Sackville-West was somewhat less fulsome, writing of her ancestor that he was: 'Lacking in charm… a personage of some solidity: weighty, Georgian solidity.' Contemporaries described him as 'a man of dignity, caution and plausibility,' but that 'in spite of the greatest dignity in his appearance, he was in private the greatest lover of low humour and buffoonery.'[8]

As a child, then styled Lord Buckhurst, the future Lord-Lieutenant of Kent was almost the death of King William III. In later life, Lionel's third son, Lord George Sackville, recalled:

My father, having lost his own mother, was brought up chiefly by the Dowager Countess of Northampton, his grandmother, she being particularly acceptable to Queen Mary, that princess commanded her always to bring her little grandson, Lord Buckhurst, to Kensington Palace, though at that time hardly four years of age, and he was allowed to amuse himself with a child's cart in the gallery.

King William, like almost all Dutchmen, never failed to attend the tea-table every evening. It happened that her Majesty having one afternoon, by his desire made tea, and waiting for the King's arrival, who was engaged on business in his cabinet at the other extremity of the gallery, the boy, hearing the Queen express her impatience at the delay, ran away to the closet, dragging after him the cart. When he arrived at the door, he knocked; and the King asking, 'Who is there?' 'Lord Buck' answered he. 'And what does Lord Buck want with me?' replied HM. 'You must come to tea directly,' said he, 'the Queen is waiting for you.' King William immediately laid down his pen and opened the door. Then, taking the child in his arms, he placed Lord Buckhurst in the cart, and seizing the pole, drew them both along the gallery to the room in which was seated the Queen, Lady Northampton, and the Company.

But no sooner had he entered the apartment than, exhausted with the effort, which had forced the blood upon his lungs, and being constitutionally asthmatic, he threw himself into a chair, and for some minutes was incapable of uttering a word, breathing with the utmost difficulty. The Countess of Northampton, shocked at the consequences of her grandson's indiscretion, would have punished him, but the King interposed on his behalf.[9]

Aged just 18 on the death of his father, Lionel became 7th Earl of Dorset and

2nd Earl of Middlesex, and, it was said, had a long and brilliant career in front of him. He took his seat in the House of Lords and in the following year Queen Anne appointed him Constable of Dover Castle and Lord Warden of the Cinque Ports, which then gave a salary of £160, positions made vacant by the death of George, Prince of Denmark. However, he was forced to resign as Constable and Lord Warden in June 1713, having been accused of drawing up the Whig address presented to The Queen in that year.

On the death of Queen Anne, Dorset was commissioned by the Regency to go to Hanover, where he had earlier accompanied an embassy, and notify her death and congratulate the new King, George I, on his succession to the British crown.

Dorset was one of four English gentlemen invited to accompany the new King back to England in the royal yacht *Pelegrine* and was appointed First Gentleman of his Bedchamber and Groom of the Stable, and, more importantly, was reappointed to his former Cinque Ports offices, sworn in as a member of the Privy Council and made a Knight Companion of the Order of the Garter.

However, in July 1717 the Cabinet refused to carry out the Hanoverian policy of the King which would have involved England in a war with Russia, and Dorset was told that the King 'has no further occasion for your service in the several different employments you held under His Majesty.' Nevertheless, five months later he was appointed Vice-Admiral of Kent and in 1720 was created Duke of Dorset.

When George I died in 1727 it was again Dorset who brought the news to the new King, and he was Lord High Steward of England at the coronation and bore St Edward's crown, 'wherewith his Majesty was crowned.' It was said that:

> 'There seems to be no doubt that Dorset was persona grata at Court, even more so with George II than he had been with his father. During the latter's reign his Grace was seldom out of office and held several of the highest posts, both about the Court and in the Government of the country, that can be held by a subject.'[10]

In 1730 he was appointed Lord-Lieutenant of Ireland and resided there from 1731 to 1736. His portrait painted at that time shows him, aged 45, bewigged, big-nosed and double-chinned. The Sackville family were the greatest of the early patrons of cricket and the 1st Duke maintained his own 'cricketing place' at Knole. 'It was the first ground to be regularly mown, rolled and cosseted in preparation for cricket.'[11]

During the '45 it was Dorset who signed an order as President of the Council to the Lord-Lieutenants of the various counties, reporting, that 'the eldest son of the Pretender hath presumed in open violation of the laws to land in the

TIMELINE

1769
2nd Duke dies and his nephew John Frederick succeeds him

1776
American War of Independence; new Militia Act

1778
Kent Militia embodied for five years

1780
Gordon Riots

1783
3rd Duke goes to Paris as ambassador and attempts to convert the French to cricket; French Revolution and Louis XVI is executed

1793
French declare war on Britain

north-west part of Scotland,' and ordering that 'all arms belonging to Papists, non-jurors, or other persons that shall be judged dangerous to the peace of the Kingdom within their Lieutenancy to be seized and secured.'[12]

Months after signing that order he was himself appointed to the Kent Lieutenancy but in 1750 was additionally re-appointed Lord-Lieutenant of Ireland, serving in that capacity until 1750. This no doubt explains why records for this period of the Kent Lieutenancy are scant.

His return to Kent was in the lead-up to the Seven Years War between Austria and Prussia and between France and Britain over colonial supremacy in India, Canada and elsewhere. In 1757, the Duke of Dorset was again appointed Constable of Dover Castle and Lord Warden of the Cinque Ports, now for the term of his natural life, and was thus totally pre-eminent military leader in the county, holding all top offices.

With many of Britain's regular troops fighting overseas and the French yet again contemplating an invasion of England, it was imperative that the Militia should be revitalised and made more efficient after many years of neglect. The Government dealt with this in the 1757 Militia Act, in compliance with which steps were taken to levy, officer, and organise the force in accordance with its provisions, which, however, 'met with considerable opposition in various localities, and numerous riots ensued…'

By earlier yardsticks the numbers to be involved were relatively light. Kent was required to provide 960 out of the total of 30,000 to be raised in England; West Kent's quota being 621 and that for East Kent and Canterbury being 339.[13] The Lord-Lieutenant moved swiftly to enact the new legislation in Kent:

> We are assured that the Duke of Dorset, the Lord Lieutenant of the County of Kent, and of the City and County of Canterbury, intends to be at Maidstone at eleven O'Clock in the Morning of that Day, in order to meet the Deputy Lieutenants, and concert measures accordingly.[14]

In 1759 Dorset, now over 70, was ordered to make preparations to repel a threatened French landing by enforcing the new Acts, and this was to spark local riots in Kent. Seizing the opportunity of the new-style West Kent Militia being in training on Penenden Heath, Maidstone, in June, the Duke inspected the regiment watched by what the *Kentish Post* recorded as 'the greatest concourse of people that was ever known on any occasion, and all the Nobility and Gentry of the neighbourhood who expressed the highest satisfaction.'

It added: 'The Duke of Dorset was so highly pleased that he ordered a handsome Present to be distributed among the men to drink the King's health.' He reported:

> In obedience to His Majesty's commands… I do hereby humbly certify that the Militia of the County of Kent with the City and County of Canterbury

A private of the reorganised West Kent Militia, 1759

consists of Two Regiments or Battalions the one stiled the West Kent Regiment, the other the East Kent Reg. Or Battalion containing 621 men have been raised and formed into Ten Companies and are Armed, Trained and Disciplined in pursuance of the Acts of Parliament… and that the officers as well as private men appeared to be completely armed and very perfect in all parts of their Exercise and Firings, and to be in readiness to be drawn out and embodied if His Majesty shall think proper and to march as occasion shall require.

And he added that he had exhorted the Deputy Lieutenants to proceed 'with Diligence and attention'.[15]

A few days later the War Office informed Dorset that the King had received intelligence of 'actual preparations making in the French ports to invade this kingdom and of the imminent danger of such invasion being attempted,' adding: 'The King orders the West Kent Regiment of Militia under your command to be embodied to march to Maidstone…' Detachments were sent to relieve regular troops guarding French prisoners at Sissinghurst and elsewhere.

At this time the *Kentish Post* was advertising a drill book for the Militia: *A Regular Form of Discipline* priced at one shilling (5p) and available for purchase from selected pubs across the county. Most movements were performed to the beat of drums and wheeling and most other movements were done in slow time, giving the Militiamen, who had previously drilled only fortnightly, a chance to keep in step.

Despite the low numbers required to serve in Kent and their satisfactory performance on parade at least, there were at first many who opposed implementation of the new Militia Acts, which required anyone balloted, rich or poor, 'to pay £10, or find a substitute, or go for a soldier, and yet he would be liable to serve again at the end of three years. The peasants became refractory beyond measure and riots were raised…'

At Sevenoaks the Magistrates called a meeting at the Crown Hotel to administer the Act's provisions, but it broke up in disorder. The mob converged on the Rectory, but the Reverend Dr Curteis, fled across the fields to the

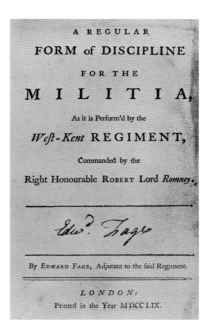

The new Militia drill book was on sale in Kent pubs for a shilling

RIGHT: Captain Smyth 'with pistol and sword charged the rabble, upon which the mob broke and fled'

Lord-Lieutenant's seat at Knole, where he reported to Captain Smyth (sometimes known as Smith), who was in charge there.

This Captain Smyth was a great character and had served under Lord George Sackville, Dorset's youngest son, the general who was subsequently court-martialled for disobedience and dubbed 'the Coward of Minden' although he later redeemed himself. While the Sevenoaks mob was rampaging, the redoubtable Smyth 'ordered the gates of Knole to be closed and barricaded and withdrew all the workmen into the house.'

Meanwhile, the mob wrecked the Rectory, drove the magistrates away in terror and then assailed the gates of Knole itself. Captain Smyth ordered his charger to be got ready, and commanded the stable gates to be thrown open, and with pistol and sword charged the rabble, upon which the mob broke and fled.[16]

What had started as a serious threat to public order ended in a farcical shambles – thanks to the heroic Captain Smyth, who proved at least on this occasion that attack is the best form of defence. He left his mark on Knole, as Vita Sackville-West describes waspishly in her book: *Knole and the Sackvilles*:

The ruins round the queer little sham Gothic house called the Bird House – which always frightened me as a child because I thought it looked like the witch's house in Hansel and Gretel, tucked away in its hollow, with its pointed gables – were built… about 1761, by one Captain Robert Smith, who had fought at Minden under Lord George Sackville, of disastrous notoriety, and who lived for some time at Knole, a parasite upon the house; they apparently purport to be the remains of some vast house, in defiance

Earliest King's and County Colours of the West Kent Militia, 1759. The regimental Colour bore the arms of the Lord-Lieutenant

of the fact that no upper storey or roof of proportionate dimensions could ever possibly have rested upon the flimsy structure of flint and rubble which constitute the ruins.

There was trouble at Ashford too, and the Lord-Lieutenant received the following alarming letter regarding the attempted swearing-in of Militiamen there:

My Lord Duke, Last Saturday being the day appointed for swearing the Militia Men of the Ashford Division, who were chosen by ballot at our meeting three weeks before, who attended at Ashford for that purpose, but met with the same Reception as once before in the Execution of the same law. We found the Street filled with men armed with Clubs and Staves who were assembled from several neighbouring parishes within ten miles, to the number of about four hundred, and there were many more in the public Houses who did not then appear.

When we went into our Room, and ordered the Constables to bring up their men to be sworn, there came upwards of one hundred and fifty of these rioters, who declared they came there to prevent every man's being sworn, and made use of their usual Threats (of pulling down and burning Houses etc) against every person who should give the Oath and all such as should take it.

We endeavoured by Argument to convince them of their Errors, but with regard to their ill-grounded opinion of the Law, and to their improper behaviour on the occasion, and to prevail upon them to disperse themselves, but all without success, therefore, after they had been in the room near an hour, we read the proclamation, upon which several went out of the room, but their places were soon supplied by others more desperate and dangerous, being many of them much in liquor, and they behaved with more riotous Insolence, breaking down the Bar betwixt us, and making use of their Clubs, striking several times Mr Sawbridge junr and once upon his head. We not being prepared with proper Force, to resist them, were obliged to retire as well as we could, they threatening to come and pull down our Houses. They staid in the Town about two hours after us and broke some Windows etc. The persons of the Rioters who came into the Room to us were chiefly Labourers, Farmers Servants, and men of very low Condition; but we have great reason to believe (almost with certainty) that they are encouraged and employed by their Masters, and many other substantial persons, who upon occasion would be ready to join them in any more desperate attempt.

We have this day consulted with several of the Deputy Lieutenants and

'We found the Street filled with men armed with Clubs and Staves'

FACTFILE

Jane Austen's
great-uncle
was clerk to the
Lieutenancy
of Kent

His duties
included
overseeing
Militia functions

Justices of the Peace of this Division of the County, who agree with us, that it is necessary to loose [sic] no time in applications for a military Force to be properly quarter'd in this riotous Country. We have therefore this day sent up a Representation of these Facts to the Secretary of State desiring an Order for a proper number of Soldiers to be quarter'd at Ashford and the neighbourhood, which we hope will meet with your Grace's approbation…[17]

The West Kent Regiment remained embodied until 1762, by which time all danger of invasion or local troubles had passed away, and Dorset was instructed that the King '…being most desirous to take the first Opportunity of relieving our Faithful Subjects from the heavy burden and Expenses occasioned by the War' ordered them to be disembodied.[18]

Meanwhile, Dorset and his Deputy Lieutenants were active regarding the East Kent Militia, as the *London Gazette* of 17 April 1762 reports:

KENT A General Meeting of His Majesty's Lieutenant, and Deputy Lieutenants for the County of Kent, will be held at the Red Lyon Inn in the City of Canterbury, on Wednesday the 5th Day of May next, at Eleven o'Clock in the Forenoon, for reforming the Battalion of Militia raised and formed in the Eastern Division of the County of Kent, pursuant to the Act of Parliament lately passed… Austen, Clerk of the General Meeting.

This was the novelist Jane Austen's great-uncle Francis Austen, a Sevenoaks attorney, Clerk of the Peace for Kent and the Duke of Dorset's agent. 'As Clerk to the Lieutenancy… Frank Austen oversaw many of the functions of the Militia, and he signed documents such as the returns made by parishes of men liable to be called up for service.'[19]

From then on the Kentish Militia regiments appear to have been assembled for 28 days' training annually, which made them a far more potent and useful force than had existed for many years.

The 1st Duke of Dorset died at Knole in October 1765. He had fulfilled his Lieutenancy duties satisfactorily, but in *Knole and the Sackvilles*, Vita Sackville-West poses the question:

Was it possible that [the Duke] would not be Lord Steward and Lord-Lieutenant of Ireland and Lord Warden and Lord-Lieutenant of Kent, did he not also happen to be Duke of Dorset? Was it possible that people such as the Sackvilles occasionally occupied positions due to their birth rather than to their intellect?

It has to be said that it was *indeed* possible, but to be fair it should be added that *noblesse oblige* – and certainly, as far as the Kent Lieutenancy was concerned, the Duke fulfilled his obligations. He was succeeded by his son Charles, Lord

Middlesex, as 2nd Duke of Dorset, who was already over 54 years of age. He had been on the usual grand tour to France and Italy and following his return, Middlesex, the title by which he was always known until the death of his father, was made Governor of Walmer Castle and family interest secured his election to Parliament. At that time he also took considerable interest in cricket and played 'in a good few matches.'

The family historian states that 'Middlesex appears to have had constant quarrels with his father the 1st Duke… and father and son do not appear to have been on speaking terms for a great part of their lives.' One reason for this was Middlesex's extravagance 'spending vast sums of money in running the Opera in London.' In 1743 Walpole informed a correspondent:

> We are likely to have no opera next year, Handel has had a palsy, and cann't compose, and the Duke of Dorset has set himself strenuously to oppose it, as Lord Middlesex is the impresario, and must ruin the House of Sackville by a course of these follies.

Later Walpole wrote:

> There is a new subscription formed for an Opera next year to be carried on by the Dilettanti, a club, for which the nominal qualification is having been in Italy, and the real one, being drunk: the two chiefs are Lord Middlesex and Sir Francis Dashwood who were seldom sober the whole time they were in Italy. [20]

Middlesex married an heiress described as 'low and ugly but a vast scholar' and Walpole commented: 'She proves an immense fortune, they pretend £130,000 – what a fund for making operas!'

In another letter in August 1746, Walpole says:

> Lord Middlesex took the opportunity of a rivalship between his own mistress, the Nardi, and the Violetta, the finest and most admired dancer in the world, to involve the whole ménage of the Opera in the quarrel, and has paid nobody… The principal man-dancer was arrested for debt; to the composer his Lordship gave a bad note, not payable for two years, besides amercing him entirely £300, on pretence of his siding with the Violetta. [21]

Nevertheless the following year Middlesex was appointed one of the Lords Commissioners of the Treasury and constituted Master of the Horse to Frederick, Prince of Wales. He cannot have been a complete fop, as he also put his name to *A Treatise concerning the Militia in Four Sections*, which was published in London in 1752, and in February 1766, as the 2nd Duke of Dorset, he was admitted a member of the Privy Council and sworn in as Lord-Lieutenant of

Charles Sackville, 2nd Duke of Dorset, succeeded his estranged father as Lord-Lieutenant of Kent

Kent.[22] The efficiency of the Kentish Militia appears to have been maintained during his three years in office, no doubt largely thanks to the zeal of his Deputy Lieutenants, and this notice gives an indication of the detailed logistical work that went into organising the annual training periods:

> Maidstone, April 8 1767 – The Deputy Lieutenants of the County, at a General Meeting held at Maidstone on the 27th Day of May, and on the 21st Day of August last, having appointed the East Kent Militia to assemble at Canterbury, on Monday, the 4th of May, for the annual Exercise of twenty-eight days, the Militia Men, belonging to the respective Companies, are therefore required to meet at the Store Room, at the Dean John near Canterbury, on the said Day, to receive their Arms and Cloaths.
>
> The Canterbury Company at Six o'Clock in the Morning; Wingham at Eight; Wye at Ten; Milton at Twelve o'Clock; Bilsington at Four in the Afternoon; *Austen, Clerk to the General Meeting*
>
> Proper Accommodations are provided at Canterbury, for the Militia-men of the Eastern Battalion, who are desirous of being inoculated; and the Sergeants when they warn the Men will direct them about the necessary Preparation.'[23]

The 2nd Duke had not long to live. Vita Sackville-West wrote quoting contemporaries of 'this proud, disgusted, melancholy, solitary man': 'He was reputed mad, "a disorder which there was too much reason to suppose, ran in the blood"'; he was certainly eccentric and there is a large picture of him in the ball-room at Knole dressed as a Roman emperor, with bare knees, a plumed helmet on his head, and various pieces of armour.'

He died in a fit at his house in St James's Street, Picadilly, in January 1769, aged 58, and Walpole wrote that he had 'worn out his constitution and almost his estate… he has not left a tree standing in the venerable old park at Knowle (sic).'[24]

His nephew, John Frederick Sackville, the 3rd Duke of Dorset, was appointed Lord-Lieutenant of Kent, aged 24, three weeks after his uncle's death and was to remain in the appointment for 28 years.

> 'For many years he mingled but little in political or busy life; his time being devoted to gallantry and pleasure among the fashionable circles, as well as in France and Italy, as in England. He was much attached to Knole, and he expended considerable sums on its repair, and internal embellishment, but would not suffer the primitive form and character of its exterior to be altered. Many of the finest plantations in the park were formed under his direction.'[25]

'What is human life but a game of cricket. And if so, why should not the ladies play it as well as we?'
3rd Duke of Dorset

LEFT: 'A good friend of the family' – Giovanna Baccelli, one of the 3rd Duke's mistresses and, reputedly, 'the love of his life'

He inherited the Sackville love of cricket and as a young man won considerable fame on the cricket field where, 'his raven locks and milk-white vest had begun to allure a crowd of feminine spectators to the new pastime.'[26] In a letter to 'a circle of Ladies, his intimate Friends,' in 1777 he asked:

> What is human life but a game of cricket. And if so, why should not the ladies play it as well as we?

His later mistresses included the flamboyant ballerina Giovanna Baccelli, subject of a much-admired Gainsborough masterpiece commissioned by the Duke, and a nude statue 'reclining voluptuously at the foot of the Great Staircase… who used to be described as "a good friend of the family" by the guides at Knole.'[27]

Although it took place far away, the American War of Independence resulted in a new Act, passed in 1776, which enabled the Militia to be called up 'in case of any rebellion existing in any territory or domain belonging to the Crown.' And two years later, with the French supporting the American cause, a warrant for the embodiment 'with all convenient speed' of all the Kent Militia was addressed to the Duke of Dorset, or 'in his absence to the Deputy Lieutenants of the said County.'

The East and West Kent regiments accordingly assembled at Canterbury and Maidstone, and the Lord-Lieutenant was appointed Colonel of the West Kents. After training the East Kents remained to serve on home territory and the larger West Kent Militia marched off westward to serve mainly in Hampshire, the *Kentish Gazette* reporting:

> The spirit of true British courage glowed in their cheeks… France may well tremble at the name of the British Militia.'[28]

Kent's Lord-Lieutenant, although dismissed by some commentators as a mere

John Frederick Sackville, 3rd Duke of Dorset, succeeded his uncle as Lord-Lieutenant

cricket-mad, gambling womaniser, appears to have had the respect of his superiors in Militia terms. Hands-on at this stage, he marched on occasion at the head of the Regiment and lived alongside the men – not always a comfortable experience. In a violent storm the Duke's marquee was washed away, 'several valuable books and manuscripts being spoiled or lost.' Camp was clearly no picnic for Kent's Lord-Lieutenant or his Militiamen.

Escorting French prisoners and helping quell the Gordon Riots in London in 1780 were the highlights of the Kentish Militiamen's embodiment. They were stood down after a five-year full-time stint, their reputation high, and in 1783 Dorset went to Paris as ambassador-extraordinary and plenipotentiary to the court of France.[29]

As well as filling his ambassadorial role with apparent dedication, he promoted cricket among British expatriates and the French with mixed success. Reporting on a match played in the Champs-Elysees, *The Times* noted, in what today might be considered borderline racist terms:

> His Grace of Dorset was, as usual, the most distinguished for skill and activity. The French, however, cannot imitate us in such vigorous exertions of the body, so that we seldom see them enter the lists.

The brief period of peace brought the usual down-grading of Britain's defences and in 1786 the Lord-Lieutenant returned briefly to oversee the reduction of the Militia's permanent staff.

He remained ambassador to France until the outbreak of the French Revolution, and on his return was a member of the committee that drew up the original laws of the Marylebone Cricket Club.

Across the Channel heads were rolling as the Terror came to a bloody climax and gave birth to the Republic, with the revolutionaries 'declaring their fraternity with all nations who wished to be "free" and offering a helping hand to assist any rebels who might prefer "liberty" like theirs to the laws and lawful Monarchs of their respective countries.'

Europe trembled, but 'the mass of the British nation, fortunately, were too well acquainted with their liberty and freedom to be deluded thus, and with eager indignation rallied round the Throne and avowed their intention to support the Constitution by all means in their power, whether against foreign foes or internal enemies…'[30]

As a precautionary measure, Dorset received an order in December 1792 'to draw out and embody such part of the Militia as was actually trained and exercised in the course of the present year,' but in fact the whole of both East and West Kent Regiments were called out – a total of 1,000 Militiamen.

The execution of King Louis XVI a month later brought matters to a head and in February the French declared war on England. The Lieutenancy was about to face its stiffest test since the Armada.

'The spirit of true British courage glowed in their cheeks… France may well tremble at the name of the British Militia'

ABOVE: The threat of invasion hung large over Kent during the Revolutionary and Napoleonic Wars. This humorous contemporary image foretold both the Channel Tunnel and aerial attacks on the Frontline County

~ ELEVEN ~

'THIS GLORIOUS DAY FOR THE COUNTY'

The French Revolution heralded two decades of war and invasion threats that turned the Frontline County into an armed camp and kept the Lieutenancy heavily involved in preparations for its defence. This involved everything from organising the Militia and other auxiliary forces to overseeing plans for a scorched earth policy involving the removal of livestock and crops from the coast. It even included regulating the amounts of bread produced by the county's bakers.

At a meeting of Lord-Lieutenants in London the precedence of the county Militias was decided by drawing lots. Fittingly for the Frontline County, Kent drew Number 1, and the newly-embodied West Kents marched away to serve mainly on the Sussex and Hampshire coast and in East Anglia before returning to Kent.

As Lord-Lieutenant the 3rd Duke of Dorset was drawn into an embarrassing public row over plans for the defence of the county

Sessions House was so crowded for the meeting that the floor appeared to be giving way and had to be propped up

Kent's light horse troops of old had long disappeared, but with the county again vulnerable to invasion mobility was crucial. This prompted the formation of an association for East Kent and Canterbury of gentlemen, yeomen and others 'willing to mount themselves on horses of not less than 14.3 (hands) high and clothe themselves at their own expense.' The committee was to consist of the Deputy Lieutenants, subscribers of £50 and the senior officer of each troop.[1]

But, according to the Yeomanry historian Lord Harris:

> The Association had been a little premature, forgetting that the enlistment of troops and the appointment of officers were rather matters for Parliament and the Crown than for independent and irresponsible bodies of civilians…[2]

The Government wrote thanking the Lord-Lieutenant for reporting the resolutions, noting the 'zeal and loyalty' of the proposers, but added that no military association which did not rest on commissions flowing from His Majesty could be countenanced. The Association was therefore dissolved. They had been commendably enthusiastic but too quick off the mark.

But in March 1794 William Pitt moved a Bill to augment the Militia and said it was contemplated that volunteer companies would be raised for local defence. The nobility, gentry and principal land owners of Kent promptly resolved that a general meeting should be held, and the Lord-Lieutenant was requested to prepare a plan for the safety and security of the county.

A meeting was duly called at which the Lord-Lieutenant found himself at the centre of an embarrassing public row:

> So great was the crowd in the Sessions House at Maidstone that it was thought that some 2,000 persons were present, and at one time people underneath the room noticed that the floor appeared to be giving way, and hastily introduced props, which fortunately had the desired effect.[3]

When the meeting got under way:

> One party vociferated that the Duke of Dorset was a 'placeman' and a 'pensioner', and not a proper person to bring forward the business. Others were equally positive that he had been requested to prepare plans, and therefore was entitled to precedence. A most violent uproar accompanied these attempts, which continued for nearly an hour and a half; at length a show of hands decided that precedence should be given to the Lord Lieutenant, but he was again prevented from speaking by shouts of 'no placemen', 'no pensioner.'[4]

The man who was to succeed Dorset in the Lieutenancy, Lord Romney:

…succeeded in pouring oil on the troubled waters, pointing out that somebody must be appointed to prepare plans, and that as His Majesty had appointed the Duke to be Lord-Lieutenant it would be 'very ungenerous to use that as a reproach which should recommend him to their esteem.' The Duke was then allowed to read his plans, which were in substance: That Volunteer Troops of Horse of 50 men each should be raised by means of a subscription, that they should not be called out of the County except in case of actual invasion, or for the suppression of riots and tumults, in which case they were to be under the Mutiny Bill and that they receive the same pay as Dragoons.[5]

Strong objections especially against forced subscriptions were led by Lord Thanet, but he was trumped by Sir Edward Knatchbull who produced a Bill which had passed the House of Commons the previous night without division, sanctioning subscriptions.

Lord Romney described the state of affairs in France, and supported the Duke of Dorset's propositions, which were then put and carried by a large majority. Mr S.Sawbridge followed with doubts as to the utility of the Volunteer Troops of Horse. 'Gentlemen,' he remarked, 'confined themselves at home to riding over hedges and ditches, but he was afraid no great reliance could be placed on them if they should be called into active service.' But others were confident the fox-hunters would soon qualify as soldiers and a subscription list was opened, which was headed by the Duke of Dorset with £500, and was so liberally supported that the total subscriptions eventually reached at least £10,000.[6]

Lord Harris records that at a subsequent meeting it was decided that 'these Troops of Cavalry to serve during the war were to consist of gentlemen and yeomen and such persons as they shall bring forward to be approved of by the Lord-Lieutenant under authority from His Majesty.'

There would be no pay unless called out; the Government would provide arms and accoutrements and pay drill sergeants; and the troops were to find their own horses and clothing. 'They were liable to be called upon by order from His Majesty or the Lord-Lieutenant or Sheriff for the suppression of riots and tumults in the country; and in such cases they were to receive pay as regular troops and to be liable to the provisions of the Mutiny Bill.'

This was the case in 1797 when the East Kent Yeomanry were for the first time called out in aid of the Civil Power.

The Mutiny at the Nore afforded the opportunity, and on Sunday, June 4th, Sir Edward Knatchbull's Provender Troop was ordered to proceed immediately to the Isle of Sheppey, and was employed in arresting seamen

A cornet of the West Kent Yeomanry Cavalry

'Whoever
appears
notoriously
drunk twice
on the days
of general
meeting, to
be expelled
the corps'

deserting from their ships… the whole coast from Sheerness and along the mainland to Faversham, through Whitstable, to the Isle of Thanet, was patrolled by troops of Yeomanry… there can be little doubt that the force was of considerable use to the Government.[7]

Resolutions adopted for Lord Darnley's Cobham Yeomanry included 'whoever appears notoriously drunk twice on the days of general meeting, to be expelled the corps'![8] This was the start of the Lieutenancy's long and close association with the Yeomanry. Not only had the Duke of Dorset initiated its formation, but the Yeomanry was to include among its officers two future Lord-Lieutenants, Camden and Sydney.

In the Revolutionary and subsequent Napoleonic Wars naval power was the key factor with British warships holding supremacy in the Channel, blockading enemy ports and bringing France and its allies to battle whenever possible. And for the first few years the main action took place well away from British shores, giving sufficient time to sort out home defence.

A professional command structure emerged with regular forces augmented by locally-raised auxiliary units which were very much the concern of the Lord-Lieutenant. He already held sway over the Militia – and later Supplementary Militia – which was reasonably well trained, usable both in and out of the county and later formed a pool in which line regiments could fish for recruits.

Associations formed by enthusiastic and patriotic Britons had raised voluntary corps, approved by the Lord-Lieutenants, for the duration of earlier threats, and early in 1794 a plan was proposed to the Lieutenants promoting the opening of subscriptions to support the formation of auxiliary units for local defence especially in coastal areas, and including Fencible cavalry in addition to the Yeomanry.

Among the additional units was the New Romney Fencible Cavalry that advertised for 'spirited young men', promising them good rations and assuring them the Regiment was not to go abroad. Nevertheless they were sent to Ireland where they served until 1800 when the unit was disbanded.

The Lieutenancies reacted positively to the call for auxiliary units and in April 1794 a distinct Volunteer Force became a reality with the passing of an Act 'for encouraging and disciplining such corps or companies of men as shall voluntarily enrol themselves for the defence of their counties, towns, or coasts, or for the general defence of the Kingdom during the present war.'[9]

Sanctioned by the Lord-Lieutenant, they were only to be called out in the event of invasion and selected their own officers.

Their magnificent uniforms disguised their utter amateurishness, inferior even to the trained Militia in readiness for combat… martial law did not apply, and the only sanction was dismissal, chronic offences included 'drinking in the ranks when at drill.'[10]

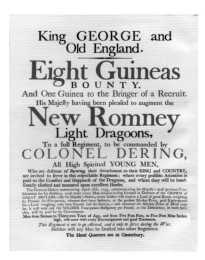

A contemporary Fencible cavalry recruiting poster

The auxiliary forces were to include Sea and River Fencibles under naval command: fishermen, boatmen – and no doubt smugglers – a kind of early Dad's Navy. Separately William Pitt, temporarily out of Government office, but still Lord Warden, raised three battalions of Cinque Ports Volunteers which he led as Colonel Commandant.

In October 1796 Spain joined France in declaring war on Britain and the following year the French determined to invade, appointing Napoleon to command the invasion force, and the forces in the Southern District under General Sir Charles Grey were put on alert. Among the enthusiastic new auxiliaries were three companies of Canterbury Volunteers, who presented the King with a loyal address tendering their services 'at this awful moment, when our daring and desperate Foes have insolently avowed their Intention of making a Descent upon our Country.'

The Volunteers pledged themselves 'to come forward with the utmost Zeal and Energy in Defence of those equal Laws, that holy Religion, and those invaluable Liberties, which all your Majesty's Subjects so eminently enjoy,' and undertook to march when ordered by the King or Lord-Lieutenant.[11] The Duke of Dorset, who had himself raised a force of 60 men – the Knole Volunteers – to protect the Sevenoaks area, was now in failing health and suffering from melancholia, and in June 1797 a new Lord-Lieutenant stepped up to the plate. Dorset's son was an infant, so this was the end of the Sackville family's Lieutenancy dynasty that had endured for more than half a century, and the Duke died at home at Knole in 1799, aged 54.

With a long and bloody war against France in its early stages the man now faced with playing a key role in the defence of the Frontline County was Charles Marsham, 3rd Baron and later as the second creation 1st Earl of Romney. He should not to be confused with Henry Sidney, the 1st Earl of Romney of the first creation in 1694.

Marsham was a happy choice to replace Dorset as Lord-Lieutenant at this critical time. He had been an active Member of Parliament for Kent, had a keen interest in the Militia, had given strong support to his predecessor in the dispute over the formation of the Yeomanry – and was ready to play a full part in overseeing the new Volunteer movement and the detailed plans that must be drawn up for coping with an invasion.

Appointed at the age of 52, his family seat was Mote Park, Maidstone, with its extensive parkland that would become the setting for the largest gathering of the county's volunteer soldiery that has ever been held. In Parliament he voted against the American war and was described by the *Public Ledger* as 'a most honest, upright, and independent Member of Parliament of Whig principles, (who) votes occasionally on each side, but most frequently in opposition.' He had a mind of his own, preferring to support 'measures not men.'

So Romney, 'an ordinary man… of good intentions and plain sense, without ornament or decoration of any kind,' was the man called upon to steer the

Cometh the hour, cometh the man: Charles Marsham, 1st Earl of Romney, followed the three Dukes of Dorset as Lord-Lieutenant of Kent

*When Men of Kent
protect our coast*

*We scorn the
threat'ning hostile
host*

*And freely cast
away our fears*

*Whilst guarded by
such Volunteers*

**From: A Song by a
Gentleman of West
Kent, 1794**

Lieutenancy through its busiest and demanding decade for more than 200 years. This time the threat lay directly across the Channel, with the French ready to cross given a window of opportunity by the Royal Navy and the right weather conditions.

This was the situation when Lord Romney was appointed and he and his Deputies were from that time on fully engaged in organising not only the Militia, Volunteers and other auxiliary forces but soon became involved in the detailed planning of many logistical contingency measures required in the then very likely event of invasion.

This planning was aimed at mobilising the population in threatened areas and assigning all able-bodied men a role. Napoleon was known to subscribe to the maxim that:

> A general should be capable of making all the resources of the invaded country contribute to the success of his enterprise.[12]

So it was decided that if an enemy were to land then:

> A policy of 'driving the country' would be followed. The coastal areas would be swept bare of any resources that might be used to support his troops. This scheme for the removal of all 'stock and produce,' had been put to Lord Romney 'for the consideration of the gentlemen of Kent' and had met with a favourable response.'[13]

These arrangements required a great deal of detailed planning and at two Canterbury meetings tracts of the county were allotted to Yeomanry troops and companies of Volunteers.

However, the immediate cross-Channel threat had diminished, Napoleon having decided that 'the pear was not yet ripe' and left to command the French Army of the Orient only to be thwarted by Nelson's great victory in Aboukir Bay in August 1798. Rebellion in Ireland supported, too late, by the French, prompted the deployment of Kent Militiamen for service there – their first overseas, every man a volunteer.

The following year began badly for the French and 'Britain was in buoyant mood and something of the spirit of this time is shown in Kent by the staging of the Mote Park Review at Maidstone in August.'[14]

This extraordinary event was made possible by the generosity of Romney, the Lord-Lieutenant, who threw open his parkland, received King George III and other members of the Royal family, many distinguished guests – some 6,000 people including the volunteers – all of whom were treated to a memorable feast watched by thousands of spectators. The scene was captured by the artist William Alexander and engraved as an aquatint.

A contemporary account captures the excitement of 'this glorious day for the

county, and an instance perhaps without parallel, when a subject at his own expence [sic] liberally entertained his Sovereign, with his Royal Consort, the different branches of the Royal Family, the great officers of state, the principal nobility and gentry of the realm, and an Army of Volunteers…'[15]

West Kent Yeomanry troops under Colonel Earl Camden came from Sevenoaks, Tonbridge and Tunbridge Wells in the west to Chislehurst, Greenwich and Woolwich in the north to the Isle of Sheppey in the east. The East Kents were from Romney Marsh to the Isle of Thanet and the villages in between. The infantry represented every town and many of the larger villages throughout the county, and the artillery corps was from Gravesend and Thanet. They began to move to the Mote at five o'clock in the morning and were all in position by nine o'clock.

There was tremendous public enthusiasm to see the King review so many Volunteers in what was an event of national importance at this time of threat.

> The crowds that thronged in from all round Maidstone to see the Review were such that the roads were rendered almost impassable; the town of Maidstone was so full the previous evening that many visitors were unable to find accommodation… the whole County of Kent seemed as it were uncommonly alive and proud on the memorable occasion.

The Volunteers provided their own transport and distinguished themselves by 'wearing oak boughs in their hats.'[16]

The wearing of sprigs of oak harked back to the time when William the Norman was confronted at Swanscombe by what appeared to be a moving forest – a Kentish army bearing boughs – with which he agreed that they could continue to enjoy their ancient liberties; hence Kent's proud motto *Invicta*: Unconquered. Honouring Kent, Pitt, the Secretary of State Dundas, and the other statesmen attending the event also decorated their hats with oak.

'This glorious day for the county, and an instance perhaps without parallel, when a subject at his own expence liberally entertained his Sovereign… and an Army of Volunteers'

'Kent Volunteers – Loyal – Brave – Free.' The triumphal arch erected in Maidstone for the King's visit

The Royal Family left London at five o'clock in the morning, breakfasted with Earl Camden at his seat at Wilderness, near Sevenoaks, and arrived at the Mote at noon. In Maidstone, where the Royal Standard was hoisted on the town hall and church, they passed under a huge triumphal arch, surmounted by a lion, unicorn and crown, bearing the proud boast: *Kent Volunteers – Loyal – Brave – Free.*

A Royal salute greeted the King's arrival at the review ground and the Queen and Princesses drove to the large tented royal pavilion where they too decorated themselves with oak sprigs.

The Volunteers, drawn up in two ranks with the Yeomanry behind, were reviewed by the King and went through military manoeuvres, each heralded by the firing of a cannon: marching and counter-marching, firing, giving general salutes and *feux de joie* with bands playing and three cheers before dinner.

> Lord Romney extended to all visitors a splendid hospitality. Tables were laid to the number of 91 and places were provided for 6,000 persons; the length of the tables, if placed in line, would have reached to 7½ miles and the value of the woodwork exceeded £2,500…[17]

Hasted claims the actual number of volunteers due to attend was 5,721, of whom he says 5,228 appeared. The sumptuous dinner served to all consisted of:

> …3 score Lambs, in quarters, making 240 dishes; 700 Fowls, three in a dish; 300 Hams; 300 Tongues; 220 Dishes of Boiled Beef; 220 Dishes of Roast Beef; 220 Meat Pies; 220 Fruit Pies and 220 Joints of Roast Veal. Seven pipes of port were bottled off by Lord Romney's butler, and what more might be wanted was ready in pipes in his lordship's cellar to be supplied. Sixteen butts of ale and as much small beer were also placed in large vessels to supply the company, and a pump was fixed outside of the house, which communicated with the cellar, for the purpose of obtaining what more might be necessary.[18]

The food on one table for 200 was left untouched and Romney ordered that it be distributed to every cottager in the neighbourhood:

> A full wagon load of it besides was sent to Maidstone, to be distributed among the poor, sufficient in quantity for 600 families.[19]

A 21-gun salute fired by the artillery volunteers signalled the Royal party's departure – and immediately General Gray offered his warmest thanks to the Lord-Lieutenant and to the Lord Warden of the Cinque Ports, the Yeomanry and Volunteers for honouring him 'by their unanimous request that he would take Command of them on this glorious and eventful day.'

A many a one who reads our bill of fare

Shall for vexation stamp and bite his lips

And hold his folly great he did not come

To Romney Park and feast with us this day

Parody of Shakespeare's Henry V speech, written by a gentleman of Maidstone[20]

In turn, the Lord-Lieutenant received fulsome thanks and praise from the King via the Secretary of State Henry Dundas:

> I have it specially in command from His Majesty to mention to your Lordship that the Military Appearance of the Volunteer Corps of the County of Kent was but one ingredient in that heartfelt satisfaction His Majesty has this Day experienced in contemplating a display of those Virtues & Manners which distinguish the genuine character of Englishmen and that however much it may be improved will never be impaired by the example of the Person to whom His Majesty has committed the Charge of this great and respectable County.[21]

Kent's Lord-Lieutenant and the Frontline County's Volunteers had triumphed, and Lord Romney's initiative in inspiring the event and his extraordinary generosity in providing hospitality for 6,000 people from the King himself down to the lowliest private – not forgetting the poor of Maidstone – would not be forgotten. Five days after the review the Court of Burghmote at Canterbury voted him the Freedom of the City:

> …in testimony of the very honourable and spirited conduct and exertions of his Lordship, in discharge of the duties of that high office, during a period which has required an attention and energy, unknown in modern times.[22]

The following month there was a meeting at Sittingbourne of a great many officers of the Volunteers to consider a lasting memorial to present to the Lord-Lieutenant to commemorate his 'unparalleled hospitality' during the review and his 'constant attention to the Volunteer Corps of this county.'

No sooner had a public subscription among the Volunteers been announced than a sufficient sum was raised for 'this truly patriotic purpose' – and a circular, stone-built pavilion in the Ionic style with eight columns was built in Mote Park, 'a short distance from the old house; and being backed by some fine trees it forms a good object from the windows of the new one.'[23]

Further recognition came in June 1801 when Romney was created Viscount Marsham, of The Mote in the County of Kent, and Earl of Romney.

This was another critical year, with military and naval preparations again afoot in French and Dutch ports, and Romney forwarded orders to the Yeomanry and Volunteers from the new commander of the Southern District. They were to 'hold themselves in constant readiness to assemble at their respective places of Parade, on the first Information of an Enemy's appearance off the coast.' Among the other roles of the Yeomanry was conveying highwaymen from Maidstone to Shooters Hill for execution, and on another occasion escorting the Irish patriot Napper Tandy under arrest to London.

The Kentish Militiamen deployed to Ireland had returned, been positioned

TIMELINE

1794
Lord-Lieutenant proposes plan for defending Kent; Yeomanry and Volunteer Force raised

1797
Nore Mutiny

1799
3rd Duke of Dorset dies; Charles Marsham, 3rd Baron Romney, succeeds him as Lord-Lieutenant; holds Mote Park Review

1801
Act of Union of Great Britain and Ireland; Romney is made an Earl

1802
Peace of Amiens

1803
War resumes

1805
Trafalgar – invasion threat recedes

1808
John Jeffreys Pratt, 2nd Earl Camden succeeds Romney as Lord-Lieutenant; Peninsular War begins

1812
Camden is made a Marquess

1815
Waterloo – war ends

The pavilion erected by the Kentish Volunteers to commemorate their Lord-Lieutenant's hospitality still stands in Mote Park, Maidstone, today

along the coast and – somewhat ominously – they and the Volunteer corps were ordered to 'practise more than has been usual in their exercise the use of the Bayonet to advance and charge in various situations on variety of ground.' The view, well before television's *Dad's Army*, appeared to be that invading Frenchmen would 'not like it up 'em!'

Despite the imminent threat, 'during the harvest one-third of the duty men in each regiment were permitted to assist in getting in the crops within twelve miles of their respective stations.' This order was soon restricted because the threat was considered too grave.[24] Nelson unsuccessfully attacked the French flotilla at Boulogne but once more the invasion threat failed to materialise and in March 1802 the Peace of Amiens between Britain and France brought at least temporary respite.

Predictably orders were sent for disembodying the Militia of Kent 'with all convenient dispatch' and with the King's thanks for their 'exemplary and meritorious services.'

Within a year of the signing of the Peace of Amiens the French were again making preparations in French and Dutch ports; in March 1803 the Militia were again embodied and in May the war resumed. A month later a meeting of Lord-Lieutenants at the Horse Guards drew lots to determine precedence among the Militia regiments and this time Romney drew not No 1, but No 57 for the Kent units, which remained in force until 1833.[25]

Towards the end of 1803 an important meeting took place at Canterbury, when Lord Romney met the captains of the Yeomanry troops 'and effected a very notable change in their Constitution.'

'It was resolved to incorporate the different Troops in East Kent into a Regt, Sir Edward Knatchbull (who had supported the Lord-Lieutenant so effectively over the raising of the Yeomanry nine years earlier) to be colonel…' Eight East Kent troops were now to be incorporated. Once again, Kent was to the fore, for it was not until the following year that the Government informed Lord-Lieutenants that it wished to encourage the amalgamation of separate troops into regiments, performing their annual 12 days' permanent duty at the same time.

With the resumption of war and the renewed invasion threat the Lieutenancy became involved in immensely detailed planning required in the event of a French landing. This included organising the evacuation of animals and crops, the raising of additional local companies to serve alongside existing armed forces, and supervising the undertaking given by bakers supplying bread.

The resulting documentation, known as the Lieutenancy Returns, survives for a number of areas. Folkestone's schedules include a 'Return of Overseers and Persons appointed for the Removal of Waggons, Cattle, Horses, and Live Stock, as well as to take charge of the Dead Stock…' There follows lists of individuals allocated specific roles for removal of different types of animals and so on.

Yeomanry troops were put at notice to escort the gatherings of livestock away from the coast. Another schedule shows the number of those aged between 15 and 60 willing to serve with arms who would agree to assemble in troops or companies should the need arise. They are listed as on horseback or foot and how armed: swords and pistols for the cavalry; firelocks and pitchforks for the infantry. The instructions were that:

> …on forwarding their names to the Lieutenancy they should propose the names of their leaders for their (the Deputy Lieutenants') Approbation, at the rate as nearly as possible of one to twenty five or at most thirty five men.

Furthermore it was:

> …earnestly recommended to all who voluntarily offer to appear with Arms, to provide a Bullet Mould for the Calibre of their Gun or Pistol, a Small Bag for Bullets, and a Powder Horn lest the bore of their [weapon] being smaller than those of the Army should Prevent their using the Ammunition made for the Kings Troops, in which case, a Delivery of Lead and Powder will be made to them.[26]

Elsewhere every man in the locality was listed with his occupation, age, marital status, number of children and role assigned. Men not suitable for fighting were to act as military pioneers, bringing with them either axe, spade or other similar tools.

The plan for securing a regular supply of bread for defending forces involved the town's 14 bakers signing their promise to deliver 'Good wholesome well baked Bread, in Loaves of three Pounds and four Pounds and a half, as our Stock of Flour in Hand at the Time may enable us to Furnish, over and above the Ordinary Consumption of our Customers' whenever required to do so and afterwards paid at rates certified to be reasonable 'by such Deputy Lieutenants or Magistrates, as may be appointed for that purpose.' For most bakers this meant doubling output in an emergency, or more with the help of an additional journeyman.

Quantities of coals and wood in the form of faggots – large bundles of brushwood brought in from the countryside around to keep the ovens constantly alight for every 24 hours – were also listed.

Many a scare kept Kent's defenders on their toes. General Sir John Moore, training the Light Infantry at Shorncliffe, wrote in October 1803: 'The signal officer at Folkestone mistook a signal, which was that the enemy's boats were out of Calais… The Volunteers, Sea Fencibles and all, were turned out, and very cheerful – not at all dismayed at the prospect of meeting the French… By the time I reached camp, the mistake was discovered.'[27]

At this time patriotic fervour was feverish and in addition to regular and

'Swords and pistols for the cavalry; firelocks and pitchforks for the infantry'

Deputy Lieutenants were to supervise bakers to ensure a regular supply of bread in the event of an invasion

Militia troops 300,000 volunteers countrywide were ready to resist an invasion. All Napoleon needed was control of the narrowest strip of the Channel – not even for days but for a matter of hours in order to launch his much-vaunted, boastfully-named 'Army of England' in their hundreds of invasion barges against the Kent coast.

Napoleon himself said in June 1805: 'It is necessary for us to be masters of the sea for six hours only, and England will have ceased to exist.'

However, the great battle for survival was not fought in the Channel, but 1,000 miles away off Spain's Cape Trafalgar. Nelson's mission was to destroy the combined French and Spanish navies and with it Napoleon's capability to invade Britain. That is exactly what Nelson did – and Napoleon's invasion army struck camp and marched away.

The Colonne de la Grande Armee erected on the outskirts of Boulogne to honour Napoleon's 'personality and works' is topped by a statue of him, not gazing wistfully at the Kent coast, but with his back turned on 'perfidious Albion.'

Having been arrayed along their native coast for that last invasion scare, Kentish Militiamen marched off to serve in East Anglia. Lord Romney was urged by government to encourage them to volunteer for the Regular Army, and a quarter of them did. Later the West Kent Militia were ordered further north to serve as far as Newcastle. Many more men volunteered for line regiments and it was not until 1814 that the Kentish Militiamen returned home as a result of the Anglo-French peace treaty. Perhaps the most important service of the Militia was that it freed regular units for service on the Continent and provided an at least partially-trained pool in which line regiments could fish for recruits.

In June 1808 the Earl of Romney had retired as Lord-Lieutenant after 11 arduous years in the post and was replaced by John Jeffreys Pratt, 2nd Earl Camden, who had entertained the Royal Family to breakfast at his seat at Wilderness on their way to the Mote Park Review.

Camden, at 49, was a well-known national figure, a friend of William Pitt the younger, a Lord of the Admiralty and later of the Treasury, a Privy Councillor and member of the Board of Trade.

He had succeeded his father as 2nd Earl Camden in 1794 and the following year was appointed Lord-Lieutenant of Ireland, where his indecision as 'a largely powerless agent faced with tumultuous political challenges' drew criticism. But he did his best and in 1798 had resigned to allow General Cornwallis to become joint Viceroy and Commander-in-Chief and enabling him to restore order after the rebellion.

Camden, 'a plain, unaffected, good humoured man, of pleasing conversation and conciliatory address' was made a Knight of the Garter in 1799. He returned to office with Pitt in 1804 and was made Secretary of State for War and the Colonies, a role in which, although it sounded vitally important at

An officer of the Kentish Militia, 1814

the height of the wars, he was in fact said to be merely a cipher because the premier handled all the important matters. Known as 'Lord Chuckle' he succeeded to the family estate of Bayham Abbey on the Kent and Sussex border, which became his principal residence, and later became Lord President of the Council.[28]

His appointment as Lord-Lieutenant and Custos Rotulorum of Kent in 1808 would have come as no surprise since he had good residential and military credentials in the county, having first been appointed as an ensign in the West Kent Militia 29 years earlier.

Lieutenancies were still worked hard at this time and between 1801 and 1814 there were no less than 51 Acts of Parliament affecting the Militia, a nightmare to administer. 'Never was the work of the County Lieutenancies more fraught with complications than during the Napoleonic Wars' and small wonder that by 1810 Deputy Lieutenants 'were on the verge of revolt in some counties.'[29] When, in 1810, Camden appointed his first new Deputy Lieutenants only one had been knighted.[30]

John Jeffreys Pratt, 2nd Earl Camden, replaced Romney as Lord-Lieutenant

Until 1829 Catholics were still debarred from office. Church of England clergy were very much involved with Lieutenancy matters as magistrates, but could not then be appointed as Deputy Lieutenants.

Predictably, no sooner had peace been signed with France than Camden was ordered 'to cause the Militia of the county to be disembodied with all convenient speed.' When the King of France left exile in England:

> The Marquess Camden, KG Lord-Lieutenant of Kent, at the head of the West Kent Yeomanry and the other volunteer regiments of the county, had the honour of receiving the King and accompanying His Majesty through the city of Rochester. The West Kent Yeomanry continued to escort the King's carriage, and the Lord-Lieutenant proceeded to Dover to pay his last respects to His Majesty.[31]

In March 1815 Napoleon escaped from Elba and rapidly attracted an army, causing the Allies to crank up their war machinery once more. In Kent, Camden was required to call out and embody the Militia, the West Kents sailing immediately to serve for a year in Ireland. But well before their return Napoleon had been defeated once and for all at Waterloo.

Wellington's despatch bearing the news of the allied victory was rowed ashore at Broadstairs and travelled by post-chaise via Canterbury, Sittingbourne, Rochester and Blackheath to London – an event being commemorated with a symbolic re-enactment in 2015.

More than 20 years of conflict that had demanded so much of the Kent Lieutenancy was at last at an end, and, through the Lord-Lieutenant, Parliament expressed its grateful thanks to the much-used Militia, the Yeomanry and Volunteers.

ABOVE: The East and West Kent Yeomanry Regiments performed their drills at a colourful review in the presence of the Lord-Lieutenant, Lord Camden, at Mote Park, Maidstone, in 1837

~ TWELVE ~
RIOTS AND AN EARLY DAD'S ARMY

ollowing two decades of war and French invasion scares Kent's Militiamen went home, the Volunteers stood down, and the Lieutenancy's workload returned once more to a routine level. It would be more than half a century before England's shores were threatened again. The next danger was to come from within.

The Lord-Lieutenant, promoted in the peerage as Marquess Camden in 1812, had retired from high political office but continued to be involved as a Tory supporter, cautiously in favour of granting Catholic emancipation and maintaining an interest in Irish affairs.

In Kent, peace meant that the annual Militia training was dispensed with until 1820 when the men exercised for 28 days, and in the 15 years after the end of the war training took place on only two other occasions: 21 days in 1821 and 28 days in 1825. There were resulting cuts in the permanent staff and the Militia were reduced to a shadow of their former strength. Camden, at the age of 68, was appointed to the largely honorary role of Colonel of the West Kent Militia in 1827.

Yeomanry activity was not at first similarly reduced. The Lord-Lieutenant had stood the West Kents by in 1815 to support the Civil Power in case 'attempts may be made in the County of Kent, to disturb the Publick Peace,'

REPRIEVE FOR GAME BIRDS – AND TENANTS?

'Notice is hereby given that the Marquess Camden (on account of the backwardness of the harvest) will not shoot himself or any of his tenants till the 14th of September' – Unfortunately-worded announcement by the Lord-Lieutenant in 1821

although nothing came of it. Again, in 1820, reliance on the highly mobile Yeomanry to aid the Civil Power in emergency is shown in Camden's instruction to the commanding officers of both East and West Kent regiments to take all necessary measures to provide prompt assistance if 'Tumults should take place.' Again, nothing materialised, but in the absence of an effective county police force the Yeomen could have proved useful if it had.

The following year the West Kent Yeomanry had the honour of escorting King George III from London to Sittingbourne, and the East Kent Regiment escorted the Royal party on to Ramsgate, winning His Majesty's warm thanks for 'their dutiful and loyal attachment.'

But in 1824 in 'a spirit of false economy on the part of the Government' the Kent Yeomanry was not called out for permanent duty and was subsequently reduced – 'a hasty and ill-advised step, for three years afterwards it had to be retraced.' Camden had the unpleasant duty of delivering news of the cuts.[1]

It seems an eternal truth that as soon as a war ends politicians seek a peace dividend and reduce the armed forces, only to have to scramble to re-form them next time the alarm bell rings. In the case of the Kentish Yeomanry:

> Whatever the cause of the Government's decision, the pendulum swung back in 1830. The distressed condition of the agricultural population led to an outbreak of the people, in the course of when private property was attacked, buildings, cornstacks, and mills were destroyed by fire, and, eventually, all attempts to protect property were practically abandoned by the local authorities.

The Lord-Lieutenant was embroiled in dealing with the Swing Riots, but was unable to call upon the Yeomanry because of Government false economy

The so-called Swing Riots, which began with the breaking of threshing machines in East Kent, were about to shake the county and country to the core.

At this point the Government appealed to the force it had disbanded three years before when it had 'no reason to apprehend under any probable circumstances, the recurrence of any necessity to call for their services.'[2] But by the time the re-formed Yeomanry troops were effective the trouble had been contained, and significantly it was regular cavalry working with magistrates, special constables, and a special Government investigator backed by some of the new London police officers – Peelers – that proved most useful in countering the machine-breakers and incendiaries. The mobility of the cavalry was key in a situation where attacks could flare up anywhere anytime.

The Lord-Lieutenant was embroiled in dealing with the riots and was in correspondence with Sir Robert Peel at the Home Office, not surprisingly concerned at the widespread incendiarism, as according to one Kentish farmer 'fires continue almost over the county.'

The radical writer William Cobbett, dedicated to opposing what he saw as a corrupt establishment, was accused of inciting the Swing crimes during a

Sir Edward Knatchbull, 9th Baronet, was considered lenient in sentencing the first batch of machine-breakers

Mysterious strangers with tricolour flags were reported among the machine-breakers and the Lord-Lieutenant blamed outrages on 'the French spirit'

lecture tour that took in Dartford, Gravesend, Rochester, Maidstone and Tonbridge before moving on to Sussex.

Lord Camden passed on a damning assessment of him to Peel:

> There never was such rank treason utter'd in any country, or at any age… he reprobated the labouring class in Sussex for not shewing the example set them… in Kent, where their fellow sufferers were asserting their rights by destroying the property of those who tyrannized over them.[3]

When the first machine-breakers were tried at Kent Quarter Sessions they were fortunate in that the Chairman was the Tory politician Sir Edward Knatchbull, the 9th Baronet, of Mersham Hatch. His late father and namesake had been a Deputy Lieutenant and former commanding officer of the East Kent Yeomanry, and the 9th Baronet had himself served in both the Yeomanry and the Militia.

He ascribed the troubles to agricultural distress aggravated by outside *agents provocateurs* and was lenient in sentencing the first batch of machine-breakers to the dismay of the Home Secretary, who believed conviction and execution of some of the troublemakers would put an end to the outrages.

Peel informed the Lord-Lieutenant that he would 'adopt any measures – will incur any Expence [sic]… that can promote the suppression of the Outrages.' He proposed that someone well versed in detecting crime, assisted by a number of the new London police officers and in close communication with the most active magistrates, should be sent to Kent.

But first the Home Secretary wanted a categorical assurance that this move would not give offence to the Kent Magistracy or lead them to relax their own efforts. Camden and a group of JPs met to give the necessary assurances and the Treasury Solicitor George Maule was despatched to Maidstone and set to work countering the attacks. He attended a meeting of more than 70 magistrates chaired by the Lord-Lieutenant to debate the causes of the trouble, which were believed to be 'over-taxation, want of work… insufficiency of wages.'[4]

Mysterious strangers and tricolour flags were reported at some of the riotous gatherings and 'Lord Camden ascribed the outrages to the French spirit…'[5]

Militia training had again been dispensed with during this riotous year, but the West Kent Militia were provided with some 500 rounds of ammunition because of 'the apprehension of riots and possible revolutions.'[6] A significant change at that time was the replacement of the sergeants' pikes with fusils – light muskets.

Three executions and a batch of transportations later the Swing Riots petered out but the county and the country had been severely shaken and reform was in the air. The 1832 Act abolished rotten and pocket boroughs, redistributed Parliamentary seats more equitably and extended voting rights. This reduced the political power of Lord-Lieutenants, but 'subsequently, the progressive abolition of so many other offices available for Prime Ministerial patronage did mean that the appointments to Lieutenancies and their Deputies were always eagerly sought.'[7]

In connection with Militia training, Camden, as Colonel, dictated the dress code for officers appearing at dinner, including: 'Each Officer is expected to have a Pair of Trousers of the Oxford Mixture according to Regulation, although the Regimental Grey Trousers without lace may continue to be worn on ordinary occasions,' and later added: 'If you happen to possess White Duck Trousers, it may be well to bring them with you'![8]

In June 1832 the East and West Kent Yeomanry were reviewed by the hero of Waterloo, the Duke of Wellington, at Camden's Wilderness Park. Following the review the Lord-Lieutenant presented troop standards to the cornets, 'called attention to their regimental motto *Invicta*, and said he hoped they would stand by the standard like their fathers of old.' A contemporary Kent newspaper report was ecstatic, and in referring to the host, Camden, said:

> …the very mention of whose name is a prelude to every thing that is loyal and patriotic… the steadiness and skill with which the manoeuvres were performed were quite surprising, considering the very few occasions which the troops have had of acting together. The Yeomen were distinguished by youth and activity, and were efficiently mounted…

Among the troop captains, it noted, was Viscount Sydney, a future Lord-Lieutenant. The excited reporter waxed lyrical:

> …the troops in the most enthusiastic style gave three cheers for the Duke of Wellington, a cry which was most cordially responded by the dense crowd of spectators, consisting of a large proportion of the gentry of the county, and of hundreds of well-mounted farmers. This cordial reception of the Hero of a Hundred Battles was not, however, confined to the thousands who had assembled immediately in rear of the saluting post; as his Grace returned to the mansion of the Noble Marquis (sic), he was accompanied by farmers and yeomen on horseback, who cheered him most heartily on his way, and gave proof most palpable of the difference of feeling which exists, as regards his Grace, between a London mob and a rural population of independent yeomen.[9]

This last was a reference to the controversy surrounding the former Prime Minister over Parliamentary reform. The feast awaiting the gathering was sumptuous if not in quite the same league as the review at Mote Park a generation earlier. Camden arranged for 200 ladies of the county to sit down to a 'very elegant cold collation, provided in the house.'

WEST KENT YEOMANRY CAVALRY, 1831-1838.
QUARTERMASTER, WITH STANDARD, AND SERGEANT'S ESCORT

West Kent Yeomanry troop standard presented by the Lord-Lieutenant, who 'called attention to their regimental motto *Invicta*'

The Lord-Lieutenant took part in the ballot that allotted the number 37 to the West Kent Militia

For the Yeomanry and the distinguished guests a large tent decorated with laurel and flags was erected in the grounds for 500 covers, the cooks carving two barons of beef, each weighing 400 pounds, and providing more than 100 plum puddings. There was a bottle of wine for each guest and barrels of Kentish ale were placed around the tent.

'When the Duke of Wellington's health was given, the yeomen could not resist the impulse – the very first intimation was received by one simultaneous burst of applause, the company standing on the chairs and benches, waving their glasses...' Tributes to the Lord-Lieutenant, who had entered the West Kent Militia fifty years before as a subaltern, were as warm.

Commenting on the Lord-Lieutenant's generous hospitality, the reporter added: '...the noble Marquess will have the satisfaction of knowing, that in adding to his well-earned popularity, he has acquired fresh claims to the approbation of his neighbours, and to the friendly terms in which he has ever lived with the county of Kent.'

The following year King William IV gave a banquet at St James's Palace for Lord-Lieutenants and colonels of Militia regiments at which another ballot was conducted to settle, permanently, the order of precedence. As a result, number 37 was drawn for West Kent and 49 for the East Kent Regiment of Militia. Training was dispensed with yet again and with only a small permanent staff the Militia remained in virtual hibernation for years to come.

It was a different story for the Yeomanry. In May 1833 the West Kent Regiment assembled at Knole for five days' permanent duty and was reviewed by Camden.

A month later the Cobham Troop was called out at 2 a.m. to deal with a disturbance caused by watermen at Gravesend, where a pier had been erected which they thought would adversely affect their work. They began to demolish it, whereupon the Mayor requested the Yeomanry to assist the civil power, 'the watermen having threatened to fire at the Customs House boats putting off to land passengers from the London steamboat.' The Yeomanry were again in attendance when there was further rioting at the opening of the new pier in July and won the appreciation of the Mayor and Corporation for the prompt way they had turned out 'which was most efficacious in keeping the peace.'[10]

Kent was in a disturbed state in 1835 when the self-proclaimed messiah Sir William Courtenay, alias John Thom, roamed the Faversham area gathering deluded rustics and leading them to a bloody encounter with regular soldiers at the so-called Battle of Bossenden Wood.

This extraordinary character had earlier caused a sensation when he stood for Parliament against the then Lord Fordwich, a future Lord-Lieutenant of Kent, in Canterbury.

Fordwich had left the Army to pursue his political ambitions. He was first returned to Parliament for the City of Canterbury in 1830, and at the 1832 general election, he stood again in Canterbury with a fellow-Whig.

There was a strong reformist element in the city at the time and the local Tories, fearing a drubbing, failed to put up candidates. But, goaded by remarks by Fordwich's prematurely exultant running-mate, the Honourable Richard Watson, some Tories bent on mischief and wiping smiles off Whig faces encouraged the flamboyant Sir William Courtenay to stand.

This larger than life character had arrived in Canterbury three months earlier posing as Count Moses Rothschild and quickly became a well-known figure as he strolled about the city, instantly recognisable from his long black hair, bushy beard and extravagant dress. Rumours spread that he was immensely rich, but in truth the money he flaunted was sponged from gullible folk on the promise of early repayment with interest.[11]

The extraordinary John Thom, man of many aliases, who stood for Parliament against Lord Fordwich, the future Earl Cowper and Lord-Lieutenant

Within weeks he underwent an astonishing metamorphosis, now claiming to be Sir William Percy Honeywood Courtenay, Knight of Malta, rightful heir to the Earldom of Devon, of the Kentish estates of Sir Edward Hales, King of the Gypsies, and King of Jerusalem.

Inexplicably this seems to have been accepted without question by the apparently then unsophisticated citizenry of Canterbury, to the extent that he could be deemed a fit person to stand for Parliament. 'Sir William, Knight of Malta', as he now styled himself, was delighted to put himself forward as an independent and his growing popularity with the local mob meant that he was sure to put Fordwich and Watson to expense and trouble in what they had thought would be an easy uncontested election ride.

This, the first election to be held under the Reform Act, took place in December 1832. Garishly dressed, Courtenay drove around the city in a barouche drawn by a pair of horses, dispensing promises and scattering coins to enthusiastic supporters. *The Times* described it as 'a scene bordering much on the ludicrous', adding, 'the gentleman is supposed to be insane…'

On election day a huge crowd filled the Guildhall and there was uproar – applause, catcalling and shouts of 'We want Courtenay!' 'Sir William' spoke, to tremendous applause, promising tax relief to the poor and industrious, and 'a return to the good old days of roast beef and mutton, and plenty of prime, nut-brown ale…'

Voting by show of hands was declared in favour of the future Lord-Lieutenant, Lord Fordwich, and 'Sir William.' But Watson's supporters protested, demanding a poll, which placed him first with 834 votes, Fordwich second with 802, and 'Sir William' third and last with a nevertheless respectable 375 votes.

Undeterred, 'Sir William' promptly stood in the subsequent election for the East Kent Division against three other candidates, but this time polled a derisory three votes out of more than 9,000.

His increasingly bizarre behaviour led to him being tried for perjury as a result of his attempt to defend a gang of Faversham smugglers during their trial at Rochester – and as a result his true identity was revealed. Hearing of the case, his wife turned up at Maidstone Gaol and unmasked the imposter,

RIGHT: The Battle of Bossenden Wood, claimed to be the last battle fought on English soil

proving beyond doubt that he was John Nichols Thom, a wine and spirit merchant, of Truro in Cornwall, with a history of previous attacks of insanity. Lord Fordwich took his seat in Parliament, and his deranged opponent was incarcerated in the Kent Lunatic Asylum at Barming.

On his release he stirred up gullible rustics and led them to the disastrous encounter – and his own death – at the so-called Battle of Bossenden Wood, claimed by some to be the last battle fought on English soil.

Of this time Lord Harris, Yeomanry historian and Deputy Lieutenant, recalls that following a riot:

> My father (who commanded a Yeomanry troop) had to escort a body of some twenty prisoners from Rodmersham to Canterbury Gaol, and he told me that he and his men were stoned all up Canterbury High Street and had to retreat into the Fountain yard and barricade themselves there.[12]

In May 1837 Mote Park was again the scene of a great entertainment given by the then Lord Romney, although not on the scale of his ancestor's event in 1799. Both East and West Kent Yeomanry Regiments, brigaded, assembled for eight days' permanent duty attended in part by the Lord-Lieutenant.

That July, the Cobham Troop took part in the procession for the proclamation of the young Queen Victoria. A new era had begun. But it began badly for the Yeomanry, with the Lord-Lieutenant being informed that the Government thought it right 'to effect every possible reduction in the public expenditure which may be found consistent with the tranquillity of the county.'

It was the same old story: a brief period of stability quickly followed by sharp reductions in force levels. And with 'great regret' Camden passed on the bad news that each regiment was to disband two troops. The Government's decision was considered an insult; there were many resignations from other troops and the effectiveness of the once strong regiments was severely reduced.

It is worthy of note that in 1839 the banker, philanthropist and politician Sir David Salomons, of Tunbridge Wells, became the first Jewish Sheriff of Kent, and later a Deputy Lieutenant and magistrate – and in 1855 became the first Jewish Lord Mayor of London.

In February 1840 Prince Albert of Saxe-Coburg and Gotha, the future Prince Consort, stayed in Canterbury on his way to London but the Kent Yeomanry's offer to escort him through the county was turned down, and the Lord-Lieutenant was told that this was because of the uncertain time of his arrival and 'the present bad state of the weather.'[13]

Camden, at 81, was by now by far Kent's longest-serving Lord-Lieutenant to date, having held the appointment for 32 years, but his health was failing. There was at that time no retirement age for Lord-Lieutenants so Camden wrote proposing that the Earl of Brecknock, who had commanded the West Kent Yeomanry, should stand in for him as Vice-Lieutenant. The response was positive and he was told: 'Her Majesty is graciously pleased to approve thereof.'

Camden retired to Wildernesse, where he died six months later in October 1840.

On Camden's death the Lieutenancy went not to Brecknock but to Henry Tufton, 11th Earl of Thanet, of Hothfield, whose mother was the sister of the 3rd Duke of Dorset. He inherited the Sackvilles' love of cricket as a talented wicketkeeper-batsman, making his debut in 1793 in a game between Surrey and Sussex and All-England at the original Lord's cricket ground, and playing in 77 major matches.

He had been arrested along with other English travellers in France when the Peace of Amiens ended, and on his return did not take up the sport again. A Whig, he served as Member of Parliament for Rochester and later for Appleby, where his family had considerable estates.

Aged 65 on appointment as Lord-Lieutenant of Kent, he took over at a time of little military activity. The Militia was still in hibernation and the Yeomanry was also at a low ebb. In 1844 the officers of the East Kent Regiment sent a circular to the gentlemen of that part of the county appealing for greater support, which, they said, if not forthcoming would force them to tender their resignations via the Lord-Lieutenant to the Government – almost certainly leading to the disbandment of the Corps.[14]

The problem was that they were well under their officer establishment, and direct appeals to individuals to fill the seven vacancies had fallen on deaf ears. The officers met at the Fountain Hotel, Canterbury, in March 1845 and agreed to send in their commissions to the Lord-Lieutenant 'it being apparent that it is no longer the desire of the gentlemen of East Kent that a Corps of Yeomanry Cavalry be maintained in this Division of the county...'

Sir David Salomons, Jewish banker, philanthropist and a Deputy Lieutenant of Kent

Henry Tufton, 11th Earl of Thanet

1844
Irish Potato famine

1852
Duke of Wellington dies at Walmer

1854
Crimean War begins

1856
Crimean War ends

1857
Indian Mutiny

1861
Prince Albert dies

1871
Lord-Lieutenants' command of the Militia is withdrawn

However, the scare tactic worked and by early 1846 new commissions recommended by the Earl of Thanet were being granted, although only two troops remained effective.

The West Kent Yeomanry also 'passed through some vicissitudes,' and lack of military activity at this time meant that 'Never before or after did the Lieutenants and their Deputies have so little to do' and, according to Lord Rosebery, their appointments had become 'positions of mere ornament and repose… '[15] Certainly in Kent the Earl of Thanet had left little mark, nor did he marry and was the last of the line, dying aged 74 in June 1849.

He had been replaced in October 1846 by George Augustus, 6th Earl Cowper, whose bizarre claim to fame was winning the 1832 Parliamentary election in Canterbury against the mad 'Sir William Courtenay'.

The Cowpers 'a family of great wealth at the centre of the Whig political, social and familial cousinhood' were well established at Panshanger in Hertfordshire and in Kent. The new Lord-Lieutenant was exceptionally well-connected: his uncle was Viscount Melbourne and his step-father was Viscount Palmerston – both in their turn Prime Ministers.

Despite his wealth and connections, and although well liked for his personal charm, he had a 'dawdling, gentlemanlike manner' and lacked self-confidence, but he travelled extensively on the Continent in his youth and acquired a love of art.

As Lord Fordwich, Cowper had served briefly in the Royal Horse Guards (The Blues), but left the army to pursue his political career.

Having been responsible for the First Reform Act, the Whigs had been returned in triumph in that first general election held under it and in 1834 Fordwich was appointed Under Secretary of State for the Foreign Department. But he served only briefly, retiring from the House of Commons at the dissolution of 1835. He succeeded to the Peerage as Earl Cowper on his father's death in June 1837 and was appointed Lord-Lieutenant and *Custos Rotulorum* of Kent nine years later.

Although Militia activity was nil, Cowper was active in his dealings with the Yeomanry, attending an entertainment for the officers and staff of the West Kent Yeomanry in 1849 at the London home of its Lieutenant Colonel, Viscount Sydney – who was to be his successor as Lord-Lieutenant – and ordering periods of training known as 'permanent duty' for both the East and West Kent Regiments.

At that time the Militia 'existed but in name,' represented only by a handful of permanent staff, and the elderly adjutant had seen the Regiment for a mere four months during his 35 years in the post.[16]

But the 1848 revolution in France and the unsettled state of Europe in the lead-up to the Crimean War led to moves to revive the Militia, still under the command of the Lord-Lieutenant, at least nominally, and to be raised no longer by ballot but by voluntary enlistment. However, balloting could still be used in the event of invasion. The county's quota was 1,000 men each for East and West Kent, with 600 for the Artillery Militia, and the normal training period was set at 21 days a year. Deputy Lieutenants now had the task of finding volunteers for the new Militia, provoking the Radical Richard Cobden to sneer:

> Have you marked the shoal of deputy lieutenants created as part of the working machinery of the law? Almost every magistrate... has been gazetted as a deputy lieutenant, and is of course entitled to appear at court with his official costume, and cocked hat and feathers. The whole of the working of the militia is calculated to foster and strengthen our aristocratic system, and to degrade the mass of the people.[17]

Officer of the newly-formed West Kent Light Infantry Militia

In 1850 the *London Standard* carried a letter about the lack of magistrates in Kent and Sussex, complaining 'The Lord-Lieutenant of Kent lives in Hertfordshire; he has a small estate in Kent, but knows very little about the county...'

However, there is no doubt that Earl Cowper was taking his Lieutenancy seriously, for example in February 1853 he applied for the Regiment to be made Light Infantry, and the reply from his step-father Lord Palmerston, then Home Secretary, informed him that Queen Victoria consented.

Two months later the West Kent Light Infantry, as it was now styled, assembled 875 strong for four weeks' training at Maidstone. The Crimean War started the following year and in April 1854 the Regiment, now numbering well over 1,000, assembled for training at Maidstone again, and through the Lord-Lieutenant expressed its readiness 'to undertake permanent service wherever and whenever it might be desirable.' Palmerston's reply to Cowper thanked the Regiment for its 'very handsome and honourable offer.'[18]

The Militiamen were indeed soon embodied, served at Aldershot where they were reviewed by Queen Victoria, and in November 1855 were posted, not to the Crimea, but to hold the fort at England's back door – in Ireland, freeing regular units for war service. Before they left Aldershot new colours were presented to replace the old ones described by Earl Cowper as 'unfit for any further service.'[19]

The Earl's Hertfordshire seat at Panshanger that housed his large collection of English portraits, Italian old masters, furniture and porcelain, was badly damaged by fire in 1855, necessitating its rebuilding. But he did not live to see the work completed. While attending Maidstone Assizes in April 1856 Cowper was suddenly seized with 'spasms of the heart' in the courthouse and was taken to a neighbouring house where he died, aged 49.

Sydney, an experienced rider, was sufficiently confident to pose on horseback for this early time exposure now in the Royal collection

Cowper's sudden death meant that there was a gap of almost two months before a successor, John Robert Townshend, 3rd Viscount Sydney, was appointed in June 1856. Despite his title, to which he had succeeded in 1831, he was not directly connected to the Sidneys of Penshurst, the family of the present Lord-Lieutenant, Viscount De L'Isle. Sydney, whose family seat was

The satirical magazine Punch ridiculed Lord Sydney for refusing to grant Volunteer commissions willy-nilly

Who is the Lord Lieutenant of Kent,

Whose business seems to be to prevent

The muster of Riflemen plucky?

Mr Punch would be very content

If that ass of a Lord Lieutenant of Kent

Were kicked from Kent to Kentucky.

**Punch
26 November 1859**[32]

at Scadbury Park, Chislehurst, had excellent credentials for the Kent Lieutenancy, having served with distinction in the Militia and the Yeomanry, and as a Member of Parliament. He took his military duties seriously, inspected the Militia on a number of occasions during annual training, and became Colonel of the Kent Artillery Militia and Captain of Deal Castle. He was well connected at Court, first as Groom-in-Waiting to George IV and then Lord-in-Waiting to William IV and Queen Victoria.

Following the Crimean War and Indian Mutiny, and ever suspicious of the French and Napoleon III's antagonistic attitude towards England, Kent was foremost in the formation of volunteer rifle and artillery corps and the Government indicated it was prepared to accept them 'provided that the proposed formation of such corps is recommended by the Lord-Lieutenant of the County, and that members provide their own equipment.'

It was to the Lord-Lieutenants, too, that the Government looked:

> …for the nomination of proper persons to be appointed officers subject to the Queen's approval… in thus giving to the LL control over the formation of a corps and the appointment of its officers the Govt seemed to be ensuring that the Force would remain socially and politically safe.[20]

This placed a tricky burden on the Lieutenancies, and led to considerable criticism of Sydney in particular for being sniffy about granting commissions to 'trade.' Each Lord-Lieutenant was in a position to affect the number and social composition of Volunteer corps in his county, but 'few seem to have been keen to exercise this power. Some seemed to be apathetic, if not hostile… in general, however, LLs seem to have preserved a discreet neutrality… It was the Lord-Lieutenant of Kent, Lord Sydney, who earned himself the most unenviable reputation for discrimination in appointments.'

In August 1859 Sydney wrote: 'We ignore all Clubs and Election of officers, neither of which the Government recognise,' and adhering to this principle and to the belief that an officer should be a gentleman, he was in constant conflict with the Volunteers in the early days.

> In Chatham he withheld a commission from the keeper of the garrison canteen on the grounds that, if appointed, he would be in command of those to whom in his employment he was subordinate. In Sheerness he objected to a solicitor, in Gillingham to a licensed victualler. Lord Sydney was perhaps exceptional, though there is evidence from elsewhere that Lord Lieutenants refused to give commissions to those in trade.[21]

Sydney was attacked by the columnist *Spectator*, who complained:

> We must have no more of that pooh-poohing of patriotic proposals for

which the Lord-Lieutenant and, it is whispered, several other Lord-Lieutenants, have been conspicuous.

The writer pointed out that to be Lord-Lieutenant was a high privilege and that the Government should take steps to see that there was no abuse of power. He accused Sydney of frustrating the advance of the Volunteer movement because 'to his little mind and purblind vision' it appeared to be 'a crude idea'. And he reminded him that he was a servant of Queen Victoria – 'and when Her Majesty… calls for volunteers, it is the duty of a Lord-Lieutenant to promote and not to obstruct the accomplishments of Her Majesty's wishes.' A Lord-Lieutenant who proved to be obstructive should be removed, he argued.

Sydney appears to have been unfazed by such attacks. It was easy to accuse him of snobbishness, but he had considerable personal military service in the Militia and Yeomanry and believed he was right not to grant commissions willy-nilly to men who, although popular, might well be totally unsuitable.

In September 1860 Lord Sydney issued a proclamation creating the 4th Administrative Battalion, Kent Rifle Volunteers, from six of the East Kent Corps. The headquarters were at Canterbury and when it was inspected for the first time, once Lord Sydney had taken post and the parade began, what transpired was near farce:

> They were naturally a raw, unvarnished set of men brought together under the gaze of the Lord Lieutenant – men unused to rifles, swords, or weapons of any sort. The ludicrous attempt they made at soldierly bearing rendered their appearance extremely comical…

For anyone who has come new to a drill square it is not difficult to imagine the chaotic scene as men in awe of the big occasion confused left foot with right, fumbled their unfamiliar rifles, and misinterpreted orders – some turning this way, and some that.

> In the absence of an imminent invasion threat the keen but amateurish volunteers did not enjoy the wholehearted admiration of the populace. At a subsequent inspection several men received injuries of a somewhat serious nature. The drilling was being conducted on the Canterbury cricket ground on a bitterly cold day and few spectators were present, with the exception of a motley crowd of roughs, who amused themselves with storming the unfortunate volunteers with turnips and missiles of a harder and more varied description. The officers experienced considerable difficulty in restraining the men from breaking the ranks and scattering the attacking force at the double; but discipline prevailed and the volunteers stood their ground unflinchingly until they were marched back to the city.[22]

An 1865 review of the Volunteers on Chatham Lines by Lord Sydney was featured in the *Illustrated London News*

'But… inspections at intervals of six months and careful drilling at home soon wore off the roughness.'

Sydney kept a close grip on the Volunteers, as evidenced by his reaction when 30 supernumaries were enrolled at Canterbury:

> …the Lord Lieutenant came down upon the ingenious commanding officer with majestic dignity. How dare he enrol these men without the sanction of the Queen's representative? A great deal of correspondence followed, but in the end Captain (George) Austin outflanked his opponent and the supernumaries were retained.[23]

Discipline was sometimes a problem and there is a familiar 'Dad's Army' ring to some incidents. Captain William Baring, of the Sittingbourne Company, a banker like the fictional Captain Mainwaring, saw a Private Dean, a tailor, in his shop making a uniform for another member of the Corps.

The officer accused Dean of charging more than contracted for by the committee and demanded by whose authority he did so. Dean retorted: 'By my own authority.' Baring warned him: 'You must remember, sir, I am your captain.' The soldier/tailor retorted: 'I am aware of that fact, and when under orders I will obey your orders; but now you have no right to interfere with my business and my customers, and I will not suffer you or any other man to do so.'

Dean was struck off the muster roll, but before long other members of the company who had been offended by Captain Baring called a meeting to decide by ballot whether he should remain in command. This prompted a letter from the Lord-Lieutenant pointing out that such action was illegal, but in the end Baring resigned anyway.

Members of the Margate Company's band were later accused by their captain of using their official-issue instruments without permission 'perambulating the country asking alms' and were threatened with dismissal.

At the 1863 Review Lord Sydney was sufficiently satisfied with progress that, according to the *Kentish Chronicle*, he 'expressed the pleasure he felt with regard to the satisfactory condition of the volunteer force – both artillery and rifles – throughout every district of the county of Kent, which had ever been foremost to evince its patriotism.'

In 1867, Dover was chosen for the now-annual Easter Monday Review, despite objections from inspection committee members who thought it 'too great a distance from the metropolis, while a great portion of the ground was arable: wholly unfit for field-day evolutions.' Whether or not a would-be invader would have agreed does not appear to have been considered. Nevertheless, the review was again judged a great success, enlivened as it was by the appearance of a *'mysterious personage.'* The *Kentish Express* reported:

> There was too, the mysterious horsewoman who now persists in making

a figure at every review and who, on Monday, faced the staff in her odd uniform of black velvet and silver badges and buttons, with a mask descending half-way down her face, and with a drawn sword held in military fashion against her shoulder.

As a matter of course, an orderly was sent to request that she should move from so conspicuous a position and, after debating the matter a little, she slowly walked her charger to the rear of the Bands. This young lady gave rise to a good deal of conversation and quizzing during the day. She was armed with two swords and rode from rank to rank and drew up with military 'sang froid' in front of each battalion, without speaking, however, or issuing any orders, until occasionally removed by means of a little persuasion.[24]

A mystery woman, masked and in military-style uniform appeared at Volunteer Corps' reviews

The East Kent Volunteers historian Charles Igglesden noted: 'It was afterwards stated that a certain officer of high rank might have solved the mystery attending this extraordinary personage.' A tomboy daughter frustrated at not being allowed to join the volunteers? After this lapse of time we may never know.

The year 1871 was a watershed for the county Lieutenancies' relations with the Militia, which in its various guises had been their *raison d'etre* for more than three centuries. With the Regulation of the Forces Act the Liberal Government introduced major reforms, including ending the purchase of commissions. Most significant for the Lieutenancies was the reversion of their military jurisdiction to the Crown, through the Secretary of State for War.

This meant that the Lord-Lieutenant and his Deputies no longer exercised any command although the right to nominate candidates for first commissions of the auxiliary forces remained – as did the entitlement to salutes and review at field days of these forces.

This loss of military authority was a crucial diminution of the authority of the County Lieutenants. It was also a practical termination of the authority of their Deputies, although they were still officially retained, with the usual property qualifications (estates of annual income of £200 or more), for the theoretical selection of men in the event of the militia ballot ever being revived.

By an Act in 1871, and subsequent Order in Council, the command of the Militia was withdrawn from the Lord-Lieutenant of each county, and the S of S was enabled to place the command in the hands of the General of the district.[25]

As Lord Chamberlain Lord Sydney was a trusted confidant of Queen Victoria

After three centuries, the military power of the Lieutenancy was reduced to little more than a cipher – and command went rightly to professional soldiers.

Kent's Lord-Lieutenant caricatured

~ THIRTEEN ~
REFORM – AND WAR

Loss of their military authority marked a fundamental change in the nature of the county Lieutenancies and in the last quarter of the 19th Century 'never before or after did the Lieutenants and their Deputies have so little to do. The office had become entirely honorific…' According to Lord Rosebery all it now did was provide 'positions of mere ornament and repose.'[1]

There were few official royal visits to counties and in their absence the Lord-Lieutenants, as Queen Victoria's representatives, 'merely by their existence, brought to their counties a comforting reassurance that the monarchy was mindful of local sentiment.' As for the Deputies, they had 'no duties what-soever, and for many of them the possession of a gorgeous uniform was their main concern.'[2]

Although Kent's Lord-Lieutenant now had few responsibilities within the county, he was fully active on the national stage. Apart from a short break, Sydney was Lord Chamberlain from 1859 until 1874, managing the Royal Household and attending many state functions.

In 1874 he was created Earl Sydney, of Scadbury in the county of Kent, and in 1880 the Queen appointed him to be Lord Steward of Her Majesty's Household, a post he held for five years.

Despite having lost command of the Militia, Sydney did not sever his links and in October 1877 was present at Maidstone when Colours were presented by his wife to the newly-formed 2nd Battalion of what was now designated the West Kent Light Infantry. It is one of the first mentions of a Kentish Lord-Lieutenant's wife being involved in such ceremonial duties – and making a speech, in which she said that those receiving the Colours 'will always show the traditional valour and loyalty of the Men of Kent'.[3]

It fell to Sydney, in September 1878, to interrupt the inquest to convey Queen Victoria's condolences to the relatives of the 658 people lost in a 'fearful catastrophe' – the collision between the *Princess Alice* and the *Bywell Castle* off Woolwich.

In 1881 the line infantry and Militia were reorganised on a county-by-county basis, the East Kent Militia being allied to The Buffs and the West Kents to the Queen's Own Royal West Kent Regiment. A further Act, in 1882, diminished the Militia's distinctiveness by encouraging officers to obtain regular commissions and offering bounties to Militiamen to enlist as regulars in line regiments.

But, importantly, it reaffirmed the statutory appointment of Lord-Lieutenants and of their Deputies, yet 'despite the fact they now had no specific responsibilities, the number of Deputies was ordered to be held at least at 20 for each county.'

'Small fry were Lords Lieutenant deemed'
WS Gilbert in The Gondoliers

That December the well-connected Sydney joined three others accompanying the Prince of Wales on a shoot at Sundridge Park, Bromley, and 'had capital sport, about 550 head of game falling to the guns.'

In 1889 another major milestone was reached with the formation of elected County Councils, which removed administration, but not legal power, from the magistrates, and lifted from the Lieutenancy's shoulders the burden of local governance it had overseen for centuries.[4] It is for speculation whether or not W S Gilbert was influenced by this when that same year he penned the line 'small fry were Lords Lieutenant deemed' in the Gondoliers. This first-word un-hyphenated plural of the Lieutenants' title was retained even by their own Association until 1976.

Early in 1890, Sydney, then in his 85th year, fell ill with bronchitis and such was his link with the Royal Family that Queen Victoria herself asked to be kept daily informed of his health. He died in February and the *Court Circular* recorded:

> The Queen received with deep concern, this morning, the news of the death of Earl Sydney, who had been for so many years attached to her person, and had held high and important offices in her household, and for whom her Majesty had the highest regard. The Queen and her family mourn in him another faithful and devoted friend.

The Queen even sent Countess Sydney a telegram asking for the funeral to be delayed so that she could attend in person. At 84, he was and remains the oldest holder of the Kent Lieutenancy, and at the time was the longest-serving, having held it for 34 years.

Sydney's memorial was placed in St Nicholas Church, Chislehurst, in the

Lady Sydney

Scadbury Chapel near the Walsingham tomb. Sir Francis Walsingham was Elizabeth I's spymaster and patron of the playwright Christopher Marlowe. Many years later there was a strange twist when the American Calvin Hoffman 'twice instigated investigations of the tomb and vaults in search of a clue which might connect Marlowe with the works attributed to Shakespeare. During one of these investigations, the effigy of Earl Sydney… was relocated to the north wall of the Chapel.'[5]

Sydney's successor as Lord-Lieutenant was Arthur Philip, 6th Earl Stanhope, of Chevening, who had deep family roots in Kent and whose family estates totalled some 12,000 acres in the county. His father Philip, the 5th Earl, an eminent historian, biographer, statesman who had played a major part in founding the National Portrait Gallery, had himself served as a Deputy Lieu-tenant during the time of the 1st Marquess Camden.

The young Arthur had a happy childhood. But at Harrow his lack of progress disappointed his father, who had only one career in mind for him, the army. This prompted objections from the 4th Earl, who wrote to Arthur's father:

> I entreat you to reconsider the project of placing A. in the army… I can only express my deep though unavailing regret, and the horror that would be felt by you, by E. [Emily Stanhope], by myself, by all your family and friends if he were to die or be disabled in a battle. Fame may be acquired by other means…[6]

Nevertheless, in 1857 Arthur was withdrawn from Harrow, transferred to a military cramming establishment and his father had to pay for his commission in the Grenadier Guards. While travelling in Switzerland before he entered the army Arthur met the Prince of Wales and they went on walking tours together. Later he wrote to the Prince:

> I can never forget the great kindness which your Royal Highness has always shown me ever since our daily rambles round Mont Blanc together.[7]

Having embarked on his military career he was still able to visit Italy and Germany and later Canada and the United States. He served with his regiment at Aldershot and in Ireland and it was there that the Prince of Wales spent several weeks in camp with the Grenadier Guards and had a brief affair with a well-known Dublin actress. Family gossip suggested that Arthur had been involved in this, and that it had been into his quarters that the actress had been smuggled, although he himself had been on leave at the time.

Royal displeasure – although presumably not that of the Prince of Wales – has been suggested as a reason for his failure to achieve advancement in the army, but as heir to the peerage and vast estates he had little incentive to exert himself and instead became a musketry instructor at Hythe where in the

Arthur Philip, 6th Earl Stanhope

railway age he was within easy reach of the family seat and the pleasures of London. The School of Musketry (later the Small Arms School), where rifle shooting became an art rather than the drill it had been with the inaccurate and now obsolete musket, had then but recently been established – in 1853 – and was to become world-famous for the excellence of its small arms training. However, the future Lord-Lieutenant was not long for the army.

It was quite clear that he would never be a full-time soldier, and so there was only one alternative occupation for him – politics. As a schoolboy he had written to his father:

> My dear Papa, All the Tories have got a half-holiday for the Queen's birthday, and so I am very glad you are a Tory.[8]

As Viscount Mahon – his title before he succeeded to the earldom – he was elected Member of Parliament for a Herefordshire constituency in a by-election and followed Disraeli in the House, but as a result of boundary changes at the 1868 general election he stood in Greenwich against Gladstone and, not surprisingly, was beaten. He resigned from the army, but retained an interest in the Volunteer movement, and became President of the National Rifle Association.

In 1869 he married Evelyn Pennefather, 'a gay person, very lively with a most engaging personality' whom his parents thought 'almost perfect,' and at their grand society wedding Disraeli himself proposed the toast to the bride and groom. The following year Mahon was elected as a Conservative MP in Suffolk, and when Disraeli became Prime Minister in 1874 was appointed a Junior Lord of the Treasury, one of the Government Whips, and remained so until his father's death in December1875. Then, as the 6th Earl Stanhope, he took his seat in the Lords and his political career was effectively at an end. His own son later wrote that he was 'a dull speaker but greatly loved.'

TIMELINE

1882
Militia Act removes most Lieutenancy military duties

1889
Kent County Council is formed

1889
Boer War begins

1890
Earl Sydney dies; succeeded by Arthur Philip, 6th Earl Stanhope

1901
Queen Victoria dies; Edward VII succeeds

1905
Earl Stanhope dies; succeeded by John Charles Pratt, 4th Marquess Camden

1908
Haldane reforms end Militias; birth of Territorial Force later known as Territorial Army

Evelyn, Countess Stanhope was a leading society hostess

Rather, his talents lay in managing his estates in Kent, Derbyshire, Buckinghamshire and Ireland. He was a good chairman and Disraeli found him a role as First Church Estates Commissioner where his good business sense was useful in managing Church of England property.

Lady Stanhope was greatly disappointed that her husband was not offered a more glamorous role, but worked out her ambitions by becoming a political hostess. Their son recalled:

> Mother… usually held three parties each season, preceded by a dinner party, and sent out invitations in her own hand to about 250 or 300 guests which included politicians and literary men as well as Society… it was possible for politicians of both parties to meet and discuss matters in private and Disraeli more than once thanked her for having afforded valuable opportunities for discussion and arrangement.[9]

Although at the time his Lieutenancy duties were light, Stanhope was deeply involved in county affairs, put himself forward when Kent County Council was set up and became an Alderman, serving as such for the rest of his life. He was the first of his illustrious line to be appointed Lord-Lieutenant and, according to the family historian, 'fulfilled admirably the largely ceremonial duties attached to that position.'

The appointment of Stanhope as Lord-Lieutenant was welcomed by the *South Eastern Gazette* as 'a very popular one in the county, as the noble earl is deservedly esteemed' It added:

> Earl Stanhope has for many years been prominently identified with the county as a landowner and a magistrate. He was a regular attendant at the meetings of the now defunct Kent General Sessions, and is a member of the County Council, serving on several committees of that body… and there are few men in the county who possess such high claims to the honour which Her Majesty has conferred upon him.[10]

One of his first public duties was the distribution of prizes at Westerham Industrial Association's annual exhibition of handicraft. In a long speech punctuated by applause and 'hear hears,' he referred to the examples of carpentry, carving, drawing, quilting, basket-making and bird stuffing exhibited by the Association's members and extolled the virtues of 'labour and perseverance and the value and advance of technical education – drawing attention to the great armour-clad ships, construction of the Forth Bridge etc.'

Public appearances by the ageing Queen Victoria were extremely rare, but Stanhope was on duty as Lord-Lieutenant in March 1899 for what was to be Her Majesty's last overseas trip – to France – in the Royal Mail steamer *Calais-Douvres*.

In 1897 Queen Victoria celebrated her Diamond Jubilee and the event was marked with many celebrations and souvenirs

When the Royal train arrived Stanhope was waiting near the gangway with a line-up of local dignitaries and as Her Majesty embarked and the great paddlewheels churned the colourful scene was 'a sight that old and young, rich and poor, will ever remember with feelings of joy…'[13]

Within two years Queen Victoria was dead – truly the end of a great era – and Edward VII came to the throne. Shortly after his accession the number of Deputy Lieutenants was regularised and the numbers tied to levels of population, thus avoiding the appointment of ridiculously large numbers that had been the practice in some counties.

Three years later the precedence of county Lieutenants and the considerably more ancient office of the High Sheriff, hitherto a subject of occasional friction, was also determined once and for all by Royal Warrant. It declared:

> …that each and every of our Lieutenants of a County… shall during his term of office and within the limits of his jurisdiction have, on all occasions, place, pre-eminence, and precedence before the Sheriff having current jurisdiction in the said County.

By the outbreak of the Boer War the Lieutenancy had no direct involvement with the Militia and Yeomanry, but, like his predecessor Lord Sydney, Stanhope maintained a close interest. The Militia were embodied for garrison duty in Malta and the county Yeomanry regiments were brought together to form the Imperial Yeomanry, seeing active service in South Africa. The Lord-Lieutenant was among those who opened a subscription fund to raise money for equipment for those going to war.[12] On their return it was Stanhope who presented them with their South African War Medals. His wife played her part in supporting the Forces of the Crown – as in 1904 when she presented HM Armoured Cruiser *Kent* with a silk ensign and Union Jack at Sheerness.

In April 1905 Stanhope died aged 66 following an operation for cancer and in its obituary the *Kent and Sussex Courier* reported:

> By his death, the County of Kent loses one of its most prominent and esteemed noblemen, who had been Lord Lieutenant of the county since 1890, and an alderman of the Kent County Council, in the work of which his lordship took a deep interest. In fact, Lord Stanhope once jestingly described his principal recreation to be county administration.

The *Kent Messenger* recorded:

> Lord Stanhope was one of the best-known men in the county. He was a staunch Churchman and Conservative, an active county administrator, a keen archaeologist, and a supporter of various charitable movements, especially in the Sevenoaks district.

TIMELINE

1910
Edward VII dies; George V succeeds

1911
Advisory Committees formed to select JPs

1914
World War I begins; Lord Harris acts as Lord-Lieutenant

1918
War ends; women over 30 get the vote

1932
Lord Harris dies

1939
World War II begins

1940
Dunkirk and the Battle of Britain

1943
Lord Camden dies; succeeded by Wykeham Stanley, 2nd Baron Cornwallis

RIGHT: An engraving
of Chevening as it was
when acquired by the
Stanhopes, whose seat it
was for 250 years before
being left to the nation

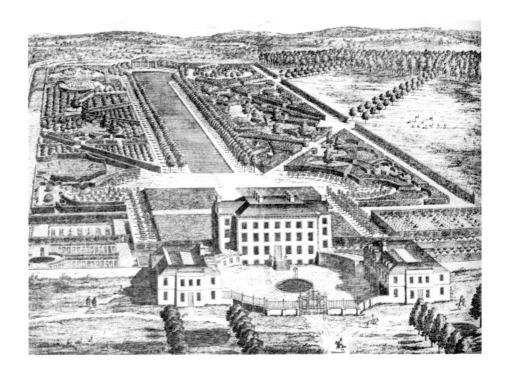

The Stanhopes' reputation as cross-party society hosts was also noted:

> He was a very popular member of society, and Lady Stanhope's receptions
> in Grosvenor Place (their London home) were generally crowded. Here
> politicians of all shades were to be met – Sir William Harcourt would be
> rubbing shoulders with Cecil Raikes, and Mr Goschen with Lord Randolph
> Churchill. The Earl himself was a very pleasant man with a genial smile for
> everyone. He was a sportsman, and on his beautiful place at Chevening,
> near Sevenoaks, there were plenty of hares to be found, even after the Hares
> and Rabbits Bill had done its worst. He will be greatly missed both by his
> tenantry and in general society. In him the Church of England loses one
> of the best friends she ever had, either in Parliament or among the laity at
> large. His death at the early age of 66 will be a sudden shock to all who
> were privileged to know him.

His son James, the 7th Earl, went on to serve with great distinction in World
War I, and, dying without issue, he left the Chevening Estate to the nation.
Under the 1959 Chevening Estate Act the Prime Minister of the day may
nominate either a Cabinet Minister or a direct descendent of King George
VI to occupy the house, and after the 7th Earl's death in 1967 it became the
country retreat and grace and favour home of the Foreign Secretary of the
day.[13] During the Coalition it has been shared by the Deputy Prime Minister
and Foreign Secretary.

Although some Kent newspapers predicted that the next Lord-Lieutenant would be Lord Harris, Stanhope's successor was John Charles Pratt, 4th Marquess Camden, who was appointed in June, 1905 at the age of 33, and was to be the county's longest-serving Lord-Lieutenant.

He knew how to enjoy himself as a keen huntsman and yachtsman, but 'not only in a personal way, but through the medium of a generous purse, the Marquess supported many works of charity…'[14] At the time of his appointment the *Dover Express* reported his visit to the harbour there 'in his yacht the *Cala Mara*… a fine vessel of 313 tons' adding that he 'is only just recovering from the results of a serious operation.'

Educated at Eton and Cambridge, he was the great grandson of the 1st Marquess who had held the Kent Lieutenancy for 32 years in the first half of the 19th Century.

The *Kent and Sussex Courier* played up the connection, stating:

> His Lordship may be depended upon to discharge the duties of his important office with the same zeal and faithfulness as his distinguished ancestor, and we need hardly add that His Majesty's choice will prove a most popular one in Kent.

Camden's portrait in his army uniform still hangs in County Hall

As a young man he had been commissioned as a 2nd Lieutenant in the 3rd Battalion of the Royal Sussex Regiment (Militia), and in 1892 joined the West Kent Yeomanry in which he served until 1916 when he retired as a major after returning from active service in Gallipoli.

In the year of Camden's appointment the great military reformer Richard Haldane was appointed Secretary of State for War and when the Liberals again swept to victory in 1906 the way was clear for him to carry out major long overdue reforms to Britain's armed forces, whose limitations had been highlighted by the South African War.

His measures included the establishment of a permanent general staff, reconstruction of the Militia as the nucleus of the regular army's Special Reserve and creation of the new Territorial Force, which became the Territorial Army.

There was opposition from the county Lieutenants, many of whom were honorary colonels of Militia battalions, but to no avail.

However, there was still to be a role for Lord-Lieutenants. Administration was placed in the hands of County Associations that would deal with all non-military matters including organisation of the units when not called out, provision of lands and buildings, assistance to cadet corps and rifle clubs – and for recruiting and liaison with employers – many of these responsibilities still handled by today's Reserve Forces' and Cadets' Associations. Under Haldane the new bodies were to include both military and non-military members – just as today – and, importantly, the Lieutenancy link that had existed for more than four centuries was maintained with the appointment of the Lord-Lieutenant as President of his County Association.

Lord Camden's fondness for yachting was a cartoonist's gift. He is shown left

Lord-Lieutenant's Flag

Haldane's far-sighted decision to retain the Lieutenancy link ensured that close territorial ties would be maintained with local volunteer forces – as they have been ever since and continue today, as strong as ever.

His measures included new criteria for the Deputy Lieutenants, who following the 1882 Militia Act had had no military duties whatsoever, and 'had been appointed by the County Lieutenant on a purely honorific basis.'[15] Now their appointment would be approved only if they were military officers of long standing, which meant that they had to have been commissioned for at least 10 years, or if they served as members of the County Association.

Although many of the county Lieutenants were against losing the Militia and argued that the new Associations were unnecessary, when the 1908 Act came into force 'they soon settled down to their new role in the Territorial Army system, and many of them must have felt relief at no longer having to maintain the charade of a largely military responsibility.'[16]

This may well have been the case with the more elderly Lieutenants, there then being no age limit – and as we have seen, Earl Sydney had still been in office in his 80s. But as Kent's new Lord-Lieutenant, Camden was not only young and already heavily involved militarily, but relished the new role and was to remain closely connected with the county's auxiliary military forces until his death during World War II. In at the start of the Haldane innovations, he remained President of the County Association from the early days of building drill halls, rifle ranges and stores all over the county, and throughout the rest of his life.

When his wife presented new Colours to the 1st Battalion, Queen's Own Royal West Kent Regiment, in August 1909, the Lord-Lieutenant 'impressed on the men to think their own Army the best in the world, their own regiment the best in the Army, and their own company the best in the regiment. It was such *esprit de corps* that often saved the situation in war.'

In 1911 the authority of the Lord-Lieutenants was further eroded by the creation of Advisory Committees which ended the sole right of recommending Justices of the Peace. However, the Lord-Lieutenant, as *Custos Rotulorum*, was Chairman of the new Committee. Much later there was a row when Camden was unwilling to take the advice of his Advisory Committee to replace his Clerk of the Peace.

On the plus side, county Lieutenants were now given permission to fly a special flag on official occasions: 'The Union Flag charged with a sword fesswise, or, and ensigned with the Imperial Crown proper.'[17]

Old turf wars were echoed in early 1914 when the *Dover Express* ranted:

In the reception of the King at Dover, it was noticed that the Lord-Lieutenant of Kent took precedence of the Lord Warden of the Cinque

Ports. Of course, this was all wrong. The Lord Warden ranks next to the King in a Cinque Port, and if such a thing had occurred some 400 years ago the Lord-Lieutenant would have been seized by the indignant Portsmen and would now have been in the dungeons of Dover Castle, or else his head on a pike over the Castle Gateway.

The legendary Kent and England cricketer Lord Harris stood in for Camden in his absence on active service

But with the assassination of Archduke Franz Ferdinand of Austria, which sparked World War I, a matter of weeks away no-one would have the time or inclination to debate such precedence issues.

The fears that had led to Haldane's Army reforms became reality with the outbreak of World War I and the Territorials were in far better shape to back up the regulars than their predecessors had been. Camden convened a meeting in August 1914 at Maidstone to arrange 'for concerted action in the county to further Lord Kitchener's appeal for 100,000 recruits for the army and to arrange a Kent War Relief Fund.'

Then, at the age of 42, Camden himself went off to serve with the West Kent Yeomanry in Gallipoli, leaving one of his Deputies, George Canning, 4th Baron Harris to act in his place.

Lord Harris was *Gazetted* Vice-Lieutenant, as it was then styled, in September 1914. He was a remarkable man. An accomplished cricketer and contemporary of W G Grace, he had captained Kent and England and his words about cricket resonate down the years and could equally stand for the way life itself should be lived as well as how the game should be played:

> It is more free from anything sordid, anything dishonourable, than any game in the world. To play it keenly, honourably, generously, self-sacrificingly, is a moral lesson in itself, and the classroom is God's air and sunshine.

Harris had served with distinction in the East Kent Mounted Rifles, becoming its Honorary Colonel and historian, and he fought as a member of the Imperial Yeomanry in the South African War.[18]

He had been Lord in Waiting to Queen Victoria, Aide-de-Camp to both Edward VII and George V, a junior Government minister, Governor of Bombay, one of Kent's first county councillors and Chairman of East Kent Quarter Sessions. During Camden's overseas service it fell to Lord Harris to form Kent's Local Emergency Committees. These were under a Central Organising Committee chaired by him as acting Lord-Lieutenant, 'to effect liaison between the civil and military authorities and make contingency plans in the event of invasion.' It was a role similar to the Lieutenancy's work during the Napoleonic Wars.

The Clerk of the County Council as Clerk to the Lieutenancy did the committee work for the central committee whose members included county councillors and the Chief Constable.[19]

'Our coast should be rendered as impossible as possible for the enemy'
Lord Harris

In the House of Lords the duties – and powers – of Lord-Lieutenants towards the civil population of their counties in the event of an invasion were questioned. The former were stated to be vague and ill-defined, while the latter were practically non-existent. In the ensuing debate Lord Harris 'the famous cricketer of bygone days':

> …had much to say of the official advice on which he had to act. Emergency committees had, however, been formed in his county, and the people had accepted their instructions in the most admirable spirit. He believed in taking the public into their confidence, and had proceeded on that principle, instead of giving such counsel as that 'if a shell comes in at the front door, it is safer to go out by the back.'[20]

Harris kept things simple, instructing the people of Kent: 'Our coast should be rendered as impossible as possible for the enemy.'

His issue of a notice about what to do in case of a raid was prophetic, presaging as it did the later bombing of Tontine Street in Folkestone. He advised people: 'Seek shelter underground – not assemble out of curiosity in the streets.'

Reporting his 64th birthday, the *Kent and Sussex Courier* reminded readers that he had earlier commanded the East Kent Yeomanry 'and his heart is with the Regiment now, only Anno Domini keeping him away from it.'

At the start of the war an Act was passed allowing special constables to be appointed for the duration, but not all were as dedicated as they might have been.

Lord Harris complained to the Chief Constable that during a Zeppelin raid on the night of 17 August 1915, he came across two cases of Special Constables who were not offering to be of any assistance in the neighbourhood. 'On being interrogated, they gave as their reason that they must stay by the womenfolk.' Lord Harris reported testily that such people were obviously useless in an emergency and suggested to the Chief Constable that 'in all probability, a weeding out of the Special Constabulary would eliminate some of these shirkers to the advantage of the whole force.'

The Chief Constable promptly sent a memorandum to the heads of Special Constabulary stating 'If this sort of thing is likely to recur, men of this description will be better out of the Force than in it and [he] hopes that Heads will make their Special Constables acquainted with the Vice-Lieutenant's remarks.'[21]

In the second year of the war the splendid scarlet full-dress Lieutenancy uniforms were mothballed in favour of khaki service dress. This was retained after the war for TA inspections and the like alongside a new modified full-dress uniform for ceremonial occasions. Simplified coats replaced those with short tails, the Deputy Lieutenants lost their hat plumes and the Lieutenancy's undress frock-coat uniform was abolished.

Camden in his scarlet full-dress Lieutenancy uniform

Back in the county in September 1916, Camden wrote to Kent newspapers 'publicly thanking Lord Harris for the very able way in which he has carried out, as Vice-Lieutenant, the many and arduous duties since the outbreak of war.' And in the same editions Lord Harris expressed his gratitude for the 'cheerful and unstinted co-operation' of all those who had helped him marshal the resources of the county for the war effort.

Marchioness Camden, as President of the Kent Voluntary Aid Detachment, was herself fully active in supporting the county's war wounded and other good works.

In 1917 Camden raised the Kent Motor Volunteer Corps (Volunteers), later called the Kent Army Service Corps (Motor Transport) and was Gazetted Lieutenant Colonel. At its height the Corps had 100 lorries, 100 officers and 1,300 men. Later, he was also appointed Honorary Colonel of the 58th (Kent) Anti Aircraft Brigade.

One of his saddest wartime duties was to represent King George V at the funeral of the many victims of a Gotha bomber raid on Folkestone in 1917.

Immediately after the war one of his tasks, delegated by the King, was to present medals of the Order of the British Empire and at one such investiture at Maidstone 16 people received the awards for bravery and devotion to duty during air raids or explosions in munition factories. One of those decorated was a Miss Spink, Matron of Margate Cottage Hospital, and the British Journal of Nursing commented:

> We think many more of these medals might be bestowed upon the nursing staffs of hospitals, who, during a long series of raids, performed their duties with the utmost courage and devotion – many of them, we know, at the expense of shattered nerves.[22]

The Order of the British Empire had been instituted in 1917 but Lord-Lieutenants were only able to submit nominations for awards for Members of the British Empire (MBE), not the OBE, the Home Office having objected on the grounds that they 'cannot possibly have any knowledge' of recipients' service in the war. In the case of hands-on Lord-Lieutenants like Camden with his own military background and involvement in county affairs at all levels, this was simply not true. Many years later, just before the outbreak of World War II, Camden told a meeting of the Association of Lieutenants of Counties that 'during the 33 years of his Lieutenancy he had never succeeded in obtaining honours for people.'

The Deputy Lieutenants Act of 1918 abolished the property qualification, tightened the residential qualification so that only those who lived in or no more than seven miles outside the county boundary could be nominated, and retained the restriction that 'the gentlemen appointed should have rendered worthy service either of a civil or military character on behalf of the Army,

'A sad wartime duty for Camden was representing the King at the funeral of victims of a Gotha bomber raid on Folkestone'

Lord Harris – 'an English gentleman of the old school'

Lady Camden's portrait in County Hall

Navy or Auxiliary Forces.' It remained very much a men only club. DLs had had no statutory duties to perform since 1882 and anything they did was on a purely voluntary basis. The theoretical duty of organising Militia ballots had long been redundant 'and was finally swept away in the Territorial and Militia Act of 1921.' They were now merely obliged to give an assurance that they would assist the Lord-Lieutenant to carry out any orders coming from the Monarch – and to report their addresses annually.

Attempts by the Association to allow some appointments whether or not those involved had the required military credentials were frustrated by the War Office, anxious to maintain support for the Territorial Army, stating in 1925:

Deputy Lieutenants are and always have been appointed under Acts of a purely military character and the duties required of them have always been of a military nature.[23]

The situation was not to change for another 40 years, and as we shall see, this created an embarrassing problem for Camden's successor.

Lord Harris, the man who had stood in for Camden during World War I died in 1932 aged 81.

Left with only periphery military responsibilities between the wars Camden found other roles suitable for his Lieutenancy. In many ways he set the pattern for the future of the ancient office, hitherto concerned solely with the organisation of auxiliary forces, county administration and local justice, by taking far more of a leading part in many other aspects of county life than any of his predecessors.

He served as president of many organisations including: the Scouts, South East District National Fire Brigades, Kent Playing Fields Association, Kent Council of Social Services, Kent National Service Committee, the Kent and Sussex Hospital, Tunbridge Wells, and the Kent Discharged Prisoners' Aid Society. A full length portrait of him in army uniform and dated 1916 is in County Hall opposite a portrait of his wife, the former Joan Nevill. She was a formidable county personality in her own right. Daughter of the 3rd Marquess Abergavenny, she involved herself in health and welfare matters, as president of the wartime Kent Voluntary Aid Detachment, the County Nursing Association, which she founded, Kent Girl Guides, and as an officer of St John. Marchioness Camden, a spirited lady who enjoyed riding to hounds, was also a member of the National Society for the Prevention of Cruelty to Children's executive committee; and her CBE was well earned.

They made a formidable couple and she was a great asset to Camden's 38-year service to four monarchs during which they attended the coronations of Edward VII, George V and George VI. It was said of him:

No other Lord-Lieutenant in the country had such a proud and interesting

record, because it was naturally to Kent that important visitors invariably came on their way to London in peacetime.[24]

He was present for arrivals and departures of a long procession of crowned heads and heads of state from British royalty to the Kings of Italy, Denmark, Belgium, Romania, Egypt, Afghanistan and Iraq, to the Crown Prince of Japan, the Empress of Russia, the German Emperor, the Shah of Persia, the French President and the President of the United States. The *Kent and Sussex Courier* recorded:

> In public life Lord Camden probably had the proudest record of all Lord Lieutenants, for when in March 1939, he went to Dover to meet the President of the French Republic it was the 50th occasion on which he had attended State visits and departures from the shores of England.[25]

Many members of the Royal Family were entertained by the Camdens at their ancestral home, Bayham Abbey, Lamberhurst, over the years and they planted trees to commemorate their visits. His unparalleled service was recognised when he was made a Knight Grand Cross of the Royal Victorian Order, which is exclusively in the gift of the Monarch.

Soon after the outbreak of World War II Clerks to the Lieutenancies were informed that the Army Council had decided that the wearing of full dress, undress and mess dress by Army officers was to be discontinued during the war – 'and that a similar rule shall apply as regards the full dress and undress uniforms of the Lieutenancy.' As in the Great War, khaki was again the only authorised uniform.

Characteristically, Camden and his wife threw themselves into war work:

'The Lord-Lieutenant's wife went shopping for troops returning from Dunkirk'

The many duties which fall upon a Lord Lieutenant did not lessen on the outbreak of the present war, and up to his last illness Lord Camden was a busy man. He gave his support to many special wartime appeals, and his name was always to the forefront in any good cause or movement for the benefit of the county.[26]

The Camdens gave first-hand support too. As the Army struggled back from Dunkirk in June 1940 a stream of trains ran through Kent stations. Local firms printed 'I'm safe' cards which were handed out by schoolchildren to troops on trains stopping at Tonbridge. All the men had to do was sign them and write their home address and the post office delivered them free. A collection was started and local people gave the men clothing and food parcels and cigarettes. 'Housewives emptied their larders and brewed gallons of tea, using jam jars when the supply of cups ran out.'

In an act typical of the veteran Lord-Lieutenant, with his fellow-feeling for Servicemen, and his wife with her dedication to the welfare of others, the couple went to Tonbridge station to welcome the troops. They chatted to the exhausted men, many with no more than they stood up in, and the Marchioness asked them what they needed and went shopping for them. One of the officers said:

> We couldn't have had a better reception if we had brought Hitler home in a paper bag.[27]

At first there was considerable uncertainty among the county Lieutenants as to what their wartime role should be. The formation of the Local Defence Volunteers – which became the Home Guard – originally involved Deputy Lieutenants in the selection of local commanders, but, this being the era of Blizkrieg, this right was soon withdrawn.

In wartime there were few statutory duties for the Lord-Lieutenant but Camden played a full part in morale-boosting and fund-raising. A typical example is in the foreword he wrote, as President of the County of Kent Military Welfare Committee, in the Autumn 1943 publication *Photography, Heritage of Kent*, that sold for half a crown (12½p), all proceeds going to the county's Military Welfare Fund. In it he recalled:

> Early in the war I made an appeal to the people of Kent to help members of the Forces stationed in the County, by entertainment in their homes – when rations permitted – by giving lifts in their vehicles, by helping in canteens, and the hundred and one ways which have made Service life more comfortable during their stay with us. The splendid response has carried on the long tradition of Kentish hospitality.

He reminded readers that Kent stood at the gateway to Britain:

ABOVE: Dunkirk veterans returning through Kent were treated with every kindness – and the Lord-Lieutenant's wife even went shopping for them

The air above it – and the waters around it – were the first to experience the turbulence of war. Its harbours and their inhabitants reached out hands of welcome to the 'little ships' returning from Dunkirk. Many of its homes are in ruins from air and long range artillery bombardment across the narrow sea, but like the Castle which crowns the white cliffs of Dover, Kent stands grim and defiant, always on the watch, and without complaint.

It was a fitting wartime tribute to the county he loved and had served so well, and it proved to be one of his last acts as Lord-Lieutenant. He was already unwell and died at Bayham Abbey a few days before Christmas.

Many handsome tributes were paid, the *Kent and Sussex Courier's* being typical:

> By his passing the whole county will mourn the loss of one of its most illustrious sons, who, as the King's representative, landowner, soldier, and sportsman, endeared himself to Royalty, potentates and statesmen down to the lowliest peasant. His 38 years as Lord Lieutenant of Kent probably establishes a record for length of service in that capacity.

It did indeed establish a record, having beaten the previous longest term of 34 years by Earl Sydney, and it remains a record that is highly unlikely ever to be equalled.

ABOVE: Battle of Britain
fighter ace Wing
Commander Robert
Stanford Tuck was in for a
surprise when he dropped
in on Lord Cornwallis

FOURTEEN

SPITFIRES AND THE
SPIRIT OF KENT

At the height of the Battle of Britain fighter ace Robert Stanford Tuck force-landed his damaged Spitfire at Horsmonden and was taken to Plovers, the nearby home of Lord Cornwallis, Vice Lord-Lieutenant of Kent and President of the Association of Men of Kent and Kentish Men, for a well-earned rest while waiting to be picked up and returned to the fray. The *Kent Messenger* reported: 'When the pilot awoke, Lord Cornwallis was able to tell him that he had the money to buy him a new plane!'

A few days earlier, by happy coincidence, Cornwallis and Lord Camden, the Lord-Lieutenant, had jointly launched an appeal via the Association to raise enough for an *Invicta* Flight of Spitfires and immediately on hearing about it a Bearsted man had sent a cheque for £5,000. Cornwallis told the *Kent Messenger*:

> The pilot was a grand fellow. Only a few days before he had received the DFC at the hands of the King and that very day he had shot down two German planes. He had a long sleep and when he awoke and we were having a meal it was a great privilege for me on behalf of the county to be able to tell him that I had the money to be able to buy him a new plane.

In no time enough was collected to pay for three aircraft, appropriately named *Man of Kent*, *Kentish Man* and *Fair Maid of Kent*. The appeal was taken up enthusiastically around the county, raising enough for a full squadron, and Cornwallis received a letter of thanks from the President of Aircraft Production, Colonel Moore Brabazon, saying:

This will be a County of Kent Squadron, and Kent will be the first County as usual to have a Squadron named after it.

The extra aircraft were named after Kentish towns and the Squadron Leader's was dubbed *The Spirit of Kent, Lord Cornwallis*. Thanking the many who had donated, Cornwallis told them:

> Just remember that when you look upward to the skies, it may be your Kent Squadron that is defending The Gateway of England and ask for God's blessing and protection for those glorious men who are riding on the wings of the White Horse of Kent.[1]

One of the Spitfires was named after Lord Cornwallis – *The Spirit of Kent*

Taking such an initiative and inspiring the Frontline County in this way when the threat of invasion was yet again very real was typical of the man who was to replace Camden as Lord-Lieutenant. Cornwallis had impeccable credentials for the appointment. He was the scion of a famous family, a war hero who had captained Kent at cricket and chaired the County Council – an inspirational leader who indeed embodied the Spirit of Kent, the affectionate title his county bestowed on him.

His ancestors included a distinguished admiral – a friend of Nelson who 'grieved much' at his death, a cavalry cornet who took part in the charge of the Light Brigade, an archbishop, and the general who surrendered to a much larger American and French force at Yorktown during the War of Independence.

Wykeham Stanley Cornwallis, the 2nd Baron, was born at the family seat at Linton Park in 1892, educated at Eton and Sandhurst, joined the Royal Scots Greys, and during World War I was wounded in the arm, leg and head at the Battle of the Aisne. He won the Military Cross for trench bombing and mining operations at Loos, was also Mentioned in Despatches, became a staff officer and eventually Aide-de-Camp to Earl Haig.

He played cricket for Kent for seven years, captained the county for three seasons, and Neville Cardus said of him: 'Cornwallis is a true Kent captain – keen, chivalrous and always in love with the game.' He rode in steeplechases and point-to-points, and enjoyed shooting, hunting, stalking, polo and football.

Between the wars he was elected to the County Council and within seven years became Chairman before resigning on the death of his father.

When World War II threatened he took on the role of Chairman of the Kent War Agricultural Committee, and said later: 'This was the biggest job in my life and I made more friends then than at any other time.'

It involved organising Kent's 11,000 farmers, ensuring that every piece of farmland was productive, and – a throwback to the Lieutenancy's invasion plans during the Napoleonic Wars – arranging for sheep and cattle to be

Wykeham Stanley, 2nd Baron Cornwallis, who, like Lord Harris, captained Kent at cricket

RIGHT: Lord Cornwallis
tries out a mini caterpillar
tractor at a War Agricultural
Committee event at
Eynsford in 1942

moved away from Romney Marsh in the event of a German invasion. Such was his leadership and power to convene that when on the eve of war he sent telegrams to 250 of Kent's largest farmers asking them to meet him at County Hall next day 249 of them turned up. Under him, Kent produced double its normal output of food during the war, despite bombing, shelling and doodle-bugs.[2]

At the outbreak of war Cornwallis addressed a special message to the Association of Men of Kent and Kentish Men urging everyone to do their bit 'for a cause that is no less than the salvation of civilisation'.

Following Camden's death in December 1943 there was a nine-month gap before his successor was appointed. When the name was eventually made known the *Kent Messenger* reported:

> The whole county… will be gratified that the King has thus honoured Lord Cornwallis, who now becomes the leading man in the county, a position richly earned by a long and notable record of public service.[3]

In truth, Cornwallis was an obvious choice for Lord-Lieutenant, an appointment he was to hold for 28 years, but the exigencies of war and the death of his first wife had delayed his appointment.

Although the war was far from over, ironically his first duty, in October 1944, a month after being appointed, was to take the salute at Canterbury at the stand-down of the Kent Home Guard, no longer needed now that, following the success of the Allies' D-Day landings, the invasion threat was past. He took the salute from a dais in Broad Street as 3,000 men marched past and at a parade at The Buffs' barracks he told them:

> It is with a feeling of great humility that on the occasion of my first public duty as His Majesty's Lieutenant of the County of Kent, I find myself

charged with the task of offering you the deep and sincere thanks of the people of Kent whom you have served so well, and for whom you were prepared to fight and die.[4]

He went on to reveal his acute sense of Kent's role as the nation's Front-line County highlighted by the Canterbury Cathedral service they had just attended 'to render thanksgiving that the horrors of invasion, bombardment and bloodshed in our county have been dispelled.' He referred to the days when the Lieutenancy organised defence:

> The history of our County is full of examples of the readiness of our citizen armies to serve in times of crisis. We remember long years ago the raising of the Trained Bands, that were the beginnings of the great County Regiment behind whose bands and drums you have marched today… All spontaneous action in defence of this old island of ours has at its commencement been of a voluntary nature, and it is therefore but natural that the Home Guard started its foundation as a voluntary body, the LDVs [Local Defence Volunteers], unarmed, except for shotguns, bottles and pikes, ready to fight with these inadequate weapons, but armed with something far greater than weapons, the spirit of free men imbued with the traditional spirit of Kent.

He reminded them of the dark days following Dunkirk when the Home Guard was rising ready to fight the threaten invasion and quoted a verse of his own:

> And had the Huns befouled our land,
> The story we could tell,
> Was that 60,000 sons of Kent
> Had sent them back to hell.[5]

Three days after the Home Guard stand-down, Cornwallis officiated at the first royal visit of his Lieutenancy when King George VI and Queen Elizabeth came to 'Hellfire Corner' to pay tribute to the people of Dover and who had endured four years of shelling, bombing and doodlebugs. They were met at Kearsney station by Cornwallis who accompanied them to see the shattered buildings and the air raid shelters which for many were now their only homes.

Their Majesties heard about the grim experiences of residents – 'people who had refused to evacuate and who had just carried on in spite of every effort by the enemy to drive them away.' Earlier Lord Cornwallis himself had a narrow escape at the top of Dover's Castle Hill when a bomb had fallen only 15 yards away.

Ecstatic crowds greeted the royal party's arrival at the Town Hall, where Their Majesties inspected a Guard of Honour composed of members of the women's services, and then their motorcade drove past throngs of cheering

King George VI is greeted by Lord Cornwallis at Kearsney for the visit to Dover and Folkestone in 1944

people standing outside their shattered homes which were covered with flags. At the caves used as shelters the Queen asked one resident: 'Do you still come down here?' The reply: 'We have to Ma'am, you see we have no homes to go to as they have been shelled.'

The King and Queen took a special interest in members of the Women's Land Army – of whom there were 4,000 in Kent – and especially in those who had worked on in the St Margaret's Bay area after Navy and Army personnel had been sent away because it was unsafe. From Dover the Royal party motored to Folkestone, visiting the worst-hit east end of the town, and everywhere among the crowds were children, former evacuees, who had come home now that the area was free from shelling.[6]

Having taken the salute at the winding up of the Home Guard, the Lord-Lieutenant accompanied the Duchess of Kent for the stand-down of Kent's Land Girls in July 1945. After a Cathedral service 1,700 of them paraded at Canterbury's St Lawrence Cricket Ground where the Duchess thanked them for their contribution to victory.

Cornwallis, in his roles as both Lord-Lieutenant and Chairman of the Kent War Agricultural Committee, had first-hand knowledge of their magnificent war work, often under fire, and told them: 'Kent is grateful to its girls in green.' It must have been particularly poignant for him because his first wife, Chairman of Kent Women's Land Army, had sadly died 18 months earlier. Ironically it was to be 60 years before the Land Girls received a special badge recognising their valuable wartime service. When recognition was finally achieved, the Lieutenancy of Kent was first to honour these heroines by inviting surviving Land Girls and Lumber Jills to civic receptions where heart-felt tributes were paid to them by the then Lord-Lieutenant Allan Willett.

Cornwallis always performed his Lieutenancy duties with appropriate decorum, but he was not above raising a laugh at his own expense – as he showed when invited to unveil the restored quintain, the only remaining one in England, at Offham Green in August 1945. Quintains, consisting of a post with a crossbeam, were used for training knights of old who rode at them attempting to strike the arm and at the same time avoid a blow from the sandbag swinging at the other end. Unskilful tilters would be knocked off their horses.

A large crowd gathered to watch as Cornwallis prepared to risk a go at the quintain after the unveiling and he told them: 'I believe a great many of you have come here today in the hope of seeing a Lord-Lieutenant being unseated from his horse, and I am going to do my best to disappoint you!'

With that the former cavalryman mounted his horse and charged, hitting the quintain with his lance – and successfully dodging the swinging sandbag. He remarked: 'Although the use of the horse and lance is now obsolete, our spirit is as unconquered as the days when knights prepared themselves for battle by tilting at the quintain.'[7] That was most certainly true of Lord Cornwallis.

A year after the war's end the King and Queen again visited Kent, this time bomb-scarred Canterbury. The Lord-Lieutenant met the royal train at Selling station and before they alighted witnessed what was described as 'a homely incident' – 'Princess Elizabeth could be seen through the train window brushing down the King's uniform.'[8]

The following month the Lord-Lieutenant was present at the installation of Winston Churchill as holder of that other ancient Kent-based office of Lord Warden of the Cinque Ports. Churchill had been appointed five years earlier, but the ceremony was postponed until after the war. It was at the Dover ceremony that Churchill used the stirring words about Kent that are still quoted today: '…this glorious foreland of England, the shrine of its Christianity, the cradle of its institution, the bulwark of its defence…'[9]

Three years later Churchill was among the new Deputy Lieutenants of Kent appointed by Cornwallis. In accepting the appointment the man known to many as 'the greatest living Englishman' was not only being honoured – he was honouring Kent, the county he had adopted.

Appointed as a Deputy Lieutenant at the same time as Churchill was Major the Right Honourable the Lord De L'Isle and Dudley VC – later 1st Viscount De L'Isle, of Penshurst Place.

Commissioned in the Grenadier Guards as a Supplementary Reservist between the wars, Sidney was called to the Colours when World War II broke out, served with the British Expeditionary Force and was one of the last to be taken off the beach at Dunkirk.

He won his Victoria Cross in Italy when, although twice wounded, he fought

'Our spirit is as unconquered as the days when knights prepared themselves for battle by tilting at the quintain'
Lord Cornwallis

ABOVE: Lord Cornwallis with Winston Churchill at the Kent County Show in 1948. The following year the great war leader became a Deputy Lieutenant of Kent

ABOVE RIGHT: Major William Sidney VC, later 1st Viscount De L'Isle, with his father-in-law Field Marshal Viscount Gort, pictured right, who had won his VC capturing a strategically-important ridge on the Western Front during World War I

off determined German attacks, dashing forward at one stage to engage the enemy with his Tommy gun at point blank range. He was asked by the Prime Minister to stand for Parliament later in 1944 as MP for Chelsea and on the death of his father in June 1945 went to the House of Lords, was appointed Secretary of State for Air by Churchill, and later became the last English Governor General of Australia. The 1st Viscount De L'Isle would undoubtedly have made a fine Lord-Lieutenant if the opportunity had arisen. It did not, but his son Philip was to win that honour for the Sidney family 60 years on.

In 1947, many of the county Lieutenants being elderly, their Association had resolved that in future they should hold the appointment only until the age of 75, then subject to annual review, and not, as formerly, 'at pleasure,' which had usually meant for life.[10]

Cornwallis was a mere 55 at that time and so it appeared he would embark on another 20 years' service, although in fact he was to serve on for no less than five years beyond the recommended date. His first wife had died during the war and in 1948 he married Lady Esme Walker who supported him in his county duties, accompanying him on many ceremonial occasions and visits, and sometimes presenting awards, until her death in 1969.

At that time Lieutenants received no expenses whatsoever to cover the often heavy costs they incurred, although remuneration for travel associated with their role as *Custos Rotulorum* was authorised from 1948. In the days before universal air travel Kent was one of the country's busiest points of arrival and departure for Monarchs and Heads of State, and the Lord-Lieutenant's commitments were heavy.

Cornwallis took up the case on behalf of all, pointing out: 'my real worry is that soon it will be quite impossible to get the right men to take on the job at all.'[11] It was an important point of principle and the Government was persuaded. Another sign of the austere post-war times was the move away from the scarlet full-dress uniform to a dark blue suit with military-style cap, similar to the army's Number 1 dress. As his Deputy Lieutenants were mostly former army officers at that time they could easily convert their military 'blues' with the appropriate Tudor rose badges and buttons. When George VI died in 1952, Lord Cornwallis was quick to promote the county's appeal for a memorial, urging all to 'prove the determination of all Kentish folk to set an example of affectionate memory and gratitude'.[12]

The following year Lord and Lady Cornwallis were present in Westminster Abbey in their coronation robes for the crowning of Queen Elizabeth II. A new Elizabethan era had begun. Ninety Lieutenants attended a Lancaster House banquet for the new Queen and *The Times* reported that:

> …the Lord-Lieutenant of today stands, first and foremost, not for anything political but for the general social life of his county.[13]

In the post-war years a succession of royal visitors and Heads of State were welcomed to Kent by Lord Cornwallis. An instruction issued in 1956 for the guidance of Lord-Lieutenants governing the composition of guards of honour mounted for The Queen and other members of the Royal Family included the blindingly obvious warning:

> Gun salutes should never be fired in close proximity to The Queen.[14]

Frequent visitors were Princess Marina, Duchess of Kent, and members of her family including – in 1953 for the first time – her son, the young Duke of Kent, who is still a regular and ever-welcome visitor today. The occasion was a rally by 10,000 members of Kent British Legion and Lord Cornwallis told them:

> It is the first time Her Royal Highness has brought her son with her on a public occasion in the County and it is fitting that he should be welcomed by the Old Brigade.[15]

Over the following six decades the Duke has visited the county many times and been welcomed by five successive Lord-Lieutenants: Lord Cornwallis, Lord Astor, Lord Kingsdown, Allan Willett – and nowadays by Lord De L'Isle. In 2006 Allan Willett presented him with the then newly-created *Spirit of Kent Award* to acknowledge conspicuous service to the county by His Royal Highness and his family over more than half a century.

Lord Cornwallis spared no effort in carrying out his Lieutenancy duties and it was said 'no ceremonial occasion in Kent is complete without him.'[16]

> You have only to attend a function of the Association of Men of Kent and Kentish Men, and to hear the applause by Kentish Fire – a special token of honour in Kent – which greets the Lord-Lieutenant on his arrival, or at the conclusion of one of his stimulating addresses, to realize the respect and esteem in which he is held by all.[17]

Lord Cornwallis in the Lord-Lieutenant's uniform adopted after World War II

The Lord-Lieutenant escorts The Queen and Prince Philip during a visit to the Royal Engineers at Brompton Barracks

The young Duke of Kent on his first official visit to the county with his mother, HRH Princess Marina, for a British Legion rally at Aylesford in 1953

Lord Cornwallis escorts Princess Margaret during a visit to Ashford where she opened new St John Ambulance headquarters

Nor was he afraid to speak his mind in defence of his county. As early as 1949 at celebrations marking the foundation of the Kingdom of Kent 15 centuries earlier, he said:

> You know, we have governed ourselves extraordinarily well during these 1,500 years, without having been planned into this and merged with that.

And in 1958 he was warning:

> I sometimes feel that those people who try to preserve the beauty, amenities and story of Kent are fighting a losing battle against the crawling octopus of London, whose tentacles seem to stretch out and take more and more of Kent's countryside.[18]

Two years later, in a House of Lords debate, he again referred to London County Council, as it then was, as 'that sprawling development of a great octopus' and voiced Kent's concern at the 'ruthless disruption of the old loyalties and county boundaries,' which were eating into the county. He argued:

> We wonder where it is all going to end. The proper geographical boundary of Kent includes Woolwich, Greenwich, Catford, Blackheath and other boroughs. In many respects these boroughs still belong to Kent.[19]

Greenwich had been lost when the County of London was created in 1889, and Cornwallis was correct in his warning of the 'sprawling octopus.' On 1 April 1965 Bromley, Beckenham, Penge, Orpington and Chislehurst became part of Greater London. He was anxious that Kent's heritage, traditions and customs – including its local dialects – should be preserved and said: 'I would rather hear the burr of the Weald of Kent than the mouthings of the BBC.'[20]

Lord Cornwallis was not a fan of the Channel Tunnel and in 1968, as President of the Kent County Playing Fields Association, was warning that development connected with it, coupled with the pressure of population, would, if care was not taken 'make it tight in Kent for open spaces.' He was especially concerned about the threat to 'the best cherry orchards in the world.'

After he had retired, when speaking at the same events as his pro-Tunnel successor Lord Kingsdown, he would contrive to bring the subject up to tease the new Lord-Lieutenant. But, Lady Kingsdown recalls, her husband knew it was coming 'and it always used to make Robin smile.'

Lord Cornwallis was acutely aware of the importance of his role as *Custos Rotulorum* and his duty to encourage the preservation of records. Promoting awareness, he said God alone knew how many documents had been lost over the years, but added: 'I do not know what the *Custus* could have done to stop it, for it was not done wilfully but through ignorance.'[21]

Cornwallis also understood the usefulness of Kent's local newspapers, trusted them, and was trusted by them. He once said: 'I have never been let down by the provincial press. They have supported me in good causes, and have always warned me when I was on a bad wicket.'[22]

He had a mutually respectful relationship with H R (Roy) Pratt Boorman, Editor-proprietor of the *Kent Messenger*, who became one of his Deputy Lieutenants and chronicled his achievements in his aptly-titled book *Spirit of Kent*.

Deputy Lieutenants' commissions had to be signed by the Lord-Lieutenant 'and sealed' which meant that his family seal had to be impressed on the document. However, this became a problem in 1960 when the then Clerk to the Lieutenancy, Geoffrey Heckles, wrote to inform Lord Cornwallis that his seal could not be found, adding:

> I am exceedingly sorry that such a thing should have happened, but unless and until the seal is found there seems to be no alternative but to ask you to sign the Commissions with the deletion of the words 'and seal.'[23]

Cornwallis replied:

> I am horrified to hear that the family seal is lost. I actually sent two to County Hall – and the one that was in use was the Personal seal of the last Earl Cornwallis and was a family treasure.

The situation reached near farce when the Lord-Lieutenant confessed:

> To add to my troubles – in the midst of the Christmas mess the container with the three commissions for General Boucher, Brig King Lewis and Col. Waring rolled on the floor and were found by my retriever puppy who chewed the end and spoilt the commissions. We shall have to begin again. I do *not* like the idea of signing *not* under seal.

Extensive searches and enquiries were made and it was ascertained that one of the seals had last been used for sealing the Warrant of the Bishop of Rochester as Deputy Lieutenant in March, 1959. But now no trace of either seal could be found and the Lord-Lieutenant could delay issue of the puppy-chewed parchments no longer. He wrote to Heckles:

> I am coming to Maidstone next Friday and will bring the Commissions with me, as I fear the damage to them is too severe for it to be possible to use them. I suppose the three unfortunate individuals have been waiting for their Charter as Deputy Lieutenants for some months now…[24]

And so new commissions had to be prepared for Colonel Arthur ('Blick')

DEDICATION FROM *KENT INNS, A DISTILLATION*

by H R Pratt Boorman and Anne Roper

To the Right Honourable Lord Cornwallis KBE MC Lord Lieutenant of Kent in grateful recognition of his personal care for his people of Kent and his vigilance in safeguarding their ancient rights and customs

The Lord-Lieutenant was embarrassed to admit that his puppy had chewed new DL commissions – an interesting variation on 'the dog ate my homework' theme!

LORD CORNWALLIS
Tunbridge Wells

Collectors' card featuring the sign of the Lord Cornwallis Hotel, Tunbridge Wells

Waring, Brigadier Humphrey King-Lewis and Major General Valentine Boucher, and signed without the Cornwallis seal.

At that time Cornwallis was officially Lord-Lieutenant both of Kent and the then County Borough of Canterbury, and he queried whether the crest of the city could be used along with the county emblem on Deputy Lieutenant commissions 'if I am allowed to use it.'

Heckles sought guidance from the Lord Chancellor's Office as to whether it was necessary or appropriate to continue to include in commissions any reference to a Deputy Lieutenant being appointed 'for the City of Canterbury in addition to the County of Kent.' The response was that Lord Cornwallis held the office of Lord-Lieutenant of the *whole* of the geographical county, including the city of Canterbury, but that DLs and their appointment were not within the province of the Lord Chancellor, but the responsibility of the Secretary of State for War. An approach to the War Office confirmed that the Lieutenancy covered the whole of the county of Kent. In the 1972 reform of local government Canterbury lost its status as a county borough and along with Whitstable, Herne Bay and the surrounding villages, became part of a district – and by Royal Charter, the City of Canterbury.[25]

Ever anxious to ensure that the Lieutenancy of Kent was following correct procedures, in 1970 Heckles set enquiries afoot to clarify the duties of Deputy Lieutenants and the resulting report is worth quoting in full:

As requested, I have investigated the statutory position with regard to duties of DLs. Section 31 of the Militia Act, 1882, provides that where the Lieutenant of a county is absent from the UK, or by reason of sickness or otherwise is unable to act, or where there is no Lieutenant for a County, Her Majesty may authorise any three Deputy Lieutenants to act as Lieutenant.

This only applies however where there is no Vice-Lieutenant and, as you know, Lord Harris [5th Baron Harris] has been appointed Vice-Lieutenant for Kent. Section 36 of the Militia Act, 1882, provides that DLs shall have such jurisdiction, duties, powers and privileges as are vested in them under any Act of Parliament in force. I have not done an exhaustive search of the statutes to ascertain the extent of such duties but one example is contained in Section 12 of the Auxiliary Forces Act, 1953, which provides that a recruit to the Territorial Forces may be attested by any DL.

Nationally, attempts to allow non-military Deputy Lieutenant appointments had been always been refused and this had sometimes led to ridiculous anomalies. One such was the blocking of the bid to appoint Walter Platts, Clerk of the Peace and of Kent County Council as a DL. Platts was an experienced and distinguished public servant who had been commissioned in the Royal Naval Volunteer Reserve during World War I and had been decorated for gallantry. Yet because he had not held sufficiently senior rank he could not be appointed. The rule was finally relaxed in 1966, but it took time for the situation to change and in a photograph of the Lord-Lieutenant with members of the Kent Territorial and Auxiliary Forces Association at their last meeting before amalgamation in December 1967, 14 of the 39 present were Deputy Lieutenants of Lieutenant Colonel level or above.[26]

They included another Victoria Cross holder, Colonel Donald Dean, from Tunstall, who in the best traditions had lied about his age to join the Artists Rifles at the outbreak of World War I. He served as a private at Ypres and the Somme, before being commissioned in The Queen's Own Royal West Kent Regiment.

Colonel Donald Dean VC – heroic Kent Deputy Lieutenant

He won the VC for 'most conspicuous bravery, skilful command and devotion to duty' in a two-day action against greatly superior numbers of Germans. At the height of one attack he was speaking to his company commander by field telephone and suddenly broke off, saying: 'The Germans are here. Goodbye.'

He was wounded four times during the war but miraculously he survived to serve again during World War II, again bravely, in the defence of Boulogne, at Dunkirk, the Sicily landings and in Italy.[27]

Also in the Kent Association group photograph was Lieutenant Colonel Angela Cobb, not yet a Deputy Lieutenant simply because she was a woman. We will hear more of her.

From 1966 persons proposed by the Lord-Lieutenant to be Deputies must now be shown to the satisfaction of the Secretary of State for Defence:

> …to have rendered either (1) worthy service as a member of, or in a civil capacity, in connection with Her Majesty's naval, military or air force, or (2) such other service as, in the opinion of the Secretary of State, makes him suitable for appointment as a DL.[28]

At first the maximum number of non-military DLs was to make up no more than 20 per cent of the active total, but this rule was scrapped in 1977.

Lord-Lieutenants are often asked to sponsor fund-raising appeals, sometimes placing them in a dilemma as they cannot support everything yet do not wish to appear churlish by declining. In 1962 the Association of Lord-Lieutenants set out its policy, advising its members only to identify themselves with purely county interests or organisations of which they might be president, making their appeals as such. They were further advised that they need not hesitate to decline to sponsor a national appeal or to explain why they are unable to do so.[29]

Although Cornwallis soldiered on as Lord-Lieutenant until he was 80, he shed some of his many responsibilities much earlier. At one time he was serving on 100 different committees in the county. In business life he became Chairman of Reeds Paper Group and Fremlins, the brewers, as well as insur-

Welcoming King Frederick of Denmark, Colonel-in-Chief of The Buffs (Royal East Kent Regiment), during a visit to Canterbury

ance companies, and was active in Freemasonry. Something had to go and after suffering four bouts of bronchitis he stepped down as President of the Association of Men of Kent and Kentish Men in 1960, saying: 'I would say to Kent that you have got to find others who will take on one or two duties, and do them properly, and not ask one man to do 40 or 50 of them.'[30] Making more active use of his Deputy Lieutenants might have helped.

The county Association, which had grown from 500 to more than 6,000 members under his leadership, made him Vice-Patron and duly found a new president.

Despite some slowing down, he continued to serve in many capacities, including Pro-Chancellor of the University of Kent at Canterbury, and President of Kent County Agricultural Society, and he continued to welcome royal visitors to the county.

Cornwallis was not above telling stories against himself and greatly amused David Seeney, who ran Kent's Special Branch until 1980, with the tale of a long journey home after an even when he asked his chauffeur to stop so that the he could change into plain clothes.

> After some miles and well out into the countryside, they stopped to make the change. His Lordship had reached the stage of being partly clothed in his underpants when a police car drove up. The rest is left to the imagination, but the police officers asked some awkward questions![31]

When David Seeney retired Lord Cornwallis asked if he could attend the farewell party at Police Headquarters and presented him with a photograph inscribed: 'To my guide, protector and friend with true gratitude – Cornwallis.'

There were further honours for the Lord-Lieutenant. He had been created a KBE in 1945 and now was made KCVO, and a Knight Commander of the Danish Order of Dannebrog.

After more than a quarter of a century in the appointment, Lord Cornwallis at last retired in 1972 at the age of 80. The following year he survived a heart attack and lived on, fit enough to open the bowling at a Linton Park charity match when he was 87. When he died in January 1982 at Ashurst Park, his home for 25 years, local newspaper headlines reported sadly: *The Spirit of Kent Dies.'*

His successor as Lord-Lieutenant, Lord Astor of Hever, described Cornwallis as a fine English gentleman, sportsman, soldier and businessman who was equally at ease with the highest and the humblest, and added: 'There are many who will remember his characteristic speeches which could fill a room with laughter or with tears.'

LEFT: Hever Castle, where
Henry VIII courted Anne
Boleyn – and later, home
of the Astor family

~ FIFTEEN ~

ENTER THE LADIES

For more than four centuries the Lieutenancy of Kent had been a male preserve, but with the retirement of Lord Cornwallis that was about to change. As early as 1953 it had been ruled that there was no legal bar to appointing women as Deputies, or even as Lord-Lieutenants. Nevertheless, for whatever reason, Cornwallis had chosen not to break the men-only stranglehold.

Perhaps not surprisingly it was one of the first acts of the *new* Lord-Lieutenant, Gavin, 2nd Baron Astor of Hever, whose aunt was the first woman to take a seat in Parliament, to appoint Kent's first female Deputy Lieutenants.

Lord Astor, who was 54 when he succeeded Cornwallis, had excellent qualities for the role, with distinguished careers in the army and in business. The eldest son of the first Baron Astor of Hever and grandson of the first Viscount, he was educated at Eton and Oxford and in World War II was commissioned in The Life Guards, serving in the Middle East and Italy where he was taken prisoner.

In 1945 he married Irene, daughter of Field Marshal Haig. They had two sons and three daughters, and lived at Hever Castle, where centuries before Henry VIII had courted Anne Boleyn.

A charming, generous and humorous man, on appointment as Lord-Lieutenant Gavin Astor made a point of explaining that it was not of his seeking nor choosing and his reaction to it was typically self-effacing: 'Naturally,' he said, 'I am thrilled at the honour of succeeding so distinguished and well-loved

Gavin, 2nd Baron Astor of Hever, in his uniform as Lord-Lieutenant of Kent

Sound the timbrel, hoist the pennant,

Gavin's now our Lord-Lieutenant.

Thane of Hever, Deal and Shoreham

He's our Custos Rotulorom.

Anonymous salute to Lord Astor on his appointment as Lord-Lieutenant

a personality as Lord Cornwallis, but somewhat overwhelmed at the prospects.'[1] He was also modest about his family's background, saying:

> I cannot claim to be drawn from one of Kent's oldest families. Two hundred years ago my ancestor was only a penniless German butcher's boy. But he became a very successful American businessman and I am grateful for the push along the road which he gave to the family. So I suppose you might say that I am a representative of the aristocracy of new capitalism rather than that of medieval lineage.[2]

The Astors did indeed have an extraordinary and romantic background. John Jacob Astor was the German butcher's boy who emigrated to America in 1783 and established a highly successful trading business, buying furs from Indian trappers around the Great Lakes and exporting the pelts.

By the end of the century he owned a fleet of a dozen ships delivering the furs to England and China and returning with manufactured goods and tea. He opened up the Pacific North West of America and founded a trapping base at the mouth of the Columbia River named Astoria in recognition of his achievement.

His profits were invested in New York real estate and after his death in 1848 succeeding generations widened the family interests to politics, hotels, newspapers, industry and agriculture. John Jacob's great grandson William Waldorf Astor loved Europe, settled in England, became a naturalised British subject, acquired Hever Castle in 1903 and was raised to the peerage.[3]

His son John Jacob won gold and bronze medals for racquets in the 1908 Olympic Games, fought with The Life Guards during World War I during which he was wounded several times, had his right leg amputated, and was awarded the Legion d'Honneur. He succeeded his father in 1959 and when he left to settle in France in 1962 his eldest son Gavin became the owner of Hever.[4]

Gavin Astor's business interests were closely involved with the press, as Chairman of *The Times* Publishing Company and Co-Chief Proprietor of *The Times* newspaper. He also became a Director of *Reuters* and Chairman and subsequently President of the Commonwealth Press Union. He was also Chairman of the Royal Commonwealth Society.

When appointed, Lord Astor wrote to The Queen personally saying how thrilled he was, adding:

> To my mind Kent is one of the most romantic, historic and vital counties in the whole of the British Isles. It will be a great privilege to become more closely identified with it and I shall always be very conscious of the tremendous honour in being your Majesty's personal representative in the county.[5]

His pride in the county was heartfelt and he wrote:

> Kent has always been in the mainstream of historical, military and spiritual events and from time immemorial the people of Kent have been to the forefront whenever our country or our county have needed them.

He announced his intention of ensuring that the Lieutenancy did not become remote from the county's communities, saying:

> The moment this office becomes impersonal to Kent it will lose a great deal of its point and purpose. In an effort to project the example of The Queen whom he represents the Lord-Lieutenant should endeavour to promote good human relations, a sense of belonging and a spirit of co-operation by the encouragement which he gives to voluntary service and benevolent organisations and by the interest which he takes in the industrial and social life of the county.[6]

Lord Astor was not one to take himself too seriously – as is clear from this Fire Service visit when he tried the headgear for size

Taking over from a man who had been steeped in so many aspects of Kent life for so long was a daunting task, and Lord Astor was under no illusion what a challenge it meant. 'Yet,' said his Vice Lord-Lieutenant, Robin Leigh-Pemberton (who was to succeed him a decade later and elevated to the peerage as Lord Kingsdown):

> …within months he had established himself in the county as a dutiful and impressive public figure and a worthy successor to Lord Cornwallis, *The Spirit of Kent*.[7]

Before long Lord Astor had become president, patron or friend of 45 Kent organisations concerned with many aspects of life in the county. His wife Irene was a great support to him in his Lieutenancy role and in her own right did an immense amount of voluntary work, notably for the Red Cross, the Order of St John, and the Royal British Legion which was founded by her father.

There is no doubt that Cornwallis had been an outstanding Lord-Lieutenant, but there was one area in which he had been backward in coming forward. Although for 20 years there had been no legal bar to women being appointed to Lieutenancies, for whatever reason Lord Cornwallis, great man that he was – yet undeniably of the old school – had not chosen to appoint any.

This gave his successor an opportunity to right a wrong and make his mark at an early stage. It was entirely appropriate that the appointment of Kent's first female Deputy Lieutenants should be made by Lord Astor, whose aunt – Nancy, Viscountess Astor – was the first woman to take a seat in the British Parliament.

The first chink in the armour of male domination of the Lieutenancies had

Irene, Lady Astor, did an immense amount of voluntary work in her own right

The then Patricia Mountbatten during her wartime naval service

appeared in Scotland in 1960 when Jean Roberts became Lieutenant for the County and City of Glasgow, but the breakthrough took longer in the rest of the United Kingdom.

To be fair, this was probably less about male opposition to female emancipation than it was about the availability of candidates who had appropriate military service. As we have seen, it was not until 1966 that the rules on the appointment of DLs were relaxed to allow a proportion of non-military appointees provided they had given significant service to their counties.

Nevertheless, when Lord Astor selected Kent's first two ladies as DLs, neither could be labelled 'token' women. Both were as well qualified as any of their male counterparts. And so history was made on 23 March 1973 when Lord Astor signed commissions appointing Patricia Edwina Victoria Knatchbull, Baroness Brabourne of Newhouse, Mersham, Ashford, and Lieutenant Colonel Angela Vera Cobb, of Birchington.[8]

Both had impeccable credentials including impressive war records and both were appointed entirely on merit. In their different ways they had both given enormous service to county and nation.

Lady Brabourne, as she was styled when appointed as a DL, was a great-great granddaughter of Queen Victoria, daughter of Earl Mountbatten of Burma, first cousin to the Duke of Edinburgh and third cousin to The Queen. She had served in the Women's Royal Naval Service during World War II, was a magistrate and was active in many national and Kent-based charitable and caring bodies and Armed Forces-related organisations.

Angela Cobb, wife of David Cobb, seventh generation chairman of his family brewing company founded in Margate in the 17th century, was, like her husband, a Territorial Army officer. Her wartime career was unusual to say the least. She joined the Auxiliary Territorial Service (ATS) – in which the then Princess Elizabeth also served – at the start of the war as a clerk with an anti-aircraft regiment, became a convoy driver and in 1941 was commissioned as a second subaltern. A keen drummer, she formed the first women's forces band which under her leadership was expanded to become a full military band and dance band. A pipe band was added including recruits from the Dagenham Girl Pipers.

They gave morale-boosting concerts throughout Britain, toured British bases in Egypt, Italy and Palestine, broadcast on the BBC's *Sunday Night Variety Bandbox*, and took part in the victory celebrations and parades in Paris and London.

She was elected as Kent County Councillor for Margate East in 1961, and later when she found she was suffering from cancer she spoke openly about the disease which at that time people spoke of in hushed tones. After major surgery she beat it, and via the Kent media urged others to consult their doctor immediately they got a warning, telling them: 'Cancer can be cured.'

She survived to continue as a Deputy Lieutenant until her death in 2006.[9]

Angela Cobb

In appointing the county's first women DLs Lord Astor was well aware that he was breaking new ground. In his letter inviting the then Lady Brabourne he wrote:

It would give me personally the greatest pleasure to have your moral support, and you are already so well identified with Kent and many worthy causes in the County that I am sure it would be a thoroughly popular appointment.

He added, reassuringly:

I have made some inquiries and am delighted to discover that even without the influence of 'women's lib' there is nothing to prevent ladies becoming DLs.[10]

One of Lord Astor's first duties as Lord-Lieutenant was to escort The Queen at Fort Halstead, Sevenoaks

She is typically down-to-earth when recalling her reaction. 'I was chuffed,' she says. Lady Brabourne succeeded her father becoming Countess Mountbatten of Burma when he was assassinated in 1979.

It is worthy of note that Kent's first two female DLs were appointed two years before discrimination on grounds of gender was made illegal in 1975, when the Equal Pay Act took effect.

One of Lord Astor's first duties as Lord-Lieutenant was to accompany The Queen on her visit to Fort Halstead, Sevenoaks. It was the first of many royal visits over the next decade, always handled with great charm and good humour.

His son Johnnie, 3rd Baron Astor and one of Kent's current DLs, recalls that when presenting a line-up of county personalities to a visiting Royal, on reaching the great Kent and England batsman and captain Colin Cowdrey, the Lord-Lieutenant said: 'And this is Denis Compton' – an equally famous cricketer.

It was simply a slip of the memory and according to the present Lord Astor: 'Colin was a real gentleman and didn't bat an eyelid or try to correct my father.'

In 1974 the Prime Minister's office wrote to the Lord-Lieutenant regarding the effects of local government reorganisation on the county Lieutenancies. Under the new Act the title Lord-Lieutenant was at last given statutory recognition and hyphenated in official documents.

Lord Astor was an insightful and often amusing speaker, using his speeches to stress the importance of community service and the development of creative pursuits and interests. At a youth event he gave wise advice that, although he was speaking three decades ago, is just as relevant today:

Lord Astor encouraged the young to strive to reach their full potential – as these Air Training Corps cadets were clearly doing

To my mind people in Britain today, especially young people, are fortunate to be living and growing up in these exciting times – to have the benefits

Lord Astor amused Prince Philip with the story of the brass cleaning order

Brigadier Maurice Atherton, who later became Vice Lord-Lieutenant, accompanying The Queen Mother at her installation as Lord Warden

and opportunities of modern technological age and to be learning to play their part in shaping the future destiny of our country. The future lies in their hands.[11]

Audiences loved to hear anecdotes about royal visits. At the Diamond Jubilee celebration of the West Kent Federation of Women's Institutes, he amused the ladies with an anecdote about a visit of the Duke of Edinburgh to Chatham Naval Base and Dockyard:

Making an inspection tour in advance of the visit the Admiral noticed that the plaque outside the medical orderly room was tarnished and an instruction was given 'Get the brass cleaned.' But the message that got through to the matron in charge was 'Get the bras cleaned.' The Duke of Edinburgh when told said: 'Good Lord, I didn't realise I'd be expected to make such a close inspection as that!'[12]

His connection with the media through *The Times*, *Reuters* and the Commonwealth Press Union made him well aware of its effectiveness in espousing good causes, and his willingness to co-operate with journalists at local level led him to ensure that lists of royal visits and his other engagements were provided regularly to the Kent media.

On many great occasions he welcomed royalty to the county, including Queen Elizabeth The Queen Mother for her installation as the first lady Lord Warden of the Cinque Ports and Prince Charles for the enthronement of Archbishop Coggan. He regularly performed half a dozen official commitments or more a month ranging from welcoming members of the Royal Family to the County Show to presenting awards, opening new public buildings, planting commemorative trees and taking salutes at military parades. In one month alone, June 1979, he carried out 16 Lieutenancy duties.[13]

In 1974 Lord Astor had been honoured by being appointed to another ancient office – that of Seneschal at Canterbury Cathedral. Seneschal is the Norman equivalent of the English steward and in the Middle Ages every great abbey and priory had one, but the office had been vacant since 1940. It was later held by Lord Astor's successor as Lord-Lieutenant, Lord Kingsdown.

Lord Astor led the 1974 Cathedral appeal that raised some £3 million – around £26 million at 2014 rates.

When Pope John Paul visited Canterbury in May 1982, Lord Astor wrote to Buckingham Palace to say that he had been invited to attend the celebration of faith in the Cathedral and pointed out that 'as no pope has ever before visited this country there can be no guidelines.'

The Queen decided it would be most appropriate for him to attend dressed as Seneschal of Canterbury Cathedral. And so it was. Nevertheless, it was Lord Astor, in his dual role as Lord-Lieutenant *and* Seneschal who received the Prince of Wales who was to attend the service.[23] Welcoming the Pope to Canterbury was one of the last official duties Lord Astor performed and he was acutely conscious of the occasion's significance, referring to it as 'a unique, unprecedented moment in history.' He recalled that one of the Papal Bulls denying Henry VIII permission to divorce Catherine of Aragon and leading to the split with Rome, was still held at the Astors' home at Hever Castle, where the King had courted Anne Boleyn, by whom he had hoped to have a male heir.[14]

By July 1982 Lord Astor had decided that after 10 years as Lord-Lieutenant he wished to hand on the torch, but before retiring he organised a great County Service at Rochester Cathedral followed by tea in the grounds of Rochester Castle. Some 900 attended, including most of his Deputy Lieutenants, Kentish Members of Parliament and civic leaders, church dignitaries, the military, members of the Judiciary and Magistracy, and representatives of many of the bodies of which he was president or patron, notably youth organisations. He met the hefty bill himself.

Of his 60 Deputy Lieutenants at that time, two-thirds had significant military service and a quarter of them were JPs. But many were getting on in years. Before giving up office, Lord Astor wrote to the Association of Lord-Lieutenants giving his views on the retirement age for DLs – favouring 75, as was by then the case for Lord-Lieutenants – to make way for younger appointees. He pointed out:

> With the removal in 1977 of all restrictions on the appointment of civilians as Deputy Lieutenants, the field is now open to a much broader range of candidates for selection. This broadening of experience in itself should help to improve the image, vitality and usefulness of the Lieutenancy, and in my view is a compelling argument for ladies or gentlemen to cease active involvement in the Lieutenancy once they have attained 75, no matter how capable they consider themselves to be at continuing to play a valuable role.

He went on to say that he was moving out of the county – to Scotland – and was retiring as Lord-Lieutenant having completed 10 years in office.

> My predecessor Lord Cornwallis held the office for 27 years, and his predecessor the Marquis [sic] Camden for 38 years. Thus in Kent, with a population of about 1.5 million, there have been virtually only three Lord-Lieutenants this century. It seems to me that this is much too exclusive to be in the best interests of the Lieutenancy, and that others should be given the opportunity and the honour of serving The Queen and the county in this office.[15]

The proposed retirement of Deputy Lieutenants at 75 was adopted, but the

TIMELINE

1973
Kent's first women Deputy Lieutenants are appointed

1977
Queen Elizabeth II's Silver Jubilee; rules for appointing DLs relaxed

1982
Pope John Paul visits Canterbury; Lord Astor retires and is succeeded by Robin Leigh-Pemberton

1983
Robin Leigh-Pemberton is appointed Governor of the Bank of England

1984
Lord Astor dies

1987
Zeebrugge disaster

'An astonishing talent for spreading happiness' – Lord Astor with Princess Margaret at a fund-raising event for Dr Barnado's

fixed 10 years for Lord-Lieutenants was not, and in fact Lord Astor's successor Robert (known as Robin) Leigh-Pemberton, later Lord Kingsdown, of Torry Hill, near Sittingbourne, was to serve for almost 20 years.

Lord Kingsdown recalled how he first became involved with the Lieutenancy:

> I remember Lord Cornwallis saying 'I want to make you DL but they're saying you are not eligible because you didn't have a regular commission.' I said, 'Well, I served in the Army for nearly four years at the end of the war' and he said 'This is what's ridiculous. We want to change this.'[16]

Cornwallis got his way and Robin Leigh-Pemberton was duly appointed as a Deputy Lieutenant in 1970. In starting the future Lord Kingsdown on the ladder Cornwallis was responsible for his devoting the next 32 years of his life to the Lieutenancy Kent – two years as a DL, 10 as Astor's Vice Lord-Lieutenant – and almost 20 years as Lord-Lieutenant.

Sadly, Lord Astor did not have long to enjoy his retirement and died of cancer in 1984, aged only 66. At his memorial service the Right Reverend Dr David Say, the Bishop of Rochester and a close friend, spoke of the universal sadness at the passing of 'so sparkling and stimulating a personality.' He added:

> We all think of Gavin as one of the kindest and most generous men we have ever met. He had an astonishing talent for spreading happiness.[17]

An Old Etonian and Trinity College, Oxford, graduate, the future Lord Kingsdown had won the Sword of Honour at Sandhurst, served with the Grenadier Guards in Palestine, and practised as a barrister before embarking on his business career. In addition to his commercial roles he had also served both as a JP and as Chairman of Kent County Council.

By the time he was invited to become Lord-Lieutenant he had been Chairman of the National Westminster Bank for five years. By any measure he was an extremely busy man and when approached by the Prime Minister's Appointments Secretary about taking on the Lieutenancy he was naturally concerned. He later recalled:

> I was rather doubtful about managing that and the other things I was doing at the same time, but I received an encouraging telephone call from the then Lord Chamberlain, Lord Maclean. He said to me quite cheerfully: 'I wouldn't be too worried about it distracting things too much. I'm Lord Lieutenant of Argyllshire but I hardly ever go there!' And he proved to be right really. I just required some assurance that I wasn't being irresponsible in trying to take on too much. When Lord Maclean said that to me I thought, well it's perfectly clear the Palace approves of me, so I'd better respond. My wife and I have a very deep affection for Kent and I suppose

ABOVE: The then Robin
Leigh-Pemberton
escorting The Queen
and Duke of Edinburgh
during their Medway
Towns visit

all those years on the County Council were an illustration of a readiness to
serve the county. So it really wasn't a difficult decision for me.[18]

Realising that the Lieutenancy is a team effort between the office holder and
their partner, before allowing his name to be put forward he discussed it with
his wife Rose. When he was Chairman of Kent County Council she had taken
over his 'extra' roles such as being chairman of school governors, and she was
already taking on many commitments as wife of the Chairman of NatWest
Bank. The Lieutenancy would make further demands on her, but her reaction
was typically positive. She said: 'I was delighted and thrilled.'

At the time of his appointment he was the first untitled person to represent
the Sovereign in Kent.

When a year later he was invited to become Governor of the Bank of
England he again asked himself 'Can I do both jobs? Then I thought to myself,
well if *she* thinks I can do both I'd better get on and do them – and that was
not The Queen but Mrs Thatcher!'[19]

Having observed Lord Cornwallis and Lord Astor in action, the new Lord-
Lieutenant had a pretty clear idea of what was expected of him in terms of
royal visits. Nevertheless it was with some trepidation that he awaited his first
visit by The Queen who came to open the new courts in Maidstone and spent
the rest of the day in the Medway Towns. He confessed:

'Lord Kingsdown presided over some 200 royal visits to the Kent'

I remember standing there waiting for the royal car to arrive and asking myself what chances had I got of just turning around and running away and escaping, but I knew in my heart of hearts I'd jolly well got to go through with it and once it had started I thoroughly enjoyed it.[20]

It was just as well that he did enjoy it because over the next two decades he was to preside over some 200 royal visits to the county.

When in 1986 Paul Sabin joined KCC as Chief Executive and took on the dual role of Clerk to the Lieutenancy he inherited a situation where there was little involvement with the Lord-Lieutenant.

I was not happy that this aspect of my responsibilities should be at such a distance and set about involving myself more in supporting the Lord-Lieutenant. Robin received virtually all his administrative support from Gill Herriot, his personal assistant at the Bank of England. She was very efficient and we developed an arrangement where the support post became two-headed to support both the Lord-Lieutenant and the County Council Chairman, and Gill took up the post at County Hall.[21]

Lord Kingsdown invited Countess Mountbatten to be his Vice Lord-Lieutenant.

I felt very honoured that she accepted the office, as it were subordinate to me, because I felt that she could very well have been Lord-Lieutenant herself. She was extremely good and there were other Deputy Lieutenants who were as well equipped in conducting a royal visit largely on account of military experience. Brigadier Maurice Atherton was a very obvious example of that and he took over from her as Vice Lord-Lieutenant when she had to retire at 75.[22]

When invited to become Vice Lord-Lieutenant, Countess Mountbatten was concerned that it might involve subsequent 'promotion' – a step she did not wish to take because of her extensive voluntary charity commitments. Reassured on that point she readily agreed and, because of Lord Kingsdown's absences overseas or on urgent business as Chairman of NatWest and then Governor of the Bank of England, was frequently called upon to stand in for him, often being on hand to greet members of the Royal Family, including her cousin, The Queen herself.

Following Countess Mountbatten as Vice Lord-Lieutenant, Brigadier Maurice Atherton, a former High Sheriff, had unrivalled relevant experience, having commanded the locally-based brigade, a role that had carried with it the appointment of Deputy Constable of Dover Castle and residence of Constable's Tower, which has been described as the British Army's finest married quarter. He had been Deputy Constable when The Queen Mother was installed as Lord Warden of the Cinque Ports and Constable of Dover Castle in 1979 and was well used to the big occasion.

The biggest royal – and international – event during Lord Kingsdown's term was the opening of the Channel Tunnel in 1994 when The Queen arrived from France in her car via Le Shuttle with President Mitterand, and was driven onto the platform at Folkestone where the Lord-Lieutenant received them for the second of the two Anglo-French official opening ceremonies. He remembered:

> The Queen had kindly made me a Knight of the Garter just before that and it was the first time that I wore my star and ribbon. President Mitterand tapped me on the ribbon and said: 'Felicitations mon enfant, felicitations.'[23]

Lord Kingsdown escorting The Queen at the opening of the Channel Tunnel

He recalled that the great opening worked reasonably well, although it was impossible to tell the Frenchmen what to do. 'They just walked about as they wanted, especially Mitterand's security men who were very intrusive.' Lady Kingsdown remembers:

> The military band did not start playing the National Anthem immediately as it was supposed to do and the Duke of Edinburgh said, in a typical Duke of Edinburgh way: 'How does the bandmaster hope to see that they've arrived – he's got his back to us!' So he sent Robin down to get them going.[24]

The Lord-Lieutenant suffered a trouser malfunction during a visit by The Princess of Wales to her namesake regiment

Lord Kingsdown did as he was told and the band struck up. During one high-profile royal visit Lord Kingsdown experienced an embarrassing dress malfunction. He was in uniform accompanying Princess Diana on a visit to her regiment – The Princess of Wales's Royal Regiment – at Canterbury's Howe Barracks when disaster struck. He recalled later:

> I drove with her in my car onto the square where the parade was all formed up and as we got out I heard a dreadful rending noise and I realised that my trousers had split in an extremely vital place. I marched along holding myself together as best I could and took my place beside the Princess on the dais and next to a very charming lady who was the wife of the Colonel of the Regiment. I said 'You must excuse me if I sit like this. It's not that I've got bandy legs but my trousers have split in a very vital place.' She said: 'I haven't been a soldier's wife for 40 years not to be prepared for this sort of thing – I've got a needle and thread in my bag.' And I had an awful vision of what might happen to me with her needle and thread if she got to work there and then – quite apart from the embarrassment of the operation being observed – so I said 'That's most kind but I think I shall be alright' and I was because as soon as the parade was over there was an

The Lord-Lieutenant accompanies Princess Anne at a Save the Children Fund event at Leeds Castle

informal stand-up lunch and a police car took me home. Fortunately I had another pair of uniform trousers to change into and when I got back to the barracks people were milling about and I got close to the Princess where I was supposed to be to make sure all was well and she said 'Oh, I'm glad to see you're back. I hear you've had a slight disaster' and I said 'I had hoped you hadn't noticed!' [25]

Lady Kingsdown remembers the occasion well:

There was a cricket match on our ground that day and I was busy up in the room where we have the lunches and heard a police car coming. I thought 'Good gracious me whatever's going on?' I heard Robin's voice and as I wasn't expecting him back until about 4 o'clock, I rushed out and said 'Goodness what are you doing at home – has there been a disaster?' and he said 'Yes – it's my trousers!' [26]

Lord Kingsdown's training in the Brigade of Guards meant that he never let the occasional mishap to faze him and treated every situation with great aplomb. Paul Sabin remembers a blistering hot day at the County Show with county dignitaries perspiring in 'full fig' at the lunch attended by a member of the Royal Family. As Clerk to the Lieutenancy he took the initiative and approached the Lord-Lieutenant at the top table to suggest that gentlemen might be allowed to take their jackets off.

After a while this was granted and Robin signalled this by taking off his own jacket to reveal a pair of bright red braces worn over a transparent shirt! [27]

On another warm official occasion the Roman Catholic Bishop of Southwark was sitting near the Lord-Lieutenant when gentlemen were invited to remove their jackets if they wished. Lord Kingsdown remembered:

The Bishop didn't take anything off at all and I said to him 'Oh dear, can't you make yourself more comfortable?' and he said: 'I knew it was going to be very hot so I haven't got anything on underneath!' [28]

Juggling the roles of Governor of the Bank of England and Lord-Lieutenant occasionally caused time clashes. Lord Kingsdown explained:

I used to go into the bank in the morning and do a certain amount of work, come down to Kent and do a public duty and then go back to the bank, change into ordinary clothes and see people and do whatever I had to do in the evening. One day I got back to the bank late and didn't have time to change, so I received the governor of some bank in Africa who was on a courtesy visit in my Lieutenancy uniform. When the interview was over this man was heard to remark 'I never knew the Governor of the Bank of England was a General!' No doubt he came from a country where they were *all* generals![29]

On one occasion Lady Kingsdown found herself standing in for The Queen, who had been due to visit a battalion of the Royal Green Jackets, then based in Dover. There was going to be a formal parade, lunch and a visit to watch training. But on the morning of the visit Buckingham Palace telephoned to say that The Queen was ill, and requested Lord Kingsdown to stand in for her.

> So I took the salute on the parade and Rose sat in The Queen's chair at lunch. It was an illustration of how The Queen fulfils her duties, because although she couldn't come that day she came down within a very short time for a quite informal visit when they were doing street fighting training. The Green Jackets were given strict instructions to carry on as if The Queen wasn't there, and the Guardsmen playing terrorists were supposed to slouch round the streets. But it was beyond any Guardsman's abilities *not* to spring to attention as The Queen appeared, even when he was supposed to be acting as a terrorist. I think The Queen was more interested in this training than a formal parade because it gave a very good impression of what life on the streets of Belfast must have been like then.[30]

Her Majesty was wearing a hat which made it difficult to wear ear defenders when the soldiers were firing, but she solved the problem by putting them on upside down.

The morale boost arising from a royal visit to any community is wonderful to observe, and Lord Kingsdown soon became aware that a visit from the Lord-Lieutenant can also have an uplifting effect, especially if The Queen's representative is in uniform, and that thanking people for community work encourages them to carry on volunteering. Lady Kingsdown observed this at first hand over a period of almost 20 years:

> The encouragement people get from those sorts of visits is huge. People really like it, and people loved it when the Lord-Lieutenant attended in uniform.[31]

Lord Kingsdown also saw the impartiality of the appointment, and what Prince Charles has called the power to convene, as of great importance. A quiet word from the Lord-Lieutenant, with no political or personal axe to grind, could often ease a contentious situation or bring opposing factions together.

> You have to be careful to make sure that you are seen to be totally impartial.

TIMELINE

1991
Opening of the QEII Dartford Bridge

1993
Robin Leigh-Pemberton is created Baron Kingsdown

1994
Opening of the Channel Tunnel

1998
Lord Kingsdown is appointed Chairman of the Association of Lord-Lieutenants

2002
Lord Kingsdown retires; Allan Willett is appointed Lord-Lieutenant

Lady Kingsdown – exactly the sort of person a Lord-Lieutenant looks for to take on important voluntary roles in the county

I once got a rap from the *Kent Messenger* for being seen to be against the creation of a Medway independent council. At the time I didn't answer it in the paper but my argument would have been that the move affected the integrity and severed an important part of the geographic county of which I was The Queen's representative. Others might argue that it was a political issue and I should not have spoken against it.[32]

In taking the stance he did, Lord Kingsdown was echoing the warnings voiced more than two decades earlier by Lord Cornwallis, who had spoken out against the 'sprawling octopus' of London swallowing parts of historic Kent, and trailing those of his own successor Allan Willett, who likened the proximity of ever-growing London to sharing a bed with an elephant.

None of the three was making a party political point, but merely speaking up for the integrity of the historic county which, as its first citizen, they saw as their duty. Miles Jebb, author of the official national history of the Lieutenancies, saw extensive changes to local government as the 'principal challenge to function of the County Lieutenancies during the second half of the 20th Century,' and the threat of regionalism as 'a constant erosion of county identity.'[33]

Lady Kingsdown not only gave great support to her husband in his Lieutenancy role but also became involved with a great many causes in her own right. She was President of the Red Cross for 12 years and at the same time was president of St John Nursing Cadets in Sittingbourne.

With a foot in both camps, she ended up chairing the joint committee that St John and the Red Cross have with the Women's Royal Voluntary Service and the military, which proved its worth providing support for Service personnel and their families during the First Gulf War. Her OBE was for her work as President of the Red Cross at the time of the Zeebrugge disaster when the organisation played a huge role, setting up a support post in Dover where all the relatives gathered.

Typically not expecting any recognition, when a letter arrived from the Prime Minister's office about her OBE she put the unopened envelope with her husband's post on a table in the hall and went out.

When I got back I said 'You haven't opened your letter from the PM's office and he said no it's for you.' Because it came from the PM's office I thought it must be for Robin![34]

A first rate administrator, Lady Kingsdown had devoted herself to voluntary work long before her husband became Lord-Lieutenant. She began working for the Mental Health Foundation and the Children's Society, which she chaired in Kent for many years, when she was in her 30s.

Through the Mental Health Foundation I got involved with a marvellous place in Staplehurst called Growing Concerns, an agricultural charity which takes mentally handicapped people and teaches them horticulture. They had a stall in the voluntary tent at the County Show and I was walking with a Lady in Waiting during a royal visit when out rushed a chap called Stephen and flung his arms round me and said 'Oh 'allo, I hope you're coming to see my cactus!' So of course we went to see his cactus.[35]

Lady Kingsdown is herself exactly the sort of person a Lord-Lieutenant looks for to take on important voluntary roles in the county. Her husband said:

> We all know what sort of people are needed but there are not so many to be found. You've got to have common sense, impartiality, a sense of drive and purpose, and be the type of person who does these jobs for the sake of it and not their own position.[36]

As chairman of the Advisory Committee on the Magistracy – and effectively the county's chief magistrate – Lord Kingsdown was involved in overseeing the recruitment of suitable people as JPs, acting as what he saw as a sieve or check on those recommended for appointment by the district magistrates' committees. He had served as a JP himself from 1961-75, so well knew the qualities required.

Among his most treasured moments during his Lieutenancy was when he took the salute at the Royal Military Academy, Sandhurst, when Territorial Army officers were passing out.

> I remember standing on the steps I had marched up years before to receive the Sword of Honour. That, and the band playing the regimental march for you personally is about as good as anything really.[37]

Maintaining the Lieutenancy's connections with the military, Lord Kingsdown was Honorary Colonel of various Territorial units including the Sharpshooters Yeomanry Squadron, as well as being President of the then Territorial Auxiliary & Volunteer Reserve Association for the South East.

His Yeomanry role provoked an amusing comment from a visitor. Lord Kingsdown remembered:

> We had a meeting of the foxhounds here at Torry Hill once, the same time that the Yeomanry squadron came down for a week-end's training. They were all out in the field with their armoured cars when the foxhounds went by and the lady riding beside me said 'Good gracious Mr Leigh-Pemberton, I never knew you had an army as well!'[38]

Greatly respected by his peers, Lord Kingsdown was appointed Chairman of

Lord Kingsdown escorting The Queen during her visit to the Royal Temple Yacht Club at Ramsgate

Lord Kingsdown presenting meritorious service awards to members of the Territorial Army and Cadets. On the right is Colonel Peter Bishop, the then Army Cadet Force Commandant who was later appointed a Deputy Lieutenant

RIGHT: Lord and Lady Kingsdown were each presented with Spirit of Kent Awards by former Vice Lord-Lieutenant Countess Mountbatten of Burma, for their conspicuous service to Kent and its people. The award was initiated by his successor as Lord-Lieutenant, Allan Willett, left, whose wife Anne is pictured, right

The Association of Lord-Lieutenants from 1998-2001. Lord and Lady Kingsdown's long record of conspicuous service to the county and its people was later acknowledged by the presentation of individual Spirit of Kent Awards to each of them – the first 'double' since its inception.

Lord Kingsdown's all but 20 happy years as The Queen's representative were nearing their end as the new Millennium dawned. It was an era of rapid and far-reaching change and the Monarchy itself was modernising and becoming more accessible to the people.

The successor chosen to take the Lieutenancy of Kent forward in the new age was about as different from the long line of predecessors as it is possible to be. He did not come from the aristocracy or landed gentry, but was a self-made business entrepreneur who had made a fortune in the packaging and coding industry – Allan Willett.

Sadly, Lord Kingsdown died in November 2013. Among the many tributes paid to his long record of conspicuous service to Kent was that of the current Lord-Lieutenant, Lord De L'Isle: 'As Lord-Lieutenant he presided over some 200 Royal visits to the county and, ably supported by his wife Rose, was at Her Majesty's side on great occasions such as the opening of the QEII Bridge and the Channel Tunnel, but still happily gave his time to attend more homely community events such as the opening of a new village hall. Whatever the occasion, his friendly manner and good-humoured style endeared him to everyone involved. All members of the Lieutenancy, past and present, join me in paying tribute to a great son of Kent who will be greatly missed.'

~ SIXTEEN ~

'THE VERY MODEL OF A MODERN LORD-LIEUTENANT'

ew Lord-Lieutenants are appointed by the Sovereign on the recommendation of the Prime Minister of the day, and as Lord Kingsdown's retirement drew near a senior civil servant was sent to take soundings in Kent regarding possible successors.

Allan Willett, businessman and founding – and then still serving – Chairman of the South East England Development Agency (SEEDA) was among the influential county personalities whose views were canvassed.

Ever progressive, he suggested the next appointee should be female, and ideally from the west of the county to ring the changes after almost 20 years of an East Kent-based Lord-Lieutenant. It was therefore to his considerable astonishment that he was then asked if he was willing for his *own* name to go forward to succeed Lord Kingsdown.

He was not from the landed gentry or aristocracy, but a self-made man from a modest farming background; his home was at Chilham rather than in West

Allan Willett's Coat of Arms

Kent, and he was clearly not a lady. The powers-that-be had totally ignored his recommendation but listened instead to the many who believed that *he* would be just the man to take the Lieutenancy forward in the new Millennium.

Born in India of tea planter parents from Kent, he returned with them when he was two and was brought up on Thanet farms during World War II. His father was an incredibly unlucky farmer – accidentally bombed out of one farm by a damaged American aircraft returning to nearby Manston, and flooded out of the second during the disastrous 1953 East Coast floods.

His parents returned to planting – this time in Kenya – and young Allan, who had played schoolboy rugby for Kent, was left, aged 17, to sell the flood-hit farm and make his own way in the world. After National Service, during which he was commissioned in The Buffs (Royal East Kent Regiment) and served with the King's African Rifles fighting the Mau Mau in Kenya, he first worked as a salesman in Canada, moved into the packaging industry and ended up creating his own company on the proverbial shoestring.

It developed the world's first micro processor-controlled labelling machine and the first inkjet printer for cartons. His entrepreneurial flair enabled him to evolve the company into Willett International Limited which became one of the largest electronic coding and information labelling players in the world. It had operating subsidiaries in 30 countries, twice won The Queen's Award for export, and for his achievements Allan Willett was made a Companion of the Order of St Michael and St George (CMG) in 1997.

In the public sector, before founding SEEDA, the lead organisation at regional level promoting wealth creation, re-generation and social inclusion in the nine South-East counties, he was Chairman of the East Kent Initiative which became the East Kent Forum – and was on the board of Locate in Kent, the inward investment organisation, and an Ambassador for Kent.

Later, *Kent Life* Editor Sarah Sturt was to write of him:

> There was something special in his make-up – an entrepreneurial spirit, a creative and decisive mind, flint-like determination and courage born perhaps of his wartime childhood and Army experiences. The fact that he has talented artists and Waterloo victor [the Duke of] Wellington in his family tree is significant. And it is appropriate that the motto on his coat of arms is: Be brave for there is much to dare.[1]

Thrilled though he was to be asked to become Lord-Lieutenant of the county he loved, he vowed only to take on the role if given the mandate to modernise the ancient office, which had become largely ceremonial, in line with the evolution of the Monarchy itself. Both Number 10 and Buckingham Palace made it clear to him that this was *exactly* what they wanted him to do. He recalls:

> This was the crucial point because I definitely would not have taken it on

under any other circumstances. Being asked to modernise the role caught my imagination and appealed to me.

Having consulted his wife Anne, who was amenable, he accepted and was duly appointed in January 2002 by Letters Patent under the Great Seal of the Realm 'to be Lord-Lieutenant of and in the County of Kent.' It was the birth of a new era for the ancient office.

This was Golden Jubilee Year, and the new Lord-Lieutenant was soon to experience at first-hand the great depth of affection in which The Queen is held among the people of Kent.

> As I travelled with David Phillips, the then Chief Constable, into Canterbury for Her Majesty's visit on Maundy Thursday, he said: 'Allan, watch people's faces – everybody's smiling when they see her.' How true. What pleasure all her hard work that year and since has given us and millions of people around the globe.[2]

Allan Willett's appointment heralded the birth of a new era for the Lieutenancy

It was the first of 95 visits to the county by members of the Royal Family during the nine years of his Lieutenancy, and he was quick to appreciate how valuable they were in lifting morale – and bringing the spotlight to bear on the good work being done in Kent's communities.

Following his appointment as The Queen's representative he consulted widely and put his business brain to work on shaping the future of the Lieutenancy. He recalls:

> As what some might call a hard-headed businessman, my gut feeling was that if this ancient office were to survive and flourish in the 21st Century it must be relevant and add value to people's lives, especially the young. Kent was facing massive forces of change. The new high speed railway, then only a twinkle in people's eyes, was going to transform East Kent into commuter country. And the great mass of London was no longer going to be a barrier that had effectively made Kent an island. That was all going to change, with train journey times slashed – both to London and to other areas of Britain, Paris and Brussels – opening up our previously isolated county. Added to this, was that London, the only true world city, could only expand, eastwards, north and south of the Thames presenting us with both opportunities and dangers.

> I saw that these changes gave this Lieutenancy the opportunity to play an increasing and significant role in keeping alive the unique spirit of Kent. As a totally independent pan-County team we could create cohesion, celebrate Kent's identity, represent its soul – and add value to its mosaic of communities.[3]

He saw, too, that if a modernised Lieutenancy were to be effective some of the initiatives he wanted to introduce would have to be funded, and this could not be by public money. Early on, following the successful sale of Willett International, he decided to set up a charitable body known as the Allan Willett Foundation, primarily aimed at 'the advancement of charitable purposes for the general benefit of persons living, working and studying in the County of Kent.' It was also to support some projects further afield, such as medical research of benefit to the population as a whole.

Launching it he said: 'I have great affection for Kent. I've been fortunate in business and I want this money to be used for the benefit of the county.'

Later, as the then Chairman of the Canterbury Cathedral Trust Fund, he was to launch the campaign to conserve and develop the spiritual home of English-speaking Christianity, and since then his own Foundation has gifted more than £2 million to this cause which is so close to his heart. Rochester Cathedral has also benefitted from Willett Foundation grants, as have important projects leading the artistic renaissance in the South East: Canterbury's New Marlowe Theatre and the Turner Contemporary gallery at Margate.

Annual donations are also made to the Battle of Britain Memorial Trust to help finance the attendance of surviving Battle of Britain aircrew – The Few – or their widows at the annual Memorial Day; to the Army Benevolent Fund, the soldiers' charity; and to the Order of St John. The Royal Engineers' Museum has been supported, as has Kent Air Ambulance with a sizeable donation. Territorial Army and Cadet units have also received grants aimed at increasing their efficiency. In all, the Foundation has given some £4 million to Kent causes and to funding Lieutenancy initiatives.

Determined to carry the modernisation of the Lieutenancy through, he formed a team with Lord De L'Isle as his Vice Lord-Lieutenant and with decorated former Army Air Corps helicopter pilot Brigadier David Ralls as Chief of Staff. David Ralls brought military-style planning to the role as well as an in-depth knowledge of Kent's local authorities gained while chief executive of a district council. The then Kent Messenger Group Chairman Edwin Boorman became media adviser and the extensive specialist experience of other DLs was drawn upon as necessary.

Standard operating procedures and a central tasking system and database were set up by the Chief of Staff and ensured timely and efficient handling of all Lieutenancy activity.

One of the new Lord-Lieutenant's first moves was to find words to describe what the modernised Lieutenancy was about and after much thought and consultation he came up with:

The aims of the Lieutenancy of Kent are to provide a focus for county identity, unity and pride, give a sense of stability, recognise achievements, success and excellence, and promote service to others. Our aspiration is to

TIMELINE

2002
Allan Willett becomes Lord-Lieutenant; The Queen's Golden Jubilee

2003
Lord-Lieutenant launches Support the Armed Forces campaign; DL badge of office created

2005
Year of Victories – VE and VJ Day 60th anniversaries and Trafalgar bi-centenary; First Civic Service celebrating community volunteers

2006
Creation of Spirit of Kent Award

celebrate Kent, its unique history and culture, serve its communities – and contribute positively to its future.

It is a mantra that has stuck and is unlikely to be bettered. Initially the word championing had been considered instead of 'celebrating' – this because some Kent newspaper headlines had referred to Allan Willett as 'The Champion of Kent'. But this was felt by some to sound rather aggressive, suggesting that the Lieutenancy was now shaping up to take on all-comers, which was clearly never the intention. The new Lord-Lieutenant was absolutely clear from the start that straying into politics and controversy was *not* on his agenda for the office.

Until those both inside and outside the Lieutenancy came to understand this and what modernisation would entail, there was some fluttering in the dovecotes and muttering in the turrets:

> I had inherited some 60 Deputy Lieutenants from across the county and I needed to get them behind the modernisation. Some were suspicious of change, no doubt wondering 'Who's this upstart businessman coming in and changing everything?' But soon they realised that we were in step with Her Majesty, shaping the Lieutenancy in the same way that The Queen wanted to shape the Monarchy. Soon that early opposition was replaced with widespread understanding and support.[4]

From the outset Allan Willett saw lack of public knowledge about the office as a major problem:

> I believed we could only modernise effectively if the people of Kent were aware of the Lieutenancy and what it was trying to achieve, so we needed to raise the profile. Many people had no idea what the Lieutenancy was, what it did, or how it was changing in order to better serve the Monarchy and Kent's communities. It was crucial to get our message across.[5]

So his team created an attractive new website, produced a flyer explaining what the Lieutenancy was about and put the message across in every speech and at every public appearance. A presentation team was formed to give talks on the Lieutenancy to varied audiences on request. Unusually for a Lord-Lieutenant he actively sought media coverage, the most important being a series of articles under his by-line in Kent Messenger Group newspapers, explaining what he was going to do and how he was going to do it. Looking back on them, they showed that the new Lord-Lieutenant not only talked the talk but walked the walk. What he said would happen *did* happen. But, he acknowledged, 'This is a marathon, not a sprint.'

Crucially, he understood that what the Lieutenancy could achieve as a whole

Raising the Lieutenancy's profile

The Deputy Lieutenants' badge of office – another first for Kent

was more important than what the Lord-Lieutenant could do alone. Therefore the appointment of new Deputy Lieutenants was a key factor. Traditionally DL appointments had become a county's way of honouring and recognising a person's achievements without expecting them to do very much. But to Allan Willett such appointments were not simply an honour. He saw them as an opportunity to select talented people prepared to play an *active* part in the life of Kent, and would not appoint anyone unwilling or unable to sign up for that.

He saw that this county-wide network of influential men and women who had made their mark in everything from commerce to the church and from medicine to the military, collectively provided an unrivalled bank of specialist and local knowledge fitting them for their role as 'the eyes and ears of the Lord-Lieutenant' and for serving the community.

From performing a handful of duties Kent's DLs were between them now expected to take on 500 or more commitments a year. But at first those carrying them out in plain clothes were unrecognised, prompting queries from others present such as 'Who's that chap (or lady) in a suit?'

So, in the interests of raising the Lieutenancy's profile and making his DLs easily recognisable Allan Willett decided to introduce a unique badge of office to be worn when attending official events throughout the county – especially important at gatherings including members of the civic 'chain gangs'. Not least, the wearing of badges of office was a visible demonstration of the Lieutenancy's interest and support.

A team including Mrs Anne Willett considered the idea and the commission to design and produce the badge was given to the highly-respected Kent jewellers and silversmiths T & B Cousins & Sons Ltd., of Sun Street, Canterbury.

The result was a diamond-shaped pendant carrying the county's rearing horse emblem above the motto: *Invicta*. In hallmarked Sterling silver gilded overall, it could be worn pinned in place or on a ribbon around the neck and was appropriate for both male and female Deputy Lieutenants. The cost was underwritten personally by the Lord-Lieutenant, although DLs had the opportunity to purchase a personal engraved insignia as a family heirloom if they wished.

The badge was well received everywhere, at least one royal visitor commenting on it positively, and although it went against the wishes of some of the 'old guard' of Lord-Lieutenants nationally it soon became the envy of DLs in neighbouring counties. But it was not until a decade later that a national badge of office was introduced.

Another of the new Lord-Lieutenant's initiatives was his series of visits to Kent County Council, Medway Council and all Kent's District and Borough Councils. These visits enabled him to brief them on where he intended to take the Lieutenancy and find out how he and his Deputies could co-operate with the elected representatives to help serve their communities. He was made welcome and the positive relationships built up were to pay off in many ways.

First among the special roles he asked selected DLs to take on was to act

Anne Willett 'totally dedicated to Kent'

as links to local authorities. This cemented the bond he had formed. Others were tasked to be the main links with the rural economy, the Armed Forces, the Magistracy, the emergency services, faith communities, youth, education, sport, and so on. He himself took on numerous extra responsibilities, as president or patron of a score of Kent organisations and voluntary bodies from the Men of Kent and Kentish Men to the Royal British Legion.

Initiating the now-annual Civic Service and thanking all those who do so much for the good of Kent and its communities was one of Allan Willett's inspired initiatives. The event rotates between Canterbury and Rochester Cathedrals and All Saints', Maidstone, and is attended by mayors, chairmen, representatives of their charities, council leaders, chief executives, and representatives from all town and parish councils throughout Kent. Also attending are representatives of the Armed Forces, Cadet and other youth movements, members of the Magistracy, the emergency services, the education and business worlds – and of course Deputy Lieutenants from all parts of the county. At the first, at Canterbury Cathedral in 2005, the Lord-Lieutenant told them:

> As I look around this iconic building, I am struck by the thought that, regardless of religion or political beliefs, the distinguished congregation gathered in the Nave today shares two things in common: dedication to your communities, and a belief in Kent and its future.[6]

A charismatic speaker, he addressed them in what some afterwards referred to as 'almost Churchillian terms' of their shared pride in the unique history of their county. He inspired confidence in its future, and thanked them with great sincerity for their sterling work for its people.

A number of those present said afterwards that they had previously given little thought to the impact or value of their work for the county, but, having been thanked personally in this inspiring manner by The Queen's representative, now felt moved to re-dedicate themselves to serving the community. The tone was set for his Lieutenancy.

The Civic Service had proved to be a great success, now repeated every year for new generations of civic leaders and community workers, and is funded by the Allan Willett Foundation as part of the legacy he created for Kent.

Throughout the years of his Lieutenancy he spoke many times to many audiences in venues ranging from cathedrals to village halls with great conviction and passion about his beloved Kent, its unique past and his hopes for its future. He would tell them:

> Let us never forget that Kent was the most powerful of the Anglo-Saxon kingdoms, founded in the 5th Century, with its influence spreading far beyond its present boundaries; the first to be converted to Christianity; the Guardian of England seeing off would-be invaders down the centuries;

TIMELINE

2007
First Celebration of Youth Achievement

2008
TA100

2010
Cadet 150; 70th anniversaries of Dunkirk and Battle of Britain

2011
Allan Willett retires; Philip Sidney, 2nd Viscount De L'Isle succeeds him

2012
Queen's Diamond Jubilee; London Olympics

RIGHT: Honouring the
Forces of the Crown with
the enthusiastic support
of Maidstone children

the most progressive, receiving, developing and passing on new agricultural
and industrial ideas and processes; and still, today, the Garden of England.

Small wonder that he never failed to send listeners away with a new-found
pride in the county and vowing to continue to do their bit for it.

From the start he introduced annual Lieutenancy meetings at which his
Deputies looked back at the impact of the previous year's activities and were
briefed on the theme and programme for the year ahead.

At the outbreak of the wars in Iraq and Afghanistan both Allan and Anne
Willett took a lead in encouraging greater public support for our Armed
Forces and their families – as they put it: 'left behind here in our care.' The
Lord-Lieutenant explained:

> We used that wording about the families left here in our care over and over
> again because it was just right and it struck a chord with people. We made
> it clear that such support is not about politics, nor whether people were for
> or against the military action. It is about fellow-feeling for those sons and
> daughters of Kent and all those based in our county who risk their lives.
> They all deserve our support and our heartfelt thanks.[7]

His DLs, a number of whom had significant military service themselves, supported the campaign enthusiastically, but he realised he also needed to get the
county's elected representatives on side.

> After my visits to the councils in which I'd explained to them what my
> Lieutenancy was about and what I was trying to achieve – the next thing
> they knew was that I was knocking on their doors again, saying 'You said
> you'd cooperate with the Lieutenancy, well, here's your chance!'[8]

LEFT: Together General
Dannatt and the
Lord-Lieutenant stood
in the rain and got
soaking wet honouring
the troops, Cadets and
veterans on parade

He told them he wanted them to sign up in full council to declarations of support for the Armed Forces, to organise welcome home parades and parties and other supportive events for the troops and their families, and that he wanted to be invited. The reaction was extraordinary and totally unprecedented. Across all party lines, every council from Kent County Council and Medway unitary down to every single District and Borough, there was not a single objection. They supported him 100 per cent.

Those were words. Now came actions. The new-style Lieutenancy took the lead in organising major parades commemorating important anniversaries from the 2005 Year of Victories to TA100 and Cadet150, and the Lord-Lieutenant issued his own Poppy Appeal Challenge to Kent's Cadet movements. Allan and Anne Willett went to wish Godspeed to various units including the Territorial Army Medical Squadron based at Ditton, which was mobilised almost in its entirety to serve on humanitarian duty in Iraq. They demonstrated their heartfelt support for the soldiers, the families, and especially their children. The presence of The Queen's representative was a great morale-booster.

True to its pledge, the County Council began a series of welcome home receptions for returning troops. The Lord-Lieutenant was at the first and told those who had been mobilised how proud the people of Kent were of them and the invaluable contribution they had made. He especially thanked the loved ones of those who had been deployed:

> We understand how coping alone while a loved one is in a combat zone is a struggle, and assure you that your personal sacrifice is recognised and appreciated. As The Queen's representative it is my privilege to thank you.

The reaction of the 'next of kin' made it clear that his words on behalf of The Queen meant a great deal to them. There were welcome home parades,

Army Cadets were highly amused to see their Lord-Lieutenant charging round on a quad bike

Sea Cadets demonstrating their first aid skills at the Trafalgar 200 event

Honouring The Few – with the Air Training Corps

freedom parades with the troops marching through Kentish towns, drums beating, bands playing, colours flying and bayonets fixed – and finally the Chief of the General Staff, General Sir Richard (now Lord) Dannatt, came down to attend the Lieutenancy's TA100 parade in Canterbury.

He was an extremely busy man, much in demand everywhere, but of all the United Kingdom, Kent was one of the few such visits he chose to make because the Frontline County had taken a lead and was doing exactly what he had been encouraging people to do nationally in demonstrating greater support for the Armed Forces. Together he and the Lord-Lieutenant stood in the rain and got soaking wet honouring the troops, Cadets and veterans.

Another great military occasion, also in Canterbury, was when the locally-based Highlanders were given the Freedom of the City. By then Allan Willett was Honorary Colonel of the 3rd Battalion, The Princess of Wales's Royal Regiment, also based there, and he told The Highlanders he was immensely proud that members of his TA Battalion had served side by side with the Argylls on hazardous operations in Afghanistan. He recalled later:

When I said: '*Our* Highlanders and *our* Men of Kent and Kentish Men – now truly brothers in arms' the effect was extraordinary and some of the Regiment's senior officers around the saluting dais were visibly moved. I was a little emotional myself![9]

Some months later the local 2 (South East) Brigade Commander, Brigadier Iain James, told guests at a Beat Retreat:

The level of public awareness of the Armed Forces is the highest we have seen for some decades, and I take this opportunity to publicly thank the Lord-Lieutenant for the very courageous and very public leadership he has shown in Kent in bringing this to the fore.[10]

His Lieutenancy also gave strong support to the Cadet Forces. Deputy Lieutenant and former TA battalion commander Richard Dixon was the hard-working link to the Cadets and fought their corner with great enthusiasm. He remembers Allan Willett's visit to Kent Army Cadet Force at annual camp where the young Cadets were highly amused to see their Lord-Lieutenant charging round on a quad bike.

In Trafalgar Bicentenary Year the Lieutenancy held a great Sea Cadet Garden Party at the Historic Dockyard, Chatham, and hundreds of Cadets came from units based all over the county to demonstrate their skills – and have fun. During the evening tattoo the skies opened but the Cadets carried on with their displays despite the rain. Allan Willett recalls:

Someone rushed up with a large umbrella for me but I waved him away. If

the Cadets were going to get soaked so was I. Just as well because someone in the seats behind me remarked loudly: 'We don't need umbrellas – we're British!'[11]

The Lord-Lieutenant was a regular attender at Battle of Britain commemoration events at the National Memorial at Capel-le-Ferne above the famous White Cliffs of Dover where he stood shoulder-to-shoulder – come rain or shine – with survivors of The Few and also met the new generation of smart young Air Training Corps Cadets.

Celebrating youth achievement was a major plank of the modernised Lieutenancy's action plan and, with DL Godfrey Linnett co-ordinating, resulted in highly successful events at the County Showground at Detling involving scores of organisations and showcasing all the positive work being done by and with young people county-wide.

Allan and Anne Willett also initiated and hosted annual receptions for incoming civic heads at their 15th Century hall house at Chilham, forming a bond between the Lieutenancy and those who would be leading their communities in the coming year.

The Willett home became the venue for dozens of other hospitality events, from the launch of a youth initiative to a lunch honouring war heroes – including Battle of Britain pilot Wing Commander Bob Foster DFC and Iraq War Victoria Cross winner Lance Corporal Johnson Beharry.

In order to make his Deputies more knowledgeable about what was going on around the county Allan Willett introduced annual awareness days involving visits *en masse* to locations ranging from the Thames Gateway to Medway, Thanet and Shepway regeneration projects, and from go-ahead Hadlow College to Kent Army Cadet Force's state-of-the-art new training centre.

ABOVE: Clockwise from main picture: Allan and Anne Willett celebrating youth achievement at the County Showground; As President of St John Kent and a Knight of Justice in the Order, Allan Willett met Badgers who had great fun demonstrating their first aid skills on him; Supporting the Armed Forces with Johnson Beharry VC

RIGHT: Allan and Anne
Willett on a community
visit to Gravesham

Another early innovation was a series of morale-boosting community visits to voluntary organisations, schools, clubs and businesses all around the county, from Romney Marsh to Swanley, and from Thanet to Gravesham.

On one of these visits, to Kemsing, the Lord-Lieutenant thanked community volunteers and afterwards one said: 'I've been doing voluntary work here for 30 years and I've never looked for thanks, but it's a great morale-booster when The Queen's representative takes the trouble to come and thank you. It makes you want to keep on volunteering.' Her remark neatly summed up the value of such visits.

The Lord-Lieutenant's ceremonial sword never failed to attract attention during primary school visits

When he visited primary schools the children were always intrigued by his sword. Asked if he had ever used it for real his laconic answer was: 'Not recently!' But his favourite memory is of another occasion when, in his uniform resplendent with medals and shiny buttons, he was confronted by a small boy who looked him up and down and asked: 'Are you real?'

As Allan Willett's modernisation took hold the then KCC Chairman John Davies put into words what many were thinking, that members of the modernised Lieutenancy were: 'true volunteers contributing enormously to the well-being of Kent and its communities. The Kent Lieutenancy is recognised throughout the country as leading the way in how a Lieutenancy should contribute in safeguarding the soul and spirit of the county.'

When the Elizabeth Cross was introduced for the next of kin of military personnel killed on active service since World War II, Lord-Lieutenants were asked to present them in their counties.

Presenting The Queen's Award to BACTEC

This involved a number of presentations dealing not only with a backlog dating back to the Malayan Emergency and the Korean War but with recent deaths in Iraq and Afghanistan.

The presentations evoked pride in long-ago sacrifices. But, although greatly valued by the families, those concerning recent fatalities were inevitably almost unbearably emotional. Allan and Anne Willett shed tears with the widows.

Queen's Awards for Voluntary Service are a valuable way of encouraging the volunteers to keep on volunteering and The Queen's representative in the county enjoyed honouring many of Kent's community organisations in this way. But it was presenting Queen's Awards for Enterprise that was a particular pleasure for Allan Willett who as a businessman had himself won two such awards for export. These awards not only raise staff morale, but have a significant spin-off in terms of raised profile and marketplace credibility. Importantly, he encouraged more firms to enter, resulting in a record five Kent winners in 2011.

As an entrepreneurial innovator, he was delighted to be able to acknowledge outstanding Kent-based companies that were knowledge-based, which is where he sees the county's future lies.

In addition to presenting these awards he created one himself. The Spirit of Kent award was designed to thank those who had given outstanding service to Kent, and it was, and is, the highest award the Lieutenancy can give.

An independent panel judges it and His Royal Highness The Duke of Kent was chosen to be first to receive it. His work as Patron of Canterbury Cathedral Trust and the Association of Men of Kent and Kentish Men made him a popular choice to receive the award, which is a work of art in itself. It incorporates a replica of the Amherst Brooch, an ancient jewel of national importance made in Kent in the early 7th Century, and the county's *Invicta* – 'unconquered' – white horse badge.

Edwin Boorman, President of the Kent Messenger Group, who sadly has since died of cancer, was the second person to receive it – in recognition for his family's long-term contribution to Kent. It was presented to him by The Prince of Wales during one of his visits to the county.

The third award went to Kent County Council Leader Lord Sandy Bruce-Lockhart. Sadly he was seriously ill and not long afterwards died of cancer. The latest awards were made jointly to Lord and Lady Kingsdown.

As nominal Chairman of the county's Advisory Committee on the magistracy the Lord-Lieutenant attended the swearing-in of new magistrates, and led a successful campaign aimed at recruiting potential new JPs. Such was the impact of the first of his calls that immediately some 60 interested people

ABOVE: The Duke of Kent accepts the first Spirit of Kent Award. Edwin Boorman receives the award from HRH The Prince of Wales. Allan Willett presents the award to Lord Bruce-Lockhart

'Just like that!' Meeting unusual characters was all part of the role, as here, at the presentation of The Queen's Award for Voluntary Service to the village tour team at St Peter's, Broadstairs

phoned in to request application forms. As the Willett Lieutenancy progressed it became universally accepted that as a result of his modernisation the office was now fully fit for purpose in the 21ˢᵗ Century. Its heightened profile meant that it was seen to be working solely for the good of the county – valuable, and valued.

Its network of hard-working DLs was being used to positive effect in every part of Kent. Its Armed Forces support, celebration of youth achievement and encouragement of community volunteering campaigns – all orchestrated and led by the Lord-Lieutenant himself – were on-going and successful.

And the Lieutenancy was taking on important new roles, notably, in partnership with Kent County Council and Medway Council, welcoming newcomers from around the world at citizenship ceremonies.

In the final years of Allan Willett's Lieutenancy he was dogged by illness, including a heart problem, prostate cancer – and more recently a form of Parkinsonism that affects his mobility. But the machinery he had put in place and his encouragement of all DLs to get involved meant that in his absences it remained 'business as usual' and not one single commitment was dropped.

An excellent example was the 70ᵗʰ anniversary two-day tour, inspired by the Lord-Lieutenant and organized by DL Group Captain Patrick Tootal, of Kentish airfields that had borne the brunt of Luftwaffe attacks during the Battle of Britain.

The Vice Lord-Lieutenant took over and, well supported by DLs at every location, ensured that the message of what Kent, the nation – and the world – owe to The Few was passed on to new generations.

To the end of his Lieutenancy, regardless of his ill health, Allan Willett carried on whenever possible – and just a few hours before his cancer operation he insisted on going to Dover to honour Dunkirk veterans returning to the beaches 70 years after the evacuation.

As he neared the end of what he described as 'a wonderful journey with the people of Kent' Allan Willett received two honours that meant a great deal to him. Kent County Council presented him with the Kent *Invicta* Award for his exceptional service to the county and he was appointed a Commander of the Royal Victorian Order (CVO) – an award entirely within the Sovereign's personal gift – in the 2011 Birthday Honours. Presenting him with the Kent *Invicta* Award, County Council Leader Paul Carter told him:

> Your charitable contribution, through setting up your own Allan Willett Foundation has been quite exceptional, as well as exceptionally generous, and has helped an enormous number of good causes and supported many, many individuals in various and different ways. In your nine years you have transformed the Lieutenancy of Kent. You have been, alongside your wife Anne, totally dedicated to the job and exceptionally generous with your time. You have touched hearts and put a smile on so many faces. And your

lead on the support to the Armed Forces in Kent and encouragement to young people has been second to none.[12]

Many more tributes were paid to him in the run-up to his retirement. Praising him for his 'energy, vision, decisiveness, clarity of thought, leadership, humanity and philanthropy' Deputy Lieutenant and former Chief Executive of Hornby plc Frank Martin said:

> The thrust of Allan's mission has been to modernize, to change things for the good and not just to be moving with the times, but to be *ahead* of them. He is truly an inspiration to us all.[13]

An affectionate tribute at Allan Willett's final annual meeting was the performance of *Invicta County Blues*, written by David Ralls and performed by him on guitar with Jools Holland on keyboard and vocal support from fellow-DLs Ros McCarthy and Ann West. The words summed up the modernisation in true blues style:

> *Woke up this morning – got the Invicta County Blues,*
> *Woke up this morning – got the Invicta County Blues*
> *Lord–Lootenant gonna be retiring – got the Invicta County Blues.*
>
> *He put his cards down on the table – way back in twenty zero three.*
> *He said: 'A modern Lootenancy – that's what we're gonna be'*
> *Lord–Lootenant gonna be retirin' – got the Invicta County Blues.*

'Relevant and visible, with a sense of history too.'
There ain't no going back now: he always said we'd see it through.
Lord–Lootenant gonna be retirin' – got the Invicta County Blues.

'Spread the word and tell the people there's an aim and there's a plan.
To all corners of Invicta County – add some value where we can'.
Lord–Lootenant gonna be retirin' – got the Invicta County Blues.[14]

At the lunch marking Allan Willett's retirement his successor, Lord De L'Isle, said he had succeeded in modernising and reforming the Lieutenancy to the point where Kent has become 'a by-word for best practice and leadership nationwide, a shining example to all other counties.' He added:

Perhaps the greatest compliment I, as the new Lord-Lieutenant, can pay to Allan is that I intend to continue to pursue the aims and aspirations he set in motion when he set out on his wonderful journey with the people of Kent.

LEFT: Stanley Blow with
Lord Cornwallis and the
Duke and Duchess of Kent

~ SEVENTEEN ~
THE EYES AND EARS OF
THE LORD-LIEUTENANT

mong the Deputy Lieutenants appointed by Lord Astor was
businessman and charity fund-raiser Stanley Blow. When in
1979 the Lord-Lieutenant invited him to take on the role he
teased Stanley, a former Home Guard corporal, by warning
him archly that 'The Queen will not approve.'

Mystified, Stanley wondered what on earth he could have done to incur
Royal displeasure, and asked with some trepidation what the Lord-Lieutenant
meant. The reply came as something of a relief:

> He said that although he did not know the historic reason, it was customary
> for The Queen *never* to approve the appointment of a Deputy Lieutenant,
> but merely to signify that 'She did not disapprove.'[1]

Today's commissions inform new DLs:

> …your name having been presented to and not disapproved of by Her
> Majesty… you are hereby required to execute the office of a Deputy
> Lieutenant within the said County of Kent and in all things to conform
> yourself to the duties thereof.

Kelvin Holford, County Commissioner for Scouts and a Deputy Lieutenant, helps further the Lieutenancy's focus on youth achievement

Frank Martin, Deputy Lieutenant and the then Chief Executive of Hornby plc, was just the man to escort HRH The Duke of Gloucester during his Thanet visit

No doubt one of the main reasons why a positive seal of royal approval is *not* given is because it would be impossible for the Palace to vet every candidate country-wide in detail, a task left to the good sense and local knowledge of the Lord-Lieutenant making the recommendation.

Stanley, born into a Jewish immigrant family from Austria and a prominent figure in the Kentish fruit industry, was duly 'not disapproved of' and following his appointment as a DL was involved in a number of royal visits. In his biography he recalled:

> I attended the Duchess of Kent when she visited the Scout Hut in the village of Matfield. A boy of about ten, wearing a somewhat bizarre hat, rushed up to her and said 'Swap hats?' To his, and my astonishment Her Royal Highness said 'Yes, I will' and took his off and put hers on his head. 'I am going to take this home for my son' she said and he, somewhat crestfallen, said 'Please can I have my hat back?' So honour was satisfied on all sides.[2]

Being appointed as a Deputy Lieutenant today is vastly different from Tudor times when they were the Lord-Lieutenant's subordinate military commanders tasked with raising, training and leading local militia forces before the days of standing armies, and carrying out a variety of local justice and government functions. In those days half a dozen prominent men were appointed for their wealth and influence as much as for their military abilities – their large estates giving them a vested interest in protecting the county from invasion and insurgency. It was for this reason that property qualifications were for many years a prerequisite for Deputy appointments, although that is no longer the case.

Historically, the survival and future prosperity of members of the Lieutenancy depended on their ability to defend the status quo – and men like Sir Thomas Scott of Armada fame and later the equally formidable Sir John Leveson clearly had what it took.

In the 17th and 18th Centuries implementing the complex and voluminous Militia legislation was often a thankless and time-consuming task and the number of Deputies was increased to cope with it. But throughout the United Kingdom in the 19th Century as the county Lieutenancies' military power declined and many of their civil duties were taken over by other bodies such as the magistracy and county councils, the importance of Deputy Lieutenants diminished to the point where in many cases their appointment became merely an honour without any real responsibilities or duties.

The major army reforms of 1871 had re-vested the Lieutenancies' military jurisdiction in the Crown and the end of the militias in 1907 further diluted their by then largely theoretical powers.

The 1966 reform had allowed for deputies to be appointed if they had rendered worthy service as a member, or in a civilian capacity, to the Forces of the Crown – or had given 'such other service as, in the opinion of the Secretary of State (for Defence), makes him suitable for appointment as a Deputy Lieutenant.'

By then there was no bar to appointing women, but the masculine reference revealed that in reality it was still a men-only organisation. A decade later the Ministry of Defence relinquished all authority for DL appointments, which first became a Home Office responsibility and, since 2005, that of the Department for Constitutional Affairs.

The loosening of the military connection meant that first Lord Astor, who as we have seen brought the first women into the Kent Lieutenancy, and then Lord Kingsdown, were increasingly able to appoint Deputy Lieutenants from the widest range of those contributing significant service to the nation and county. Their successors Allan Willett and Lord De L'Isle have continued the trend and currently only a quarter of Kent's serving DLs have significant military service. A further quarter are women.

Ironically, as responsibilities diminished, the number of DLs in all counties grew. Yet throughout the 20th Century, countrywide, there were many honoured with the post-nominal DL who were seldom – if ever – called upon to perform a Lieutenancy duty.

But now the wheel has turned full circle and before being appointed new Kent Deputies are asked if they share the Lord-Lieutenant's aims and aspirations – and if they are willing and able to assist with or carry out whatever public duties he requests them to undertake. A 'no' would result in no appointment. There are no passengers now.

Today's Deputies – some famous, but many *unsung* – are honoured for their contribution to county and nation and chosen for what they can bring to the Lieutenancy team. They can be nominated by anyone other than themselves and are selected by a panel of experienced DLs chaired by the Lord-Lieutenant himself.

To be appointed is an honour which binds the recipient to the county and a wide cross-section of people with experience of many facets of its communities is required nowadays to carry out the Lieutenancy's duties and pursue its modern aims and aspirations.

Many already have extensive patronages, presidencies or memberships of both national and Kent organisations and voluntary bodies – or, once they have joined the Lieutenancy, soon will have.

Nowadays it is said, rightly, that where once they raised, trained and served in armed forces to protect county and nation, Deputies now encourage and serve armies of volunteers working for the benefit of all Kent's communities, no matter what their political, religious or ethnic background.

Deputies come from all areas of the county and a great variety of specialisations. And, importantly, they are the eyes and ears of the Lord-Lieutenant. A recent Parliamentary answer explained:

Deputy Lieutenant and National Care Association Chairman Mrs Nadra Ahmed. From a men-only Lieutenancy until 1973, a quarter of today's Kent DLs are women

Allan Willett Esquire
Companion, Order of St Michael and St George,
of Cumberland House, Chilham in the County of Kent
Her Majesty's Lord Lieutenant of the ancient and ceremonial
County of Kent

To

Barry Duffield Esquire

By virtue of the power and authority in me vested
I do hereby constitute, nominate, appoint and grant Commission to you

Barry Duffield

to be a Deputy Lieutenant of Kent (your name having been presented to
and not disapproved of by Her Majesty) and you are hereby required to
execute the office of a Deputy Lieutenant within the said County of Kent
and in all things to conform yourself to the duties thereof.

Given under My Hand this Nineteenth day of August
Two Thousand and Eleven

Her Majesty's Lord Lieutenant of Kent

A Kent Deputy Lieutenant's commission

'The Lord-Lieutenant leads up to 70 influential Deputy Lieutenants county-wide, honoured for their positive contributions to the county and the nation, who use their local and specialist knowledge and experience for the benefit of Kent's varied communities'

The primary criterion for appointment as a DL is that of 'appropriate service', including military service together with residence in or within seven miles from the boundary of the relevant county or area. In choosing DLs Lord-Lieutenants are expected to interpret widely 'other suitable public service' which can qualify someone for appointment. In particular they should be looking for people well known in their locality for the service they have or are giving through public life, charitable activity, voluntary service or the uniformed services. The overall aim is that within each county or area DLs should be widely representative of the county or area's life in social range, gender, community background, ethnic mix and service to the community.[3]

This produces a pan-county, non-partisan force for good, collectively providing a great depth of specialist and local knowledge and experience that can be used to positive effect in key sectors ranging from education to youth services, and from business to the rural economy.

Becoming a Deputy Lieutenant can cost a good deal in both time and money. They fund their own duty travel and subsistence, pay for their badge of office and – in the case of male DLs who wish to acquire them – buy their own uniforms. However, they do not *have* to buy badges as the Deputy Clerk can loan them one from a pool purchased by the Lord-Lieutenant – and no-one *has* to have a uniform. Also, it is said that the cost of being a DL is proportionate to the pleasure derived from carrying out duties, as often they are asked to cover events they would like to attend anyway.

So why would anyone want to do it? Most would answer, not only for the honour, but for love of county and a wish to 'put something back.' In the modern Lieutenancy this is no cliché.

In recent years Kent's DLs have included the near legendary soldier, politician and *Daily Telegraph* editor Bill Deedes, and Bernard, later Lord Weather-ill, a former Speaker of the House of Commons, whose obituary recorded that he 'will be remembered as the first Speaker to chair televised sessions of the Commons, a development he had long advocated.'

Other prominent DLs, now on the supplementary or retired list – having reached the age of 75 – include a former Attorney-General, the Right Honourable Lord Mayhew of Twysden, former Navy Minister Sir Keith Speed, and the founder of the MORI polls, American-born Sir Robert Worcester.

But in addition to the well-known names, there are today many less high profile but nevertheless valuable DLs in Kent, from diverse backgrounds covering every aspect of modern society and doing far more than their bit for the county's great variety of charitable and community organisations.

In his 2007 book *The Lord-Lieutenants and Their Deputies*, Miles Jebb singles out Kent for special mention in this regard:

> The multiplicity of charities and good causes in all Lieutenancies is always impressive, the magnitude and the range naturally varying with size and population. Kent is a populous county with a vigorous Lieutenancy which has evolved the concept of networks within county activities, with a DL leading each sector.[4]

And he goes on record a long list of Kent causes and organisations that individual Deputy Lieutenants have supported ranging from ex-Service bodies to nature reserves, community trusts and youth movements. There can be few such organisations in the county that do not have the Lord-Lieutenant himself or one of his Deputies as patron, president, member or voluntary worker.

Although most DLs are involved in a wide variety of charities it is firmly *not* the Lieutenancy's role to raise funds for charities. It could not possibly help all the many hundreds seeking funds and it would be totally invidious to support some and not others.

Quite unfairly, it could be argued in these days of gender equality, national Lieutenancy rules only allow for a male DL uniform, although lady DLs who have previously been commissioned in one of the Forces of the Crown may wear the uniform of their rank and arm of service on appropriate occasions.

The male DL uniform is a version of the Army's navy blue barathea Major-General's tunic. It is worn, mainly although not exclusively, by those with a military background. They wear it with a brown leather Sam Browne belt and infantry pattern sword rather than the crimson and silver sash and General's pattern sword with curved blade worn by the Lord-Lieutenant. Among the other differences the Lord-Lieutenant, unlike his Deputies, has a crown above the Tudor rose on his badges of rank.

As we have seen, it was Allan Willett who introduced the Invicta badge of office for his Deputy Lieutenants. It rapidly became the envy of DLs in other

BBC TV MASTERMIND QUESTION

Who is the keyboard player and presenter appointed a Deputy Lieutenant of Kent?

Answer: Jools Holland OBE

How the uniform of a Deputy Lieutenant of Kent should be worn. Brigadier Trevor Minter at Dover Castle, where he was formerly Deputy Constable and Commander of 2 (South East) Brigade

The new national badge for Deputy Lieutenants

counties and pressure built for similar insignia elsewhere. In 2012 the Association of Lord-Lieutenants, never in favour of individual county insignia, introduced a national badge for all counties and this has been adopted for use in Kent by new Deputy Lieutenants. Those in possession of a Kent Badge continue to wear it when in plain clothes on appropriate occasions, but no new *Invicta* versions will be produced.

The new national badge is in the form of a large red enamelled Tudor Rose. Male Deputy Lieutenants wear it on a broad ribbon around the neck, and lady DLs may wear it similarly or mounted on a court bow worn on the left breast. Its purpose is to indicate that the Deputy Lieutenant is representing the Lord-Lieutenant.

The role and functions of DLs are not specified in the Lieutenancies Act but they are expected to support their Lord-Lieutenant by carrying out tasks that including acting as his eyes and ears throughout the county, keeping him informed and suggesting ways in which the Lieutenancy can support Kent's varied communities and promote and reward voluntary service.

This includes commending to him suitable candidates both voluntary and professional for invitation to a royal garden party, assessing nominations for The Queen's Award for Voluntary Service, participation in citizenship ceremonies, and myriad other duties. Collectively Kent's DLs perform some 500 Lieutenancy duties each year, ranging from paying morale-boosting visits to Cadet units, liaising with local authorities and presenting awards, to giving talks about the Monarchy to schoolchildren.

Taking part in citizenship ceremonies held by both the Kent and Medway authorities is a popular duty with many DLs, as Sir Robert Worcester recalls:

I was astonished to receive Allan Willett's telephone call that that he would like to put my name forward to the Palace to be a Deputy Lieutenant. 'You can't', I told him. 'Why not?' 'Because I'm an American'. 'Oh, I didn't think of that. I'll have to put it forward to the Palace and see what they say.'

Three weeks later Allan rang again: 'It seems there is no bar to it.' I was duly appointed and a year or so later I was chairing a dinner of the Pilgrims' Society of Great Britain at which The Princess Royal was our speaker. I related the above and she was, typically, quick to remark: 'Oh, we got over that a long time ago!'

When the Lieutenancy began taking part in citizenship ceremonies, the Lord-Lieutenant was back on the phone:

He said: 'As you've just become a citizen I thought it would be suitable if you were to do the first ceremony'. I didn't know quite what to expect but I pitched up at County Hall and joined the about-to-be citizens for a cup of

tea. I liaised with the Chairman of Kent County Council who gave them their charge before the Registrar took the oath and I was then called upon to welcome them on behalf of the Lord-Lieutenant and encourage them to take part in community life. The spirit of the new citizens and their families was truly heart-warming. Pleased and proud, they all had their story to tell of the country they were from and our new, adopted country.[5]

Citizenship ceremonies were also the favourite regular duty of former diplomat Sir Alistair Hunter:

They have made such a difference to the significance of becoming British. I was always amazed at the variety of new citizens involved. One winter day, the registrars pointed out to me before the ceremony a new citizen of Chinese race, a lady probably in her late 30s, who had cycled 25 miles through the snow. For my generation, a Chinese resident probably runs a takeaway. 'Where do you come from?' I asked her, trying not to sound patronising. 'Taiwan.' 'And how long have you been here?' 'Ten years.' 'And why did you come to Britain?' 'To do a PhD in Mediaeval History.' Collapse of stout party![6]

Former head teacher Mrs Ros McCarthy recalls being told by many of the new citizens how extremely moving they find the ceremonies, and how important it is to have a formal occasion where they can make their promises in front of witnesses – almost like a wedding with buttonholes and a small reception – and be welcomed on behalf of Queen and county. 'The official photographs are treasured too.'[7]

Magistrates Bench Chairman and former deputy head teacher Mrs Ann West believes:

The Lieutenancy's involvement in citizenship ceremonies is very much

RIGHT: Former head teacher Mrs Ros McCarthy is a member of the team of Deputy Lieutenants giving presentations on the Monarchy to schools pictured here with Sandgate Primary School pupils

appreciated by the Registrars and by the new citizens taking part in the last piece of the jigsaw of becoming a British citizen. To show young people the importance of creating and welcoming new British citizens the ceremonies have occasionally been held at a secondary school. However, these ceremonies need to be held in central, prestigious and impressive settings as they are so important to our new citizens, but recognising the importance of senior students learning more about British Citizenship, schools are now invited to send small groups to observe the ceremonies.

Ann West believes awareness of the Lieutenancy among the general public is still limited and therefore involvement with schools is very important.

With the introduction of 'Citizenship' as a recognised topic in the school curriculum it is possible to include information on the Lieutenancy. In the build up to the Queen`s Jubilee, Deputy Lieutenants gave presentations on the Monarchy to some 100 primary schools throughout Kent and Medway. Head teachers welcomed these as they fitted in extremely well with the schools` plans for celebrating such an important and exciting national event. As a follow up to this involvement the schools and the Lieutenancy are now enjoying closer links with more talks and presentations on the Lieutenancy in Kent.[8]

The talks generate many questions from the schoolchildren. DL, businessman and public sector agency chairman John Ogden recalls being asked: 'Does the Queen have a Nan?'

I had made quite a play on the fact that The Queen was an amazingly fit

In his DL role John Ogden fostered strong links with Gravesham's Sikh community

and active 86-year-old and we all hoped that she would live at least until a
Platinum Jubilee which elicited this question from an eight-year-old sitting
cross-legged on the floor just in front of me with his elbow on his knee who
said quizzically, 'You know how The Queen sends a card when you are 100,
well, will she have to send herself one when she gets to 100?'

After I got back from giving a talk at Meopham Community Academy, I
got a text from a young friend in Meopham Players who has a six-year-old
daughter at the Academy: Her daughter had told her: 'Mummy, your friend
Mr Ogden visited school today. He is related to Her Majesty you know!'[9]

As a former Royal Air Force pilot, Group Captain Patrick Tootal is seldom lost
for words, but was almost stumped when asked: 'How many bathrooms are there
in Buckingham Palace?' He thought for a moment before answering: 'Lots!'[10]

Sir Alistair Hunter recalls numerous occasions when he thought the Lieutenancy was doing a worthwhile job. One notable example was the Battle of
Britain 70th anniversary ceremonies in 2010.

> The one at Manston was well attended, clearly striking a real chord among
> those old enough to remember, and marking out the county of Kent as the
> one over which most of that titanic struggle took place. Promoting pride in
> one's locality is an important ingredient in creating a sense of community
> and improving quality of life, and the Lieutenancy is very good at doing that.

His most enjoyable event was presenting Duke of Edinburgh's Awards in
the Winter Gardens in Margate – this because of the historical association
of the venue.

RIGHT: Richard Dixon in
'DL camouflage uniform'
at Kent ACF annual camp

Hard as it is to imagine 60 years later, the Winter Gardens were where the Conservative Party had held its annual conference in 1953 – Winston Churchill's last. That autumn, after the Coronation, the Cabinet had been racking their brains about how to keep The Queen's male consort occupied, and, as I told the participants, it had surely been a topic of conversation in the very room where the 2009 awards ceremony took place. Someone said: 'I think the young man has an idea of his own' – and thus the Awards were born.[11]

Lieutenancy links with the Forces of the Crown, the Cadet movements and ex-Service charities are important and strong, and take many forms. The Lord-Lieutenant himself has served as Honorary Colonel of Kent's Territorial infantry unit and the Army Cadets, and several of his Deputies have held both executive or similar honorary appointments.

For many years Lieutenant Colonel Richard Dixon, a former commanding officer of the 5th (Volunteer) Battalion, The Queen's Regiment, chaired the County Committee for the Reserve Forces and Cadets, an important appointment now held by his former Kent ACF Commandant Colonel Robert Murfin, a DL for the London Borough of Bromley. Colonel James Partridge, a Kent DL, is currently Chairman of South East Reserve Forces' and Cadets' Association at Aldershot. Colonel Godfrey Linnett, who preceded Richard Dixon as Chairman of the County Committee, is also a former Kent ACF Commandant, as is another Deputy Lieutenant, Colonel Peter Bishop.

The Lieutenancy's ability to bring competing interests together to achieve consensus was demonstrated by Jeremy Leigh Pemberton as Chairman of the Lord-Lieutenant's Year of Victories Welfare Fundraising Co-ordination Committee. He persuaded an extraordinary gathering of the many Kent-based

Service charities to agree to share the fund-raising effort – and the resulting money – donated by the public at anniversary events. He remembers: 'I have seldom enjoyed a role more. It was an enormously gratifying job not least because it put me in contact with some wonderful people, including one who reminded us on more than one occasion which the Senior Service was!'

It was an excellent example of what the Lieutenancy, without any axe to grind, is able to achieve in bringing people or organisations together and getting them to agree to an unselfish course of action.

One of the most poignant roles for the Lieutenancy was when in 1998 surviving veterans of World War I from any Allied country who had fought on French soil were made Chevaliers of the Légion D'Honneur as part of the commemoration of the 80th anniversary of the war's end.

The Royal British Legion took on the task of organising presentation of the medals to surviving veterans and its then Kent Field Officer, Patrick Tootal approached Lord Kingsdown to see if he would like to present them.

Group Captain Patrick Tootal, in RAF rather than DL uniform, during a visit by HRH Prince Michael of Kent

> Robin agreed and most other Lord-Lieutenants followed his example. His only caveat was that he would not kiss the recipients on both cheeks! At that time there were 17 World War I veterans in Kent. The youngest was 99, having lied about his age on enlistment, and the oldest was 112.

The Lord-Lieutenant was not available for the first presentation so Godfrey Linnett took his place. He remembers: 'The recipient was at the time in Farnborough Hospital and he and his relations were delighted to have a presentation, but sad to say he died a couple of months later.'

For the other presentations Patrick Tootal drove the Lord-Lieutenant in full uniform to each venue.

> I was armed with the medals passed to me from the French Embassy and a posh red cushion which I offered to Robin who duly pinned the medal on each recipient after he had said a few words. Venues ranged from private homes to nursing homes.

> One in Tunbridge Wells was a major event. It was a very moving experience and for their ages all were most articulate. One stood up and said he went 'over the top' three times and by rights should not have survived. There were plenty of tears.[12]

There is often confusion when Group Captain Tootal appears in his DL uniform. Some comment: 'I didn't know that Army officers could wear RAF Wings!'

There was confusion of a different sort when Brigadier David Ralls represented the Lord-Lieutenant at a 60th anniversary commemoration at the Battle of Britain National Memorial at Capel-le-Ferne. He was wearing his

Brigadier David Ralls at the Battle of Britain National Memorial at Capel-le-Ferne

Her Majesty advises Dick Tapp not to get caught hunting with dogs

DL uniform with, among his decorations, the Distinguished Flying Cross awarded during his service with the Army Air Corps.

An elderly lady asked if he had fought in the Battle of Britain, and, not wishing to wrong-foot her, he said he was flattered to be asked but regretted he had missed it. In fact he had missed it by three years, not having been born – in North London during the Blitz – until 1943!

An important role for DLs is taking soundings in their communities and the voluntary organisations with which they are involved to recommend worthy people to receive a once-in-a-lifetime invitation to attend a Buckingham Palace Garden Party – truly special and memorable events.

SSAFA-Forces Help Kent stalwart Suresh Khanna recalls that one charity volunteer he had recommended for a garden party wanted to go again the following year because 'I really enjoyed it'.

> Another couple, in their 80s, produced an illustrated booklet to send to their friends and relations after attending a Buckingham Palace Garden Party – an indication of how much people cherish these occasions.[13]

He has also witnessed how highly Queen's Awards for Voluntary Service are valued.

> While waiting for the results of the assessment the Chief Executive of a Maidstone group had an accident and broke his leg. Undeterred he turned up on crutches for the Lord-Lieutenant's presentation of the award. Winning it had been his ultimate ambition to get further funding from the Government and Kent County Council. He succeeded and having achieved this summit and ensured the future of the voluntary organisation he retired, as he was planning to do. A marvellous outcome.[13]

Occasionally, Kent's Deputy Lieutenants can find themselves unexpectedly thrust into the limelight.

A few weeks after being appointed as a DL, agricultural business director Dick Tapp was telephoned from the Lord-Lieutenant's office and informed that he had been selected to sit beside The Queen at the lunch following the 2002 Maundy Thursday ceremony at Canterbury.

> This was something of a shock to the system as I had no idea how to handle what seemed to be the tricky task of keeping Her Majesty interested and amused during lunch! My wife, Tessa, was to be seated on the right-hand side of the Lord-Lieutenant with a Bishop to her right.

> I had been informed that The Queen would start a conversation if she wanted to and that I was to call her Ma'am (to rhyme with spam). Of

course she asked me what I did and where I did it and luckily this brought the rural scene into the conversation with no trouble. We briefly discussed various farming issues and then moved on to country pursuits.

I did not hold my own on horses but from shooting we followed on to dogs which was a very good subject. When I informed Her Majesty that I usually went for a daily farm walk not only with my dog but also with my daughters' three dogs I was warned in the nicest possible way and with a twinkle not to get caught 'hunting with dogs'![14]

Lieutenancy duties occasionally have a humorous side. James Bird, former chairman of a Sandwich-based engineering business that won five Queen's Awards for Export Achievement, recalls being asked by the Lord-Lieutenant's office to present a cheque and congratulate a ladies' rowing four for winning a national championship:

James Bird

> The event was to be held at their winter training area on the river Stour and my wife Jenny said that nobody would turn up so she declined to accompany me. I was keen as it was different to other events I had attended such as the funerals of other DLs!
>
> When I arrived at the boat house I was surprised at how many people had turned up. I introduced myself and suddenly two large doors on the boat house swung open and out trotted four extremely nubile young ladies in small, tight singlets and tiny shorts carrying their triumphant skiff.
>
> I said a few words of congratulation and they gathered round me as I presented the cheque. A glass of champagne was thrust into my hand and the next thing was the flash of cameras. I duly returned home, didn't say much to Jenny until the local paper came out and there was a large photo of me surrounded by the four attractive and semi-attired young girls, a large smile on my face and a glass of champagne in hand. Jenny was not impressed and said she would in future accompany me on such outings. I was not to be trusted!'[15]

All part of the myriad duties of today's hard-working Deputy Lieutenants…

ABOVE: The Lord-Lieutenant takes the salute on his first day in office

~ EIGHTEEN ~
THE LIEUTENANCY TODAY

Diamond Jubilee preparations were high on the agenda when Viscount De L'Isle took office as Lord-Lieutenant of Kent. But his first assignment, on the very day he took up his appointment, was a reminder of the Lieutenancy's historic role.

He took the salute as the locally-recruited 2nd Royal Tank Regiment exercised the Freedom of Maidstone, marching through cheering crowds in the town centre in accordance with tradition, with drums beating, band playing, Colours flying and bayonets fixed.

'Today,' he told the Regiment, 'is a very special day for you – and for me. You are rightly being honoured by the people of Maidstone, our County Town. And it is a great honour for me to be invited to salute you on this, my very first day as Lord-Lieutenant and Her Majesty The Queen's representative in our Frontline County of Kent.'

He explained how, historically, the Lieutenancy was responsible for organising the defence of the county, adding although that responsibility now lay elsewhere the close relationship with the Forces of the Crown remains strong. He added:

Kent is part of your recruiting area and we are proud of our special link with your Regiment, the oldest Tank Regiment in the world – and of the fact that in your short history you have won 73 battle honours and six soldiers from the Regiment have been awarded the Victoria Cross. You may be called the 2ⁿᵈ Regiment, but you are second to none!'[1]

Sadly the Regiment's proud title disappears due to the latest army reorganisation.

The Maidstone event was the start of an extremely busy period for the Kent Lieutenancy and Lord De L'Isle announced from the outset that its aims would remain unchanged. It would be: 'More of the same, but achieved slightly differently.' He is conscious that the office has been evolving since Tudor times and will go on evolving, nowadays in close step with the Royal Family itself.

In his first message to the county, Lord De L'Isle pointed out that Kent had led the way in encouraging greater public support for Service personnel and their families, and he urged everyone to continue to give this campaign their undivided attention. Importantly, he also confirmed his support for that other army – of the county's thousands of community volunteers:

> Across the county and in Medway we are blessed with an army of volunteers who tirelessly work supporting others and particularly assisting our youth, the seed corn of tomorrow's Kent. I look forward to visiting and working with these charities. We face changing times in the field of youth employment and it is my hope the Lieutenancy can work with all the agencies involved to ensure our children can find work suited to their set of skills.[2]

The new Lord-Lieutenant was soon to turn these words into action but with no Lieutenancy budget available for such initiatives he decided to work with Kent's local authorities on events like Kent Choices 4 U Live at the County Showground.

This was staged jointly by Kent County Council and the Kent Messenger Group, and the Lieutenancy was able to give it a tremendous boost and raise the profile by delivering a royal visitor – His Royal Highness The Duke of York – and support it with active participation from Deputy Lieutenants including Jools Holland, who encouraged job-seekers and thanked exhibitors for taking part.

Opening the event the Lord-Lieutenant said:

> We all need to achieve a high level of skills and be prepared to constantly re-train as technology and the speed of change transform our working lives.

Thousands of young people and jobseekers of all ages attended and Prince Andrew made a point, in an exclusive interview with Kent Messenger Group

RIGHT: The Lord-Lieutenant escorting the Royal couple during their visit to Thanet

Business Editor and Deputy Lieutenant Trevor Sturgess, of saying how impressed he was with the concern being shown about creating opportunities for young people and encouraging them to get jobs in Kent.

Two great events were to dominate the first 12 months of Lord De L'Isle's Lieutenancy – the celebration of Her Majesty Queen Elizabeth's Diamond Jubilee and of the Olympic Games to be staged on Kent's doorstep in East London. But first the county was to host a visit by The Queen herself to the Isle of Thanet. It was a family joke that if Lord De L'Isle got this first VVIP visit wrong he might well end up in Her Majesty's Tower of London, and it certainly looked as if it had disaster potential when he arrived at Manston to be told that owing to thick low cloud it was touch and go whether or not the royal aircraft would be able to land. Lord De L'Isle confesses:

> The thought crossed my mind that if the visit was cancelled I would have to go into the centre of Margate to tell the thousands of people waiting there 'the show's over!'

To everyone's relief there was a break in the cloud and the aircraft landed safely. If it had not at least part of the visit would have gone ahead anyway, because there is always a contingency plan to take account of Britain's capricious climate.

The official lunch took place at the Turner Contemporary, alongside Margate's Lifeboat Station, and Lord De L'Isle recalls:

> During lunch the silhouette of the lifeboat came along the window which much amused The Queen, who said: 'I don't often share my lunch with a lifeboat!'[3]

The whole visit was a huge success. Excited flag-waving children lined the route and everywhere The Queen and Duke of Edinburgh were greeted by cheering crowds, said to be the biggest they had encountered on such a visit for a very long time. The royal couple were visibly delighted and the Lord-Lieutenant was safe from incarceration in the Tower!

Representing the Monarch in the county could be said to be in Lord De L'Isle's DNA, having experienced Government House life when his late father was Governor-General of Australia, and his service in the Household Division during his time in the Grenadier Guards.

Both, by extension, involved him with the Royal Family, and fitted him well for that important part of his role as Lord-Lieutenant.

That background and standing in for the former Lord-Lieutenant during his illness, meant that he had, in his words, 'already got my head around it' before taking on the appointment.

Whether or not a Lord-Lieutenant's partner chooses to involve him or herself is entirely up to the individual, but Kent is fortunate that Lady De L'Isle, willingly and with great charm and good humour, plays a full part helping to carry out her husband's Lieutenancy duties.

Born Isobel Compton, she is the daughter of Britain's first Parliamentary Commissioner, or Ombudsman, Sir Edmund Compton. A Cordon Bleu cook, she started her own cookery school and was secretary to two charitable trusts before marriage in 1980. Since then she has held important appointments at regional level with the National Trust and as Chairman of the Rural Development Commission Committee for Kent, Sussex and Surrey. She has been President of the League of Friends at Pembury Hospital since 1992.

Visitors to magnificent Penshurst Place and Gardens beside the Medway

ABOVE LEFT: Lord and Lady De L'Isle at their Penshurst Place home

RIGHT: South Front of Penshurst Place. Home of the Sidney family for over 460 years

ABOVE LEFT: Lord De L'Isle accompanying The Queen during her visit to The 5th Battalion, Royal Regiment of Scotland (Argyll and Sutherland Highlanders) at Canterbury

RIGHT: The Porcupine is the sinister supporter and crest on the Sidney Coat of Arms, which is a Pheon or Broad Arrow. The statue pictured was sculpted by Robert Rattray, Lord De L'Isle's nephew

near Tonbridge are often surprised to learn that it is still very much a family home as well as being an award-winning tourist attraction and wedding venue.

Remarkably, it has been in continuous occupation by Lord De L'Isle's family – the Sidneys – for more than 460 years. The house itself dates back nearly seven centuries and periods of what he terms 'genteel poverty' preserved it from rebuilding mania. Although it has been close to ruination twice and was damaged by Hitler's doodlebugs it remains the best-preserved example of a defended manor house in England.

It retains its medieval feel and its mellowed stone exudes history. But the De L'Isles see themselves as custodians of Penshurst's future as much as of its past, and are determined to ensure its continuity for future generations. Their children, Sophia and Philip, share their vision.

When not performing official Lieutenancy duties, Lord De L'Isle can be found at Penshurst taking a close personal interest in the challenges and finer points of running the house, gardens and 2,600-acre estate. Uniquely for a peer of the realm, he has also been the Penshurst village sub postmaster. This and other initiatives such as encouraging job creation in estate buildings, and hosting the farmers' market on the Penshurst car park, are evidence of Lord and Lady De L'Isle's passionate determination to support the hard-pressed rural economy and maintain local facilities.

Effectively, as the Sovereign's representative, the Lord-Lieutenant is the senior person in the county and needs to lead by example and use his considerable influence for the good of its varied communities.

Lord De L'Isle's mantra is that Kent is best talked about as a whole rather than the sum of its parts. He firmly believes in what he calls 'a united front for Kent.'

However Lord De L'Isle is acutely aware that the Lieutenancy must avoid politics and controversy. Potential 'Pooh traps', such as backing one town, business venture or cause against another or appearing to support a political party's line, are not always obvious. A simple guideline is: would The Queen do or say this?

There is occasionally disappointment among those who fail to win Lieutenancy backing, or by the local media, who – innocently – ask for comments on whatever controversy pops up. But it has to be remembered that Lord-Lieutenants are the representatives of the Sovereign, not 'rent-a-quote'.

An early event of Lord De L'Isle's Lieutenancy was the 70th anniversary commemoration of the devastation of the village of Sturry, near Canterbury, by a wartime bombing raid that killed 15 people and injured more than 30 others. The Lord-Lieutenant told those attending the commemoration:

> We must never forget that – especially in this Frontline County – the civilian population, men and women, boys and girls on the Home Front were themselves often in the front line. It is fair to say that in a relatively small population every single person suffered loss or was touched by this horrendous event. Yet did they cower and whine? No they did not. They immediately set about rescuing the trapped and injured and in the dark days that followed they helped one another. It was the strength of the community that carried the people of Sturry through those dark hours, and by your presence here today each and every one of you is demonstrating that this is still a strong community.[4]

As The Queen and Duke of Edinburgh had been such recent visitors to Kent, Her Majesty asked The Earl and Countess of Wessex to visit the county as part of the Diamond Jubilee regional visits programme. And, appropriately in such a significant year, one of the happy venues was Royal Tunbridge Wells.

That June in towns and villages throughout the county people joined together for community 'big lunches', and another of the Jubilee celebrations harked back to the early days of the Lieutenancy and the lighting of the beacons, although this time as a celebration – not a warning.

They were part of a chain of more than 2012 beacons across the United Kingdom the Commonwealth and Protected Territories and the Lord-Lieutenant himself lit the Penshurst blaze while elsewhere across Kent his Deputies helped send the symbolic message on its way marking the Sovereign's 60 years of devoted service to her people throughout county, nation and Commonwealth.

The county was also represented in the great Thames Pageant, with the Lord-Lieutenant flying the Kent flag, appropriately in one of the Dunkirk Little

The Lord-Lieutenant flew the Kent flag in the Dunkirk Little Ship *Hilfranor* in the Thames Pageant in 2012

Ships, the 42ft *Hilfranor*, commanded by Simon Palmer. Deputy Lieutenants Douglas Horner and David Ralls accompanied him and Douglas recalls:

> We were smartly dressed in blazers and accompanied by uniformed Naval personnel, but just as we passed The Queen who was taking her salute, the heavens opened with an almighty downpour. The Lord-Lieutenant and the rest of us got absolutely soaked and frozen, but it was a great occasion![5]

The full and varied programme of events supported by the Lord-Lieutenant and his Deputies continues apace with more royal visits, including those of The Prince of Wales for the enthronement of the new Archbishop of Canterbury and the Whitstable Oyster Festival, presentations of Queen's Awards for Enterprise and for Voluntary Service, the swearing-in of new magistrates, citizenship ceremonies, investitures at Penshurst Place for the presentation of the British Empire Medal and the Elizabeth Cross, presentations of Meritorious Service Awards for the Volunteer Reserves and Cadets, receptions for newly-appointed civic leaders, and myriad other events from symbolic tree-plantings to the Blessing of the Waters.

Initiatives currently underway include the resumption of talks on the Monarchy by Deputy Lieutenants to schools, joint action with the Shrievalty in promoting greater understanding of the principle of restorative justice, major involvement in three events marking the centenary of the commencement of World War I, and in 2015 the bi-centenary of Waterloo and the 75th

anniversary of the Battle of Britain. Administration of a busy Lieutenancy like Kent's requires a good deal of behind-the-scenes work, especially when it comes to planning royal visits to make sure that everything runs smoothly on the great day. Lord De L'Isle is very much a hands-on Lord-Lieutenant and leads from the front with the assistance of his own private office at Penshurst – and the Clerk and Deputy Clerk to the Lieutenancy based at County Hall.

The link with Kent County Council, of which both Lord Cornwallis and Lord Kingsdown have been Chairman, harks back to the civil administration elements of the Lieutenancy's role in years past.

Latest in a long line of Clerks to the Lieutenancy is Geoff Wild, Head of Governance and Law at the County Council, whose role there is to maintain probity and standards, ensuring that it acts lawfully and properly within its powers in a fast-changing world – making him, in effect, 'keeper of the council's conscience'. Of his Lieutenancy duties he explains:

> As a lawyer, the first thing I did when additionally appointed Clerk to the Lieutenancy was to ask for the terms of reference, but I was told that effectively there were none. It is very much down to the individual relationship you build up with the Lord-Lieutenant and to the particular county style that has been built up over the years. If the bank of tradition in a county is largely ceremonial then it's likely to stay ceremonial, but if it's more businesslike as it is in Kent it's likely to carry on that way.[6]

The Government sets out limited guidelines as to its expectations of Lord-Lieutenants, but these are minimal and Geoff Wild believes that is how it should be. 'There needs to be scope for flexibility and individual style. It would be a sad day if civil servants were to dictate how a Lieutenancy should operate in the minutest detail.' Although KCC and Medway Council share many of the Lieutenancy's aims and aspirations for the good of the people of Kent it would be quite wrong for either to be 'in each other's pockets.' The

Lieutenancy must remain totally apolitical. What is his take on his appointment as Clerk?

I see my role as being to facilitate and ensure that the Lord-Lieutenant
has an infrastructure of support, administration, research or whatever he
needs around him to do his job properly. No-one at the County Council is
appointed to serve the Lieutenancy. The support we give in addition to our
other work represents a tiny part of one per cent of the council's £2 billion
budget, but the impact it has on the county and the importance the County
Council places on its relationship with the Lieutenancy as a force for good
working for the people of Kent makes it extremely good value for money.

You just need to look at the programme of events the Lieutenancy
undertakes in engaging with community groups from schools to the elderly
and promoting the county and its many unsung heroes to understand that
this is something far more than going round in uniform during a Royal
visit. It is hugely influential, but not widely enough known. Some might
wonder why we have up to 70 Deputy Lieutenants, but if you multiply that
figure by the ten or more organisations with which each of them is actively
engaged, and multiply that by the number of individuals who benefit from
the work of those organisations the figure reaches hundreds of thousands.

With today's limited budgets the County Council could not possibly engage
with all these community organisations. Increasingly we have to rely on the
third sector, the voluntary and community bodies, and the Lieutenancy is a
key player in that area.

It is an ancient office and that's important because Kent is staunchly proud
of its position, status and history, more so than other parts of the country.
The Lieutenancy keeps alive that feeling of Kentishness, but the fact that

it is being constantly modernised and updated brings a fresh approach and real drive that makes it absolutely relevant today.[7]

Daily interface with all members of the Lieutenancy, the Royal Family's private offices and the county at large is the Deputy Clerk, Joanne Holmes, fount of all knowledge on protocol and every aspect of Lieutenancy activity from doing 'recces' for royal visits to arranging for Deputies to represent the Lord-Lieutenant at all manner of events.[8]

She explains that the main ways in which the Lieutenancy can help Kent's communities are:

- Where appropriate, suggesting that a visit to the organisation might be included in the programme of a visiting member of the Royal Family.
- Arranging for a Deputy Lieutenant to visit, suitably badged and identifiable, to acknowledge the work going on and provide feedback to the Lord-Lieutenant.
- Advising on procedure for The Queen's Award for Voluntary Service.
- Advising on how any member of the public can nominate a key player for an honour, and supporting the honours nomination when referred back to the Lord-Lieutenant for comment.
- Celebrating and encouraging volunteering.
- Supporting youth organisations.
- Supporting youth employment initiatives.
- Attending Citizenship Ceremonies.

Up-to-date news, information on etiquette, protocol and honours nominations together with contact details for the Lieutenancy of Kent can be found at: www.kent-lieutenancy.org.uk

From Tudor times the Lieutenancy has played a major, although often behind-the-scenes, part in the lives of successive generations of the people of Kent. There is no doubt that the ancient office has an extraordinary past, but has it got a future?

Few could doubt that its modern role of providing a focus for county identity, unity and pride, recognising achievements, success and excellence, encouraging community volunteering and promoting service to others, adds value to the lives of its people.

In celebrating the Frontline County's unique history and culture and serving its communities the Lieutenancy is contributing positively to future success – and keeping the spirit of Kent alive.

As Geoff Wild puts it: 'If the Lieutenancy did not exist we would need to invent something very like it.'

'If the Lieutenancy did not exist we would need to invent something very like it'

LIEUTENANTS OF KENT
Later known as Lord-Lieutenants

Commissions of Lieutenancy were issued, renewed and terminated at erratic intervals according to political exigencies until the defeat of the Spanish Armada, after which the appointment became permanent. Among the early commissions granted were:

1512 George (Neville) 3rd Baron Bergavenny (Abergavenny)

1547 and 1551 Sir Thomas Cheney

1558 Sir Henry Jerningham

1559, 1569 and 1585 onwards William (Brooke) 10th Baron Cobham

1597 Henry (Brooke) 11th Baron Cobham

1604 Edward (Wotton) 1st Baron Wotton

1620 George (Villiers) 1st Marquess of Buckingham

1620 Ludovic (Stuart) 2nd Duke of Lennox (1st Duke of Richmond 1623)

1624 Philip (Herbert) 1st Earl of Montgomery (4th Earl of Pembroke 1630)

1642 Robert (Sidney), 2nd Earl of Leicester (Parliament-appointed)

1642 Philip (Herbert) 4th Earl of Pembroke (Parliament-appointed)

Interregnum

1660 Heneage (Finch), 3rd Earl of Winchilsea

1662 Thomas (Wriothesley) 4th Earl of Southampton

1668 3rd Earl of Winchilsea and Charles (Stuart) 3rd Duke of Richmond

1672 3rd Earl of Winchilsea

1688 Christopher (Roper) 5th Baron Teynham

1688 Louis (de Duras) 2nd Earl of Feversham

1689 3rd Earl of Winchilsea

1689 Henry (Sidney) 1st Viscount Sidney

1692 1st Viscount Sidney and Vere (Fane) 4th Earl of Westmorland

1693 1st Viscount Sidney (1st Earl of Romney 1694)

1704 Charles (Finch) 4th Earl of Winchilsea

1705 Lewis (Watson) 3rd Baron Rockingham (1st Earl of Rockingham 1714)

1724 John (Sidney) 6th Earl of Leicester

1737 Lewis (Watson) 2nd Earl of Rockingham

1746 Lionel (Sackville) 1st Duke of Dorset

1765 Charles (Sackville) 2nd Duke of Dorset

1769 John Frederick (Sackville) 3rd Duke of Dorset

1797 Charles (Marsham) 3rd Baron Romney (1st Earl Romney 1801)

1808 John Jeffreys (Pratt) 2nd Marquess Camden (1st Marquess Camden 1812)

1840 Henry (Tufton) 11th Earl of Thanet

1846 George Augustus (Cowper) 6th Earl Cowper

1856 John Robert (Townshend) 3rd Viscount Sydney (1st Earl Sydney 1874)

1890 Arthur Philip (Stanhope) 6th Earl Stanhope

1905 John Charles (Pratt) 4th Marquess Camden

1944 Wykeham Stanley (Cornwallis) 2nd Baron Cornwallis

1972 Gavin (Astor) 2nd Baron Astor of Hever

1982 Robert (Robin) Leigh-Pemberton (Baron Kingsdown 1993)

2002 Allan Robert Willett

2011 Philip (Sidney) 2nd Viscount De L'Isle

DEPUTY LIEUTENANTS

Mrs Nadra Ahmed OBE DL
Involved in social care since 1982: she is the Chairman of National Care Association since 2001: Patron of Rockdale Housing in Sevenoaks & President of Hi-Kent. Also a trustee of Royal British Legion Industries and Parkinson's UK. She was awarded the OBE in 2006 for her services to Social Care.

Mr Jacques Arnold DL
Former Member of Parliament for Gravesham, and now an international adviser on Latin America. Formerly Chairman of Kent County Scout Council. A Trustee of the Constitutional Monarchy Association and author of a series of books on Royal genealogy and on the history of parliamentary constituencies.

Lord Astor of Hever DL
Served in The Life Guards 1966-70; currently Parliamentary Under Secretary of State for Defence; active with a number of Kent charities, and a Kent Ambassador.

Mr James Bird DL
Formerly Chairman of Sandwich engineering company that won five Queen's Awards for Export. Was involved in the public sector as Chairman of K&C Hospital Trust and South Kent College, Vice-Chairman of Canterbury Festival and Treasurer of the University of Kent. Former Trustee of Canterbury Cathedral Trust.

Colonel (Retd) Peter Bishop OBE DL
After operational service in Aden, Cyprus and Northern Ireland was senior military public information officer, HQ UK Land Forces. Later Chairman Challenger UK/World. A former Colonel Commandant, Kent Army Cadet Force, he is President of The Queen's Own Buffs (The Royal Kent Regiment) Regimental Association.

Mr Peter W Blackwell JP DL
A retired human resources manager born and educated in Kent. Appointed a magistrate in 1971, and has held prominent positions in the Magistracy at Bench, county and national levels. Involved in several Tunbridge Wells based charities and voluntary organisations.

Major (Retd) Dennis Bradley BEM DL
Served in the Grenadier Guards. Past Mayor of Hythe, President of East Kent Branch Grenadier Guards Association. President and Director of Hythe Festival Company, involved in a wide range of military charities.

His Honour Judge Jeremy Carey DL
Practising barrister from 1974 to 2002. Now Resident Judge at Maidstone Crown Court and Honorary Recorder of Maidstone. Special interest in Kent Magistracy. Member of the Parole Board and Deputy High Court Judge (Court of Appeal Criminal Division).

The Lady Clarke DL
Chairman of the Blantyre House Vocational Fund and on the Council of the Old Bailey Charity The Sheriffs' and Recorder's Fund. Former Kent Magistrate and IMB member of Blantyre House.

Mr John (Algy) Cluff DL
Served in the Grenadier Guards 1959-65; President Kent Wing Air Training Corps; Vice President, Kent Army Benevolent Fund; Chairman of the War Memorials Trust. Was Chairman of the Spectator for 25 years and is currently Chairman and Chief Executive of Cluff Natural Resources and the National Army Museum Foundation.

Mr Bill Cockcroft DL
Senior Partner of a Quantity Surveying Practice. Former Chief Commissioner of England for the Scout Association. Chairman of the organising committee of the 2007 Centenary World Scout Jamboree held in the UK. President of Kent Scouts. Patron or Trustee of several Kent Charities.

The Lady Colgrain DL
Chairman of Kent Community Foundation, Kent Visitor for The Henry Smith Charity and previously a volunteer for many years with Sevenoaks Citizens Advice Bureau. Currently employed by an inner City CAB and partner in an 800 acre family farm in West Kent.

Lord Condon QPM DL
Former Chief Constable of Kent and Commissioner of the Metropolitan Police. He is currently active in police charities.

Mrs Amanda Cottrell OBE JP DL
Former High Sheriff and Magistrate. Chairman, Visit Kent, Board member Visit England and Patron of Produced in Kent. Trustee of Canterbury Cathedral, Vice President, Kent Wildlife Trust and Canterbury Festival, County President of the Guide Association and President of East Kent Stroke Association.

Sir Roger De Haan CBE DL
Retired as Chairman of Saga Group in 2004. He is engaged in charitable projects designed to make Folkestone and surrounding areas better places to live and work. Sponsor and Chair of Governors of two Kent Academies. Chair of The Creative Foundation and The Roger De Haan Charitable Trust.

Lieutenant Colonel (Retd) Richard C B Dixon TD DL
Born and educated in Kent, his Territorial Army service included command of the 5th (Volunteer) Battalion, The Queen's Regiment. A retired company director, he is active in various military charities including The Army Benevolent Fund, The Soldiers' Charity and The Royal British Legion.

DEPUTY LIEUTENANTS

Mr Barry Duffield DL
Served in the RAF, is a former deputy chief photographer with the Kent Messenger Group and now runs his own public relations photography business. Joined Kent Army Cadet Force in 1975 recently retired as Lieutenant Colonel heading the Media Team. President of Medway Town Sea Cadet Unit.

Mr Alister Dunning DL
Held senior legal and management positions with Pfizer in UK and United States; Legal and Public Affairs Director Pfizer Ltd Sandwich 1975-98. Voluntary appointments include Treasurer, University of Kent (1998-2004), and Treasurer (1998-2009) and President Kent County Cricket Club (2010).

Mrs Rosemary Dymond DL
A practising Headteacher for over 26 years, Chairman of the Thameside Schools Music Association and Trustee of the Local Learning Partnership also serving on local sports bodies. Trustee of Cobham College and Chairman of the Friends of Cobham Hall.

Mr Bill Fawcus DL
Former General Manager of Property and Planning at Dover Harbour Board and Chairman of South Kent College. Has various charitable and voluntary interests around Dover.

Colonel Peter Gilbert TD DL
Link DL for Reserve Forces and Cadets. A GP in Rochester, he served in the Regular Army and TA, commanding the UK Field Hospital in Afghanistan before being Deputy Commander of 2 (SE) Brigade. Selected for promotion to Brigadier as Deputy Director of Army Medical Services, April 2014

Colonel (Retd) Jo Gunnell OBE DL
Regular Army Infantry Officer from 1966 to 1995. Bursar The Royal School for Deaf Children 1996 to 2001. Army Welfare Support Officer Kent 2001 to 2012. Joined SSAFA 2001, Chairman SSAFA Kent since 2007.

Mrs Valerie Hale JP DL
Former teacher, School Governor, small business owner, Non – Executive Director with the Kent and Medway Partnership Trust and Deputy Chairman of the East Kent Bench. Currently Lay Chair with London and KSS Deaneries and closely involved with local Charities.

Mr Philip Harland DL
Former partner with Cluttons and now consultant with Smiths Gore specialising in land/estate management. Vice chairman of The Avante Partnership and trustee/ committee member/volunteer with other charitable organisations.

Dame Pauline Harris DBE DL Involved in wide range of causes, especially health and education. On the Board of the Harris Federation. Fellow of Oriel College, Oxford. President of Harris HospisCare, Bromley.

Mr Richard Henderson JP DL
A JP on the East Kent Bench and represents Kent's Magistrates on the National Council of the Magistrates Association. He is a former Director of investment managers Henderson Group plc and served on the National Trust's Regional committee for the South East as Chairman of its Finance Committee.

The Reverend Martin Henwood DL
Vicar of Holy Trinity, Dartford and Bishop of Rochester's Advisor for Thames Gateway. Founding Member of The Guild – in the Business of Now – a societal, systemic and experiential approach to transforming organisations. Former Chair of Dartford, Gravesham and Swanley Primary Care Trust.

Mr Kelvin R Holford DL
Former Kent County Commissioner Scout Association 2002-2012. Currently charity trustee for Buckmore Park and other local youth charities. Professionally a project manager.

Mr Jools Holland OBE DL
Musician and big band leader, he hosts BBC 2's music programme Later with Jools Holland as well as his own Radio 2 Show. Appointed OBE in 2004 for his services to music. Keen on the preservation and prosperity of Kent.

Mr Douglas Horner DL
Widely involved in business and rural affairs including with the NFU and Kent County Agricultural Society. Founding Chairman Kent Economic Forum, former Vice Chairman SE England Regional Assembly, and serving member Kent Economic Board, SE Local Enterprise Partnership and SE Council of the CBI.

Mr George Jessel DL
Short service Commission with 15/19th Hussars. Partner in 1,200-acre family farm. Honorary Life Governor of the Kent Agricultural Society, Chairman Trustees Wye Agricultural Museum. Past Chairman Kent CLA and NFU member. Patron, Hadlow College and Governor, Hadlow Rural Community School.

Mr Suresh K Khanna CBE DL
Former Royal Engineers' officer; and now a Fellow of the Institution of Royal Engineers; Department of Trade 1978-2000, retiring as Director Middle East and Africa. Currently a volunteer for SSAFA-Forces Help Kent; Member of the Rochester Diocesan Synod (1999-2012); former Chairman, Bredhurst Parish Council.

DEPUTY LIEUTENANTS

DEPUTY LIEUTENANTS

RETIRED DEPUTY LIEUTENANTS

In line with national practice, Deputy Lieutenants are placed on the Retired, or Supplemental, List when they reach the age of 75. However, they remain members of the Lieutenancy, retain the post-nominal letters DL – and are still sometimes called upon to represent the Lord-Lieutenant at events that match their areas of local and specialist knowledge. Occasionally Deputy Lieutenants under the retirement age are placed on the Supplemental List if they move away or for any other reason are unable to undertake further Lieutenancy duties.

Mr Robert Alston CMG QSO DL

Brigadier Maurice Atherton CBE JP DL

David G W Barham Esq FRICS JP DL

Tim Brett Esq JP DL

Richard Carr Esq TD DL

Commandant Elizabeth Craig McFeely CB WRNS (Rtd) DL

The Baroness Emerton DBE DL

Dame Peggy Fenner DBE DL

Mrs Elizabeth Fleming DL

Peter Hardy Esq DL

John Hosking Esq CBE JP DL

Sir Alistair Hunter KCMG DL

C John Jennings Esq MBE JP DL

Ivor Jones Esq DL

Jeremy Leigh Pemberton Esq CBE DL

RETIRED DEPUTY LIEUTENANTS

Michael Lewis Esq DL

Colonel (Retd) Godfrey Linnett TD DL

Simon macLachlan Esq MBE DL

The Rt Hon Lord Mayhew of Twysden QC PC DL

Colonel (Retd) David McDine OBE DL

The Rt Hon Countess Mountbatten of Burma CBE MSC CD JP DL

Sir John Mummery PC DL

Robert Neame Esq CBE DL

William V Newman Esq DL

Sir Graeme Odgers DL

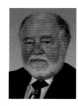

John A Ogden Esq DL

Brian H Pearce Esq CBE DL

Wing Commander Ronald Powling DL

His Honour Giles Rooke TD QC DL

Mrs Tricia Shephard MBE DL

Sir Keith Speed RD DL

John A Spence Esq OBE DL

Sir John Swire CBE DL

RETIRED DEPUTY LIEUTENANTS

Dick Tapp Esq MA DL

The Right Reverend Dr Michael Turnbull CBE DL

The Right Reverend Dr Stephen Venner

Mrs Mary Villiers OBE DL

Sir John Wells DL

Mrs Ann A West MBE JP DL

Sir Robert Worcester KBE DL

Lieutenant Colonel U H B Alexander MBE DL DCL

Colonel David R A Barnes JP DL

Kenneth McAlpine Esq OBE DL

The Lord Northbourne DL

Major General (Retd) John Badcock CB MBE DL

Lieutenant Colonel (Retd) Robert Simpson OBE TD DL

Colonel (Retd) James Ogilvie OBE TD DL

Sadly a number of active and retired list Deputy Lieutenants, all of whom gave conspicuous service to county or nation, have died in recent years. They include:

Major Malcolm Bains JP DL

Mr Stanley Blow OBE DL

Mr Edwin R P Boorman OBE DL

Mr Edward St J Brice DL

Mr Charles Busby CBE DL

Mr David Clark DL

The Lord Cornwallis OBE DL

Lt Gen Sir Napier Crookenden KCB DSO OBE DL

Mr Alan Day MBE DL

Lord Bill Deedes MC DL

Mr Alex de Gelsey CBE DL

Lieutenant Colonel Garth Doubleday TD JP DL

Mr David Downes DL

Rear-Admiral Colin Dunlop CB CBE DL

Captain Robert Evans

DL The Viscountess Falmouth OBE DL

Mr Geoffrey Fletcher MBE TD JP DL

Lieutenant General Sir Martin Garrod KCB CMG OBE DL

Sir Brandon Gough DL

Major General David Grove OBE DL

Sir John D Grugeon DL

Air Chief Marshal Sir Lewis Hodges KCB CBE DSO DFC DL

Brigadier John Holman CBE DL

Wing Commander Dennis Jackson OBE DL

Lord Hugo Kindersley DL

Brigadier Charles Millman OBE DL

Colonel Gerald Mullins DL

Mrs Paddy Nesham DL

Lord Michael Nolan DL

The Lady Julia Pender OBE DL

Lt Colonel John A Porter TD JP DL

Mr Andrew Rowe DL

Mrs Penny Stubbs MBE JP DL

Colonel Frederick Theobald DL

Major-General The Viscount Monckton of Brenchley CB OBE MC DL

Mrs Sarah Ward OBE DL

The Rt Hon Lord Bernard Weatherill DL

SOURCE NOTES

The redoubtable Sir Roger Twysden, 17th Century scholar, constitutional historian, magistrate and sometime Deputy Lieutenant of Kent intended to write a history of the Lieutenancy and collected papers concerning the office with that aim in mind. He wrote: 'I have an intention, God inabling me, to say somewhat of the first raising of Lord Lieutenants and Deputy Lieutenants… and for that purpose doe have the sheetes before here clear, but that I may not forget what happened in my time and that I was an actor in, being now fresh in my memory…' Sadly, his attention was drawn elsewhere and the sheets that followed remained blank. Much water has flowed down the Channel since then and the Lieutenancy has been inextricably tied up in the Frontline County's eventful history ever since – hence this book.

Fortunately along the way a handful of other researchers and writers have examined aspects of Lieutenancy history closely and published the results. The earliest was Gladys Scott Thomson who edited *The Twysden Lieutenancy Papers* and also wrote on the office in the 16th Century. A special debt is owed to J J N McGurk, who wrote on *Lieutenancy in Kent 1580-1620, Armada Preparations in Kent, Lieutenancy and Catholic Recusants in Elizabethan Kent, Rochester and the Irish Levy of October 1601* – and calendared the *Letter Book Relating to the Lieutenancy of Kent, 1604-28*. A M Everitt's *The Community of Kent and the Great Rebellion 1640-60* has been invaluable, as has Colonel J Bonhote's mammoth *Historical Records of the West Kent Militia*. The late Editor-proprietor of the *Kent Messenger*, H R Pratt Boorman's Kentish books, especially *Spirit of Kent*, have been heavily drawn upon. Sir John Sainty's impeccable research and listings of the *Lieutenants of Counties 1585-1642 and 1660-1974* is gratefully acknowledged, as is that of Miles Jebb in his book covering the national scene: *The Lord-Lieutenants and their Deputies*.

The quirky spelling in historic quotes has been retained, although in the main text the modern form of surnames and place-names has been used.

The author is grateful to all those whose work is acknowledged in the following source notes.

Chapter 1: 1 J J McGurk, Lieutenancy in Kent c1580-1620, p.237; 2 Ministry of Justice protocol 2009; 3 Paul Millward and the Civic Secretaries Group, Best Practice Guide to Civic Life

Chapter 2: 1 Gladys Scott Thomson, Lords Lieutenants in the 16th Century p.14; 2 Ibid, p.45; 3 Colonel J.Bonhote, Historical Records of the West Kent Militia p.2; 4 Duncan Harrington, Lost Sandwich Muster Records and Other Records; 5 Bygone Kent, Vol 21 No 7; 6 Scott Thomson, Lord Lieutenants in the 16th Century p.24; 7 Bygone Kent Vol 21 No 7; 8 Scott Thomson, Twysden Lieutenancy Papers, Archaeologia Cantiana Vol X p.6; 9 Ibid; 10 Scott Thomson, Lords Lieutenants in the 16th Century p.41; 11 State Papers Domestic Elizabeth l xxiv, no. 34; 12 Scott Thomson, Twysden Lieutenancy Papers p.7; 13 Ibid; 14 John Knox Laughton, State Papers relating to the Defeat of the Spanish Armada, Vol I p.142; 15 Kent Archives KG LAM pp.63/64/65; 16 Bonhote p.31

Chapter 3: 1 Oxford DNB; 2 Scott Thomson, Lords Lieutenants in the 16th Century p.123; 3 McGurk: Armada Preparations in Kent, Arch Cant Vol 85, p.73; 4 Northamptonshire Lieutenancy Papers 1580-1614; 5 Harrington, Lost Sandwich Muster Records and Other Records; 6 Hunter's History of London; 7 James Renat Scott, Memorials of the Family of Scott; 8 Ibid p.195; 9 Ibid; 10 McGurk, Armada Preparations p.83; 11 Ibid p.87; 12 State Papers Domestic Elizabeth 1581-1590, Armada correspondence; 13 Laughton, Defeat of the Spanish Armada Vol II p.93; 14 David A Thomas, Armada Handbook p.159; 15 Ibid p.160.

Chapter 4: 1 McGurk, Armada Preparations p.91; 2 Sir John Smith's Instructions, Observations and Orders Militarie p.183; 3 McGurk, Armada Preparations pp.92/93; 4 McGurk, Lieutenancy and Catholic Recusants in Elizabethan Kent pp.157-170; 5 Ibid; 6 Ibid; 7 Ibid; 8 Scott, Memorials of the Family of Scot, pp.195-206; 9 Alastair Bruce, Keepers of the Kingdom; 10 Peter Ackroyd, Shakespeare the Autobiography; 11 Ibid; 12 McGurk, Lieutenancy in Kent p.89; 13 Oxford DNB; 14 Ackroyd, Shakespeare the Autobiography; 15 Oxford DNB; 16 Ibid; 17 McGurk Lieutenancy in Kent p.94; 18 Ibid p.96; 19 Ibid p.99; 20 McGurk, Rochester and the Irish Levy of October 1601, The Mariner's Mirror, Vol 74, No 1; 21 Ibid; 22 Ibid; 23 Oxford DNB; 24 A Weldon, Court and Character of King James; 25 Thomas Carte, A General History of England 1747-55; 26 Oxford DNB; 27 Ibid; 28 Ibid; 29 State Papers Domestic 1619-1623; 30 Privy Council letter 1 July 1603.

Chapter 5: 1 Oxford DNB; 2 McGurk, Letter Book relating to the Lieutenancy of Kent 1604-1628, Arch Cant Vol 82; 3 Scott Thomson, Lords Lieutenants in the 16th Century; 4 Arch Cant Vol 82; 5 Alan Stewart, Philip Sidney – A Double Life; 6 Oxford DNB

Chapter 6: 1 Chambers Biographical Dictionary p.224; 2 State Papers Domestic 1619-1623; 3 Oxford DNB; 4 State Papers Domestic 1619-1623; 5 Victoria County History Vol 2 p.290; 6 M A Gibb, Buckingham 1592-1628 p.236; 7 Arch Cant Vol 82; 8 Oxford DNB; 9 State Papers Domestic 1619-1623 p.149; 10 Ibid p.151; Ibid p.599; 12 Ibid p.600; 13 Chilham Castle leaflet; 14 Oxford DNB; 15 J C Sainty, Lieutenants of Counties 1585-1642, Bulletin of the Institute of Historical Research, Special Supplement No 8; 16 Oxford DNB; 17 Ibid; 18 Frank W Jessup, Sir Roger Twysden 1597-1672; 19 Bonhote p.44; 20 Mark Charles Fissel, War and Government in Britain, 1598-1650 p.204; 21 Ibid, p.221; 22 A E Everitt, Community of Kent and the Great Rebellion1640-60; 23 State Papers Domestic 1638-39 p.514; 24 Oxford DNB; 25 Jessup, Sir Roger Twysden; 26 Bonhote p.53; 27 Alan Bignell, Kent – a Place in History; 28 Oxford DNB; 29 Everitt, p.100

SOURCE NOTES

Chapter 7: 1 Victor L Slater, Noble Government –The Stuart Lord Lieutenancy and the Transformation of English Politics; 2 Everitt, Kent and the Great Rebellion, p.14; 3 Ibid; 4 Oxford DNB; Michael G Brennan, The Sidneys of Penshurst and the Monarchy 1500-1700; 6 Oxford DNB; 7 Everitt, Kent and the Great Rebellion p.108; 8 Slater, Noble Government; 9 Oxford DNB; 10 Everitt, p.108; 11 Ibid p.112; 12 H F Abell, Kent and the Great Civil War p.79; 13 Everitt, Kent and the Great Rebellion pp.114/5; 14 Hasted Vol IV p.146; 15 Abell p.87; 16 Northbourne Sources, Thomason Tracts; 17 Brennan, The Sidneys of Penshurst and the Monarchy; 18 Oxford DNB; 19 Slater, Noble Government; 20 Everitt, Kent and the Great Rebellion p.129; 21 Everitt, The County Committee of Kent in the Civil War p.21; 22 Everitt, Kent and the Great Rebellion p.129; 23 Ibid p.133; 24 Everitt, The County Committee of Kent in the Civil War p.16; 25 Everitt, Kent and the Great Rebellion; 26 Ibid; 27 Ibid; 28 Everitt, The County Committee of Kent in the Civil War; 29 Ibid; 30 Everitt, Kent and the Great Rebellion p.197; 31 Ibid p.199; 32 Ibid p.217; 33 Ibid p.204; 34 Austin Woolrych, Battles of the English Civil War p.99; 35 Bonhote p.57; 36 Everitt, Kent and the Great Rebellion p.234; 37 Bonhote p.57; 38 Everitt, Kent and the Great Rebellion p.255; 39 Ibid p.259; 40 Oxford DNB

Chapter 8: 1 SPH Statham, History of the Castle, Town and Port of Dover, pp.118/19 (Minutes of the Common Assembly of Dover; 2 Bonhote p.65; 3 Clarendon, History of the Rebellion, vol VI p.233; 4 Oxford DNB; 5 Ibid; 6 Complete Peerage, XII, ii, p.778n; 7 Oxford DNB; 8 Scott Thomson, Twysden Lieutenancy Papers, Arch Cant Vol X p.37; 9 Jessup p.174; 10 Sir Hughe Knatchbull-Hugessen, Kentish Family pp.27/28; 11 Scott Thomson, Twysden Lieutenancy Papers, Arch Cant Vol X p.52; 12 Bonhote pp.67/68; 13 State Papers Domestic 1667; 14 P G Rogers, The Dutch in the Medway p.134; 15 Oxford DNB; 16 Ibid; 17 M M Reese, Goodwood's Oak p.19; 18 Oxford DNB; 19 Scott Thomson, Twysden Lieutenancy Papers p.56; 20 Ibid

Chapter 9: 1 Everitt, Kent and the Great Rebellion, p.303 (The Complete Peerage XII, ii, p.778n); 2 David Constantine, Fields of Fire p.56; 3 Oxford DNB; 4 Jebb, The Lord-Lieutenants and their Deputies; 5 Slater, Noble Government, p.147; 6 Bonhote p.70; 7 Peter Earle, Monmouth's Rebels: The Road to Sedgemoor 1685; 8 Richard Holmes, Marlborough – Britain's Greatest General, p.119; 9 Slater p.170; 10 Oxford DNB; 11 Slater, p.175; 12 Knatchbull-Hugessen pp.61/2; 13 Bonhote p.71; 14 Ibid; 15 Ibid p.72; 16 Oxford DNB; 17 The Viscount De L'Isle, Jamestown Speech, 2009; 18 Luttrell's Diary ii p.459; 19 London Gazette June 4-7 1694; 20 Philip Sidney, The Sidneys of Penshurst; 21 Bryan I'Anson, History of the Finch Family, p.56; 22 Jebb, The Lord-Lieutenants and Their Deputies; 23 London Gazette 30 June 1713; 24 J R Western, The English Militia in the 18th Century, p.53; 25 Ibid p.52; 26 London Gazette 25 February 1716

Chapter 10: 1 Bonhote p.77; 2 Ibid p.78; 3 London Gazette 10 December 1745; 4 Bonhote p.79; 5 Ibid pp.79/80; 6 Western, The English Militia in the 18th Century; 7 Lord Edmund Fitzmaurice, Life of William, Earl of Shelburne; 8 J Bridgman, Sketch of Knole 1817; 9 Charles J Phillips, History of the Sackville Family, Vol 2 p.1; 10 Ibid p.20; 11 John Major, More Than a Game p.50: 12 Phillips, History of the Sackville Family, Vol 2 p.45; 13 Bonhote p.82; 14 Kentish Post 2-6 July 1757; 15 Ibid 13 June 1759; 16 Phillips, Kentish Homes, p.66; H Walpole, Memoirs of the Reign of George II Vol III p.40; 17 Phillips, History of the Sackville Family Vol 2 p.71; 18 Ibid; 19 Works of Jane Austen, Cambridge Edition; 20 Phillips, History of the Sackville Family, Vol 2 p.86; 21 Ibid; 22 London Gazette No 10599; 23 Kentish Post 22-25 April 1767; 24 Phillips, History of the Sackville Family, Vol 2 p.97; 25 Brady, Guide to Knole, 1839; 26 Horace Bleakley, Ladies, Fair and Frail; 27 Robert Sackville-West, Knole Kent; 28 Kentish Gazette 2 May 1778; 29 Bonhote pp.134/5; 30 Ibid p.145

Chapter 11: 1 Colonel Lord Harris, A Century of Yeoman Service p.3; 2 Ibid; 3 Ibid p.5; 4 Ibid p.6: 5 Ibid; 6 Ibid, p.9; 7 Ibid p.13; 8 Lieutenant Colonel J F Edmeades, West Kent Yeomanry – Some Historical Records p.6; 9 Glenn A Steppler, Britons To Arms! p.14; 10 Jebb, p.77; 11 London Gazette 15 October 1796; 12 Jay Luvaas, Napoleon on the Art of War p.107; 13 Peter Bloomfield, Kent and the Napoleonic Wars, Kentish Sources X; 14 Ibid; 15 Hasted, Vol 3; 16 Harris, p.15; 17 Hasted pp.446-452; 18-22 Ibid; 23 Edward Wedlake Brayley, Beauties of England and Wales, Vol VIII (Kent), 1808; 24 Bonhote pp.195/6; 25 Ibid p.206; 26 Folkestone Lieutenancy Papers, Schedule 3; 27 Bloomfield, p.76; 28 Oxford DNB; 29 Jebb, The Lord-Lieutenants and their Deputies; 30 London Gazette 27 February 1810; 31 London Gazette April 27, 1814

Chapter 12: 1 Harris, p.29; 2 Edmeades, p.30; 3 Roger Wells, Mr William Cobbett, Captain Swing, and King William IV, Agricultural History Review p.36; 4 Ibid p.38; 5 J L and B Hammond, The Village Labourer, p.309; 6 Bonhote p.238; 7 Jebb, The Lord-Lieutenants and their Deputies; 8 Bonhote, p.239; 9 Edmeades, p.35; 10 Ibid; 11 P G Rogers, Battle of Bossenden Wood; 12 Harris, p.38; 13 Ibid, p.45; 14 Ibid, p.46; 15 Jebb, The Lord-Lieutenants and their Deputies; 16 Bonhote p.245; 17 Jebb, pp.99/100; 18 Bonhote, pp.251/260; 19 Ibid; 20 Hugh Cunningham, The Volunteer Force, pp.8/9; 21 Ibid; 22 Charles Igglesden, History of the East Kent Volunteers, p.7; 23 Ibid; 24 Ibid; 25 Bonhote, p.7

Chapter 13: 1 Jebb, pp.93/4; 2 Ibid; 3 Bonhote, p.272; 4 Jebb, pp.94/102; 5 St Nicholas Church website; 6 Aubrey Newman, The Stanhopes of Chevening; 7-9 Ibid; 10 South.Eastern Gazette 15 April 1890; 11 Felix, Rambles Around Folkestone; 12 Bob Ogley, Kent, A Chronicle of the Century Vol 1 1900-24 p.4; 13 Brian Bond, War Memoirs of Earl Stanhope 1914-18; 14 Kent Messenger 17 December 1943; 15 Jebb, p.103; 16 Ibid, p.105; 17 Ibid, p.114; 18 Kent Messenger 26 March 1932; 19 Elizabeth Melling, A History of the KCC 1839-1974; 20 Newcastle Journal, 8 January 1915; 21 Roy Ingleton, Policing Kent 1800-2000 p.78; 22 The British Journal of Nursing 7 June 1919; 23 Jebb, p.112; 24 Kent Messenger, 17 December 1943; 25 Kent & Sussex Courier, ditto; 26 Kent Messenger, ditto; 27 Kent and Sussex Courier, ditto

Chapter 14: 1 H R Pratt Boorman, The Spirit of Kent p.93; 2 Ibid pp.97/11; 3 Ibid p.113; 4 Ibid p.115; 5 Ibid p.118; 6 Ibid, pp.120/123; 7 Ibid p.130; 8 Ibid p.130; 9 Ibid p.135; 10 Jebb p.126; 11 Ibid p.128; 12 Pratt Boorman, The Spirit of Kent p.183; 13 Jebb p.130; 14 Cornwallis/Heckles correspondence, Kent Archives; 15 Pratt Boorman, The Spirit of Kent pp.198/200; 16 Ibid, p.232; 17 Ibid, p.457; 18 Ibid p.272; 19 Ibid p.273; 20 Ibid p.373; 21 Ibid p.261; 22 Ibid p.293; 23 Cornwallis/Heckles

SOURCE NOTES

correspondence, Kent Archives; 24 Ibid; 25 John Boyle, The Illustrated Portrait of Canterbury, p.178; 26 Pratt Boorman, The Spirit of Kent p.362; 27 Roy Ingleton, Kent VCs pp.93/95; 28 Jebb p.137; 29 Jebb p.159; 30 Pratt Boorman, The Spirit of Kent p.382; 31 David Seeney, At Your Service

Chapter 15: 1 Astor Lieutenancy Papers; 2 Ibid; 3 Gavin Astor, Hever Castle booklet; 4 Ibid; 5 Astor Lieutenancy Papers; 6 Ibid; 7 Kent Messenger 6 July 1984; 8 London Gazette 3-6 April 1973; 9 Kent Messenger 15 October 1976; 10 Astor Lieutenancy papers; 11 Ibid; 12 Ibid; 13 Ibid; 14 Ibid; 15 Ibid; 16 Lord and Lady Kingsdown interview; 17-26 Ibid; 27 Paul Sabin interview; 28 Lord and Lady Kingsdown interview; 29-32 Ibid; 33 Jebb; 34 Lord and Lady Kingsdown interview; 35-38 Ibid

Chapter 16: 1 Kent Life July 2011; 2-5 Allan Willett interview; 6 Allan Willett, Civic Service speech 2005; 7 Allan Willett interview; 8-9 Ibid; 10 Brigadier Iain James, Beat Retreat speech July 2009; 11 Allan Willett interview; 12 Paul Carter, Invicta Award speech October 2011

Chapter 17: 1 Stanley Blow, Act Imaginatively; 2 Ibid; 3 Parliamentary Question; 4 Jebb; 5 Sir Robert Worcester interview; 6 Sir Alistair Hunter interview; 7 Mrs Ros McCarthy interview; 8 Mrs Ann West interview; 9 John Ogden interview; 10 Group Captain Patrick Tootal interview; 11 Sir Alistair Hunter interview; 12 Group Captain Patrick Tootal interview; 13 Suresh Khanna interview; 14 Dick Tapp interview; 15 James Bird interview

Chapter 18: 1 Lord-Lieutenant's 2 RTR speech September 2011; 2 Lieutenancy news release September 2011; 3 Lord De L'Isle interview; 4 Lord-Lieutenant's Sturry speech November 2011; 5 Douglas Horner interview; 6 Geoff Wild interview; 7 Ibid; 8 Joanne Holmes interview

ACKNOWLEDGEMENTS

Grateful thanks are due to Allan and Anne Willett and the Trustees of the Allan Willett Foundation for recognising the value of recording the hitherto unpublished story of the Frontline County's Lieutenancy and making this publication possible.

The author is also most grateful to the present Lord-Lieutenant, Lord De L'Isle, and all members of the Lieutenancy, past and present, for their enthusiastic support and contributions. Invaluable help was given by Lord and Lady Kingsdown, although sadly he died in the run-up to publication, by Countess Mountbatten of Burma, and by Lord Astor of Hever, who granted full access to his late father's Lieutenancy papers. Sir John Mummery kindly read the draft and commented on it wisely, and both the Clerk to the Lieutenancy, Geoff Wild, and his Deputy Joanne Holmes have given sterling assistance.

Kent Messenger Group Chairman Geraldine Allinson, whose late father and grandfather were both long-serving Deputy Lieutenants, has been a stalwart supporter, notably providing free access to the Group's newspaper and photographic archives. Trevor Sturgess, in both his Kent Messenger Group and Deputy Lieutenant hats, has been of enormous help. Thanks are due, too, to Kent Messenger Group legal advisor Norman Smith for his advice and interest.

Jan Powell and Madeleine Duffield deserve special mention for their skill and patience in undertaking picture research ranging back over five eventful centuries and obtaining permissions to publish.

Kent County Council Archives and Libraries and many other repositories have been unstinting with their assistance, as have all other institutions and individuals approached during the research phase of *Unconquered*, too many to mention all by name. The author is grateful to them all.

PICTURE CREDITS

We acknowledge the help of Kent County Council (portraits), Dover District Council (stained glass and portraits), Godington House (wooden friezes) and Maidstone Museum (Battle of Maidstone artifacts) in enabling us to photograph and to use images of items they hold.

All Original Artwork: Richard Barton

All Special Photography: Barry Duffield DL

With the exception of:

Chapter 1: p.1 & p.5 (top): Kent Messenger Archives.

Chapter 3: Musketeers of the Trained Bands, p.30 & Pikemen of the Trained Bands, p.33: by kind permission of Viscount De L'Isle from his private collection at Penshurst Place, Kent, England; Elizabeth I Armada Portrait, p.38: with thanks to W. Tyrwhitt-Drake, Esq.

Chapter 4: William Brooke and family, p.40: reproduced by permission of the Marquess of Bath, Longleat House, Warminster, Wiltshire; Sir John Leveson, p.50: reproduced by permission of the Sutherland Trust; King James I, p.52: reproduced by permission of Knole Estates.

Chapter 5: Sir Philip Sidney, p.57: by kind permission of Viscount De L'Isle from his private collection at Penshurst Place, Kent, England.

Chapter 7: Robert Sidney, p.82 & Penshurst Place, p.83: by kind permission of Viscount De L'Isle from his private collection at Penshurst Place, Kent, England; Leeds Castle, p.88 & Lord Fairfax, p.96: courtesy of the Trustees of Leeds Castle Foundation.

Chapter 8: Sir Norton Knatchbull, p.103: by permission of the Hon. Timothy Knatchbull; Dutch on the Medway, p.107: Maidstone Museum.

Chapter 9: James II's capture, p.112: Look and Learn; Henry Sidney, p.119, Arrow, p.121 & John Sidney, p.124: by kind permission of Viscount De L'Isle from his private collection at Penshurst Place, Kent, England.

Chapter 10: Knole House, p.125 & John Frederick Sackville, p.137: © National Trust Images; Lionel Sackville, p.128 & Charles Sackville, p.135: reproduced by permission of Knole Estates; Giovanna Baccelli, p.137: Photographic Survey, The Courtauld Institute of Art, London. Private Collection.

Chapter 11: 3rd Duke of Dorset, p.140: © National Portrait Gallery; Sessions House, p.140: Maidstone Museum; Charles Marsham, p.143: © Trustees of the British Museum; John Jeffreys Pratt, p.151: by permission of Brecknock Museum.

Chapter 12: Sir Edward Knatchbull, p.154: by permission of the Hon. Timothy Knatchbull; John Thom, p.157: by permission of Fleur De Lis Museum; Battle of Bossenden Wood, p.158: courtesy of the Council of the National Army Museum, London; Sir David Salomons, p.159: permission of Salomons UK Ltd; Henry Tufton, p.159: reproduced by courtesy of Abbot Hall Art Gallery, Lakeland Arts Trust, Kendal, Cumbria; Sydney on Horseback, p.161 & Lord Chamberlain, p.165: Royal Collection Trust/© Her Majesty Queen Elizabeth II 2013.

Chapter 13: Lady Sydney, p.167: Royal Collection Trust/© Her Majesty Queen Elizabeth II 2013; 6th Earl Stanhope, p.168: © National Portrait Gallery; Lord Camden Cartoon, p.174: © reserved, photograph National Portrait Gallery, London; Cricketer Lord Harris, p.175: by permission of Kent County Cricket Club; Bayham Abbey, p.179: by permission of The Weald Organisation; Dunkirk Veterans, p.181: Kent Messenger Archives.

Chapter 14: Robert Stanford Tuck, p.182: © Imperial War Museum (CH1680); Wykham Stanley, p.183: by permission of Kent County Cricket Club; The Spirit of Kent Spitfire, p.183: Barry Duffield Archive; Lord Cornwallis, p.184, 185, 187, 189, 190, 194: Kent Messenger Archive; Winston Churchill, p.188: Barry Duffield Archive; Major William Sidney, p.188: by kind permission of Viscount De L'Isle from his private collection at Penshurst Place, Kent, England.

Chapter 15: Lord Astor, p.197: by permission of Lord Astor of Hever; Lady Astor, p.197: image Madeleine Duffield; Patricia Mountbatten, p.198: by permission of Countess Mountbatten of Burma; Angela Cobb, p.198: by permission of Mrs Carolyn Ernest Jones; Lord Astor, p.199 & Air Training Corps, p.199: Sevenoaks Chronicle; Lord Astor, p.200, p.202, Brig. Maurice Atherton, p.200, Robin Leigh Pemberton, p.203, p.205, Princess of Wales, p.205, Princess Anne, p.206: Kent Messenger Archive.

Chapter 16: General Dannatt, p.219: image Roger Tutt; Allan Willett on Quad Bike, p.220: image Madeleine Duffield.

Chapter 17: Stanley Blow, p.227: Kent Messenger Archive; Dick Tapp, p.238: by permission of Dick Tapp..

Chapter 18: Thanet Visit, p.242: image reproduced by permission of Manu Palomeque; Penshurst Place, p.243 & Porcupine, p.244: by kind permission of Viscount De L'Isle from his private collection at Penshurst Place, Kent, England; Royal Visit, p.244: Kent Messenger Archive; the Hilfranor, p.245: Maryann Webster; Enthronement Service, p.247: © Lisa Emanuel/Canterbury Cathedral.

INDEX

INDEX

INDEX

INDEX

HEADLEY BROTHERS
Kent-based Printers of *Unconquered*

ABOVE: The Lord-Lieutenant
of Kent passes the first
printed sheets with
Headley Brothers' managing
director Roger Pitt and
author of *Unconquered*
David McDine

The printing of this publication was provided by Kent printing company, Headley Brothers Ltd.

The Ashford-based printing company Headley Brothers started life as The Invicta Press, founded in 1881 by Herbert and Burgess Headley in a small room above their father's grocery shop at 46 High Street. The enterprising brothers offered a printing service of paper bags, bill heads and circulars to local traders, and were an immediate success. In 1892, a factory was built behind the High Street and after Burgess Headley visited America on a fact-finding tour, Headley Brothers pioneered monotype in Europe.

In 1906 a disastrous fire destroyed the whole works, but within a fortnight, the entire staff was back at work at a temporary premises. A new site was built at the lower end of Queen's Road, Ashford, where the factory still stands today. During the 1970s the company made the big step from Letterpress to Litho and in 1976 installed its first Web press. This coincided with a move into magazine production, which now accounts for more than 80% of the

The Lord-Lieutenant sends the first pages of *Unconquered* to press

ABOVE: The staff at Headley Brothers warmly welcomes the Lord-Lieutenant and Viscountess De L'Isle to the premises

company's output. The company continued its ethos of continuous, intelligent investment in the latest technologies over the following decades; investments which ensured that the company could always provide to its customers the most efficient and high quality service. The company's many developments included the launch of its digital printing arm of the business in 2004, enabling the company to diversify to cater for customers' requirements for short-run printing, and customised marketing collateral.

Chief executive Roger Pitt says: "The company's focus has always been on investing in its equipment and its people, to ensure that we can consistently provide a flexible, cost-effective and efficient service to our customers. Each decade has seen Headley Brothers significantly invest in new machinery and building expansion, in addition to staff training and development. The company's ISO 9001 (quality assurance) and Investor in People accreditations underline this.

"From digital, sheet-fed and web printing to finishing and fulfilment, mailing and dispatch services, our company is well-placed to offer a quality solution to any print requirement – for a range of products including business cards and stationery through to customised marketing communications and magazine and brochure production; for print runs of as little as one copy. Simply put, no job is too small."

Today, Headley Brothers is still an independent family company celebrating a fantastic 133 years in the business. The company's continued ethos of investment in its staff, machinery and processes ensures that it remains a specialist in the magazine printing domain, and a trusted supplier of printed material to the Kent business community.